CW01664944

Stanley Spencer

Heaven in a Hell of War

Paul Gough
Amanda Bradley
David Taylor
Katy Norris
Simon Martin
Jamie Hacker Hughes
Jenny Beddington

edited by Amanda Bradley
and Howard Watson

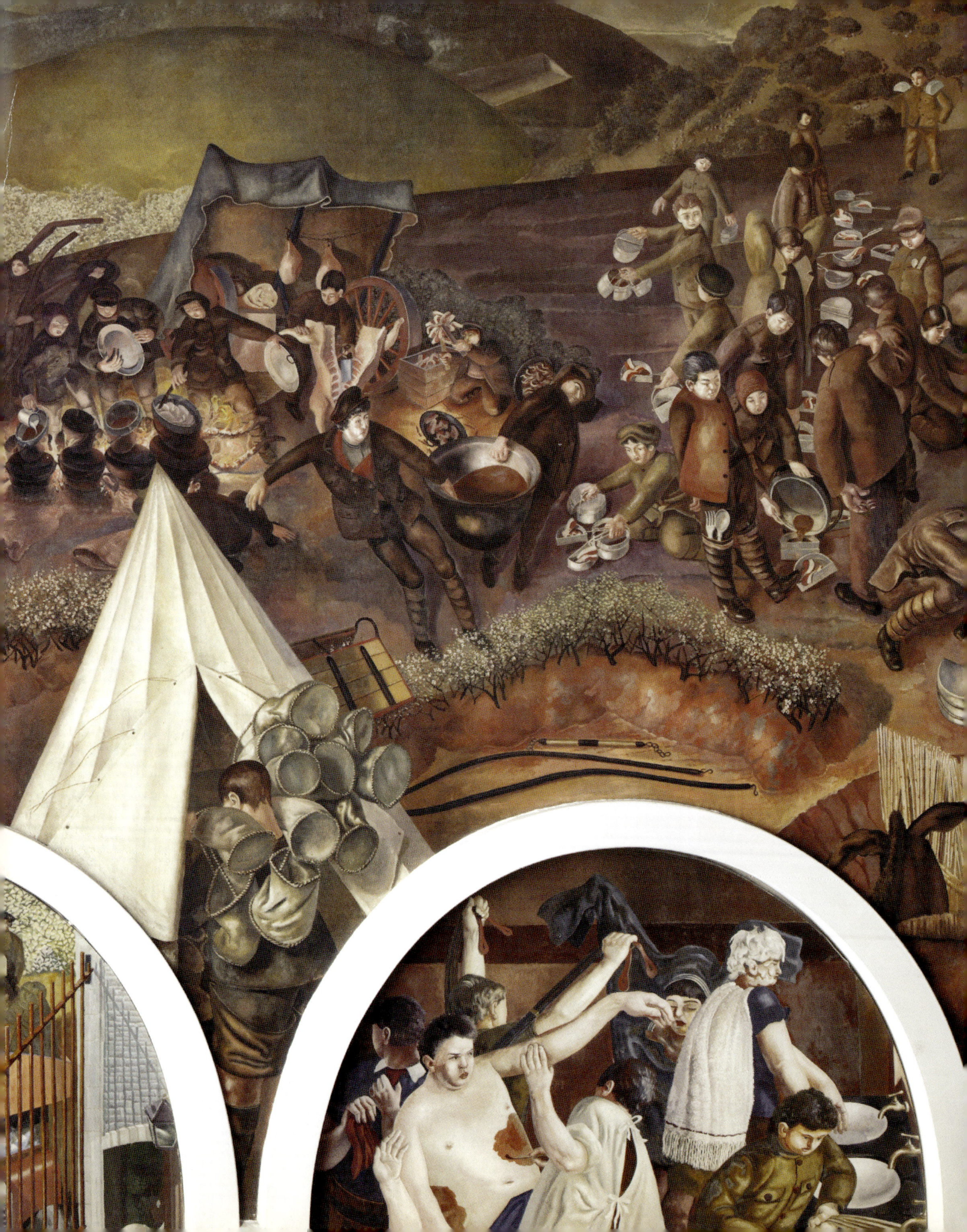

Stanley Spencer

Heaven in a Hell of War

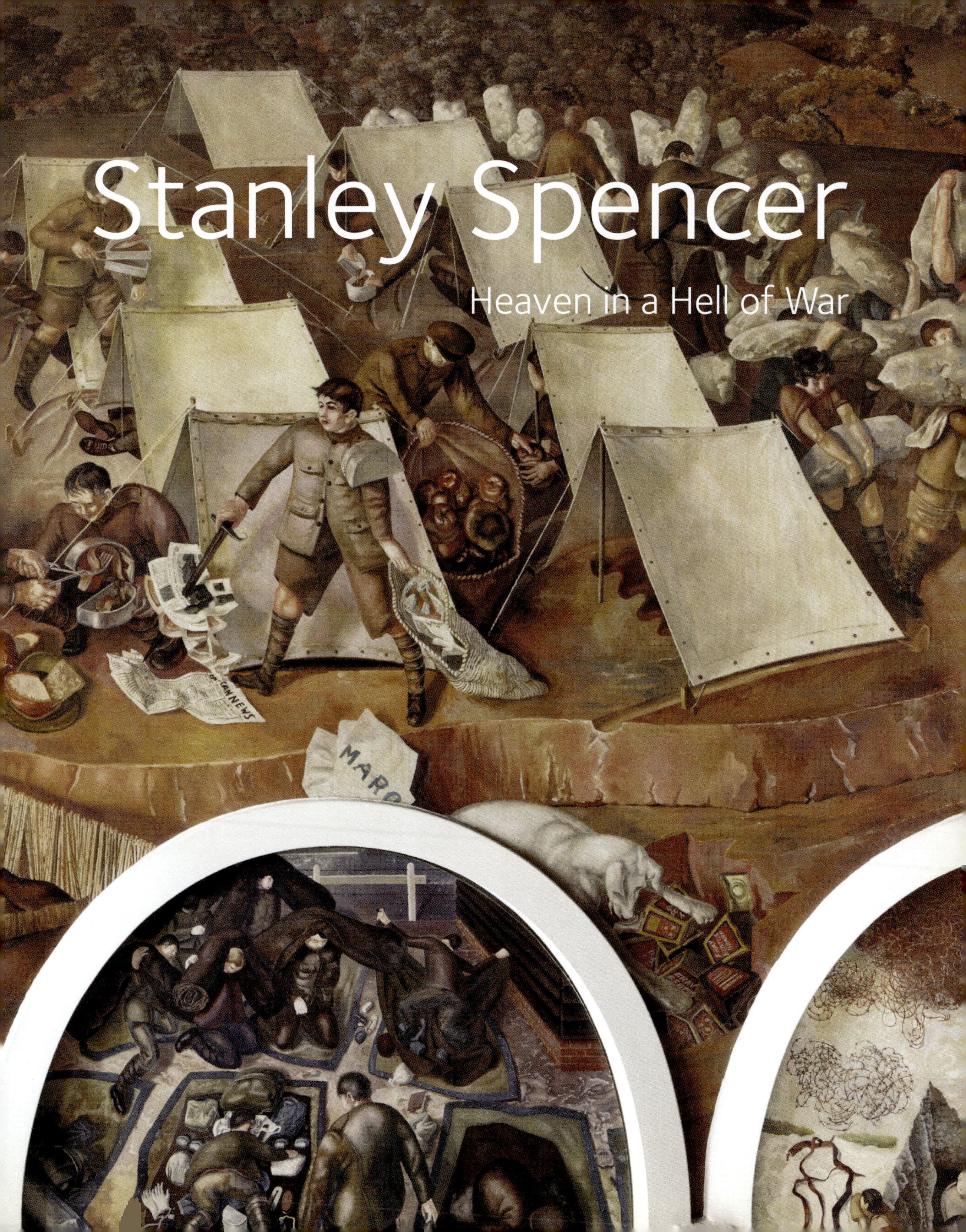

Published to coincide with the exhibition
Stanley Spencer: Heaven in a Hell of War
co-curated by Amanda Bradley and David Taylor

Somerset House, London
7 November 2013 – 26 January 2014

Pallant House Gallery, Chichester
15 February – 15 June 2014

Supported by Toovey's and
The Stanley Spencer Supporter's Circle

First published in 2013 by
Pallant House Gallery
in association with The National Trust

Pallant House Gallery
9 North Pallant
Chichester
West Sussex
PO19 1TJ
United Kingdom

www.pallant.org.uk

Edited by Amanda Bradley and Howard Watson
Production Manager: Harriet Judd
Designed by David Wynn
Set in Foundry Sterling by The Foundry, London
Printed by Selsey Press Ltd

Text © The authors, 2013
Works by Stanley Spencer © The Estate of Stanley Spencer 2013. All rights reserved DACS.
Additonal image copyrights see p. 111.

All rights reserved. No part of this publication may be reproduced, stored in a retrieval system or transmitted in any form or by any means, electrical, mechanical or otherwise, without first having permission of the copyright owners and publishers.

The authors assert their rights under the Copyright, Designs and Patents Act, 1988, to be identified as the Authors of this Work.

ISBN: 978-1-869827-13-7

British Library Cataloguing in Publication Data.
A catalogue record of this book is available from the British Library.

Front cover: *The Resurrection of the Soldiers* (detail) on the East Wall at Sandham Memorial Chapel

Back cover: *Poppies*, 1938. Newark Town Council

p. 2 and 3: *Camp at Karasuli*, a panorama above the bay divisions on the North Wall at Sandham Memorial Chapel

p. 70 and 71: *Riverbed at Todorovo*, a panorama above the bay divisions on the South Wall at Sandham Memorial Chapel

Contents

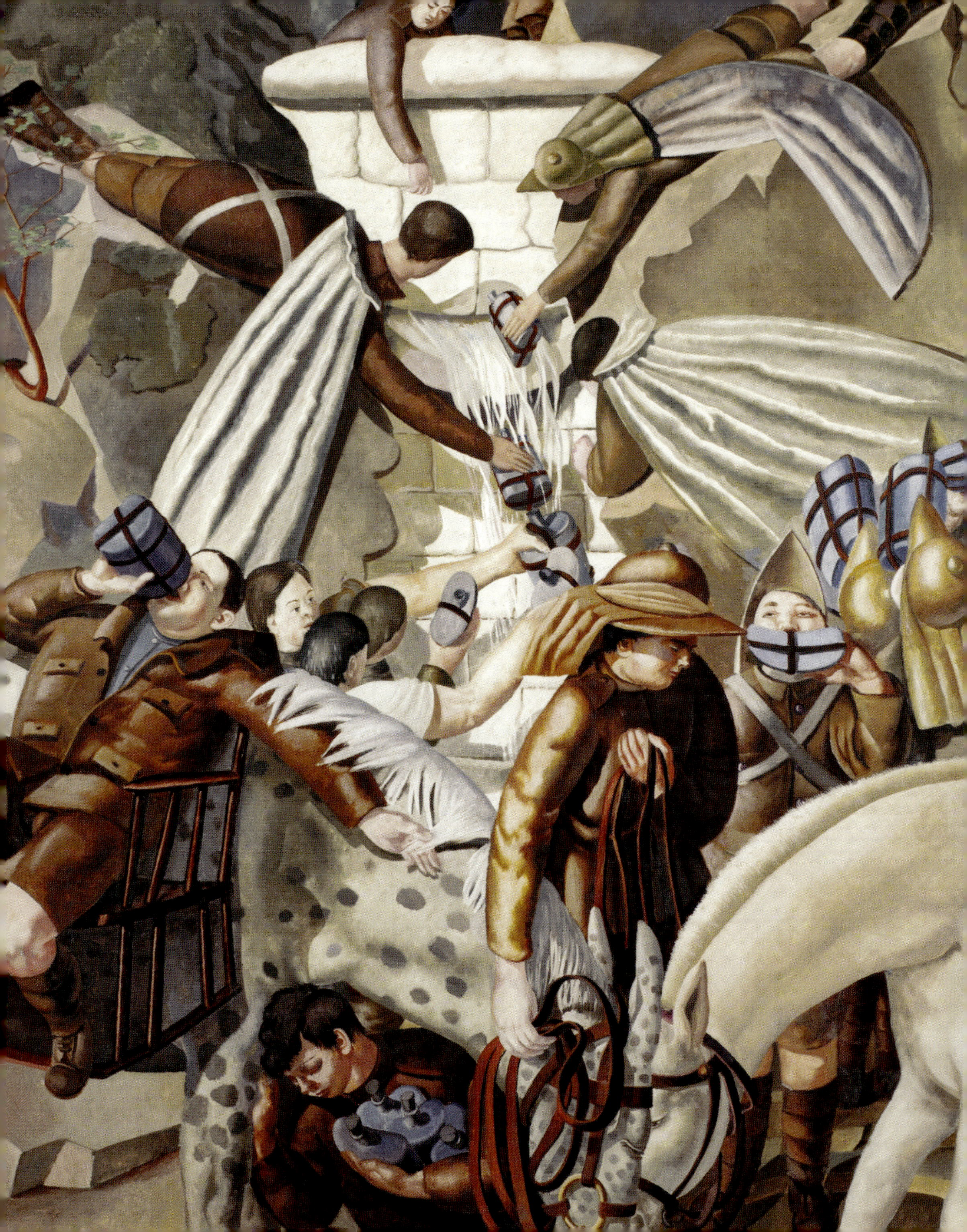

Foreword from the National Trust
Dame Helen Ghosh
Director-General

Sandham Memorial Chapel is a rarity amongst National Trust properties. The Trust looks after very little in the way of Modern British art, partly because families from large estates now in Trust ownership had little or no money to spare in inter- and post-war years to spend on what was then contemporary art. Notable exceptions are the Derek Hill collection at Mottisfont, examples at Dudmaston and Chartwell, and the *trompe l'oeil* murals by Rex Whistler at Plas Newydd. Stanley Spencer's canvases inside the chapel are arguably his greatest artistic achievement, and this jewel-like interior is exceptional in the history of Modern British art for both its form and content.

The National Trust relies on the generosity of donors and the public, and the gift of the chapel to the Trust in 1947, with an endowment, from its sponsors, John Louis and Mary Behrend, was an act of characteristic but exceptional generosity. We are delighted to be able to bring the canvases from the chapel to a wider audience, who might not otherwise be able to visit them *in situ* at Burghclere. Spencer himself requested that the canvases might be temporarily exhibited in London and was confident that they would 'blow the "Gallery" atmosphere to the four corners of the heavens'. We are extremely grateful to Gwyn Miles at Somerset House and Gregory Perry at Pallant House Gallery for enabling this exhibition to take place, and for all their colleagues who have brought the project to fruition.

The exhibition is the first of the Trust's commemorative events to mark the centenary of the beginning of the First World War. The Sandham canvases are based on Spencer's experiences of war, firstly in Bristol as a medical orderly, and later on the forgotten Macedonian front. The chapel was dedicated to Harry Sandham, who also served in Macedonia, but died from a war-related illness on his return.

The exhibition coincides with a major restoration of the fabric of the chapel and of the garden at Burghclere. The project will enable more visitors to enjoy what Spencer called the 'Holy Box' in perpetuity.

Filling Water-bottles (detail)
Sandham Memorial Chapel
(South Wall) See Cat. 12

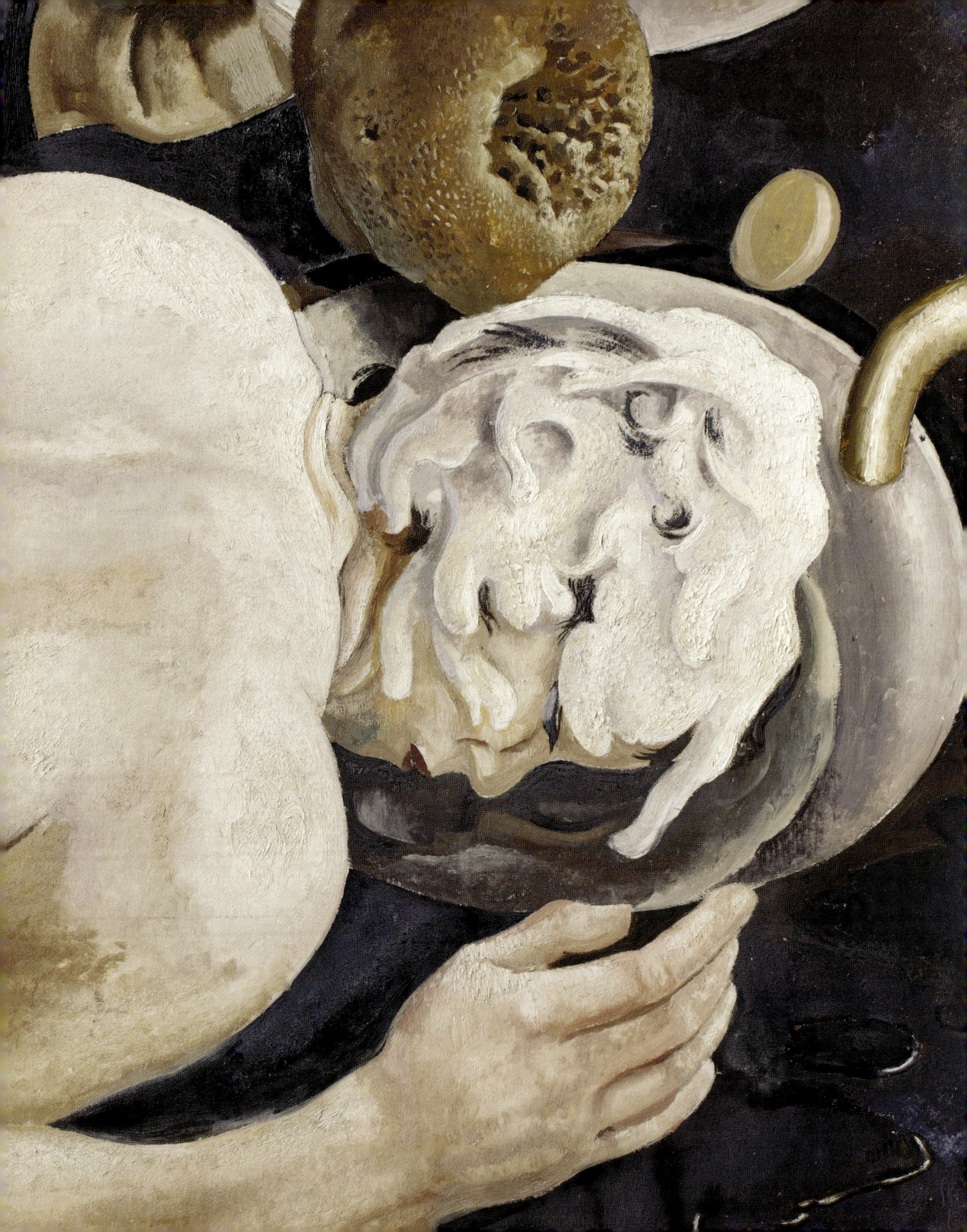

'That vile place': The Beaufort War Hospital, Bristol, as a Source of Inspiration for Stanley Spencer

Paul Gough

> *After the War I can see myself doing some strange things. It will be something like this – I arrive home, two days after get in a train for Bristol, get out at Bath, stand on the Railway platform & look towards a certain loathsome suburban church standing in the side of big hill. Take notes & get back into train. Get out at Bristol, on tram up to Fishponds. Go up a certain hill, a slummy street on left; small cottage, window-sill, on the windowsill earthenware animals & flower pots, on the other side of house small cottage garden on a steep slope, on opposite slope little orchard. Take notes and return to Cookham.*
> Stanley Spencer[1]

Today, a substantial stone reception lodge still stands at the gateway that first confronted Stanley Spencer as he entered the Beaufort War Hospital on an autumn day in 1915, having already enlisted in the Royal Army Medical Corps (RAMC). This was the 'male' entrance; the 'female' gate was further down Blackberry Hill. Across the lawns lay the sprawling conurbation of the military hospital, 'the Bristol Lunatic Asylum' as it had been known since it opened in 1861.[2]

Spencer's view would have been dominated by 'a mad looking tower'; under the daunting gaze of its four huge clock faces lay a solid two-storey administrative block covered in ivy creeper (Fig. 2).[3] Stemming from these central offices emerged two wings each linked by corridors and internal passageways: the west wing housed female residents, the east wing males. Transecting the wings at various points were the two-storey ward blocks, and in between them a warren of connecting corridors, verandas and loggias that enclosed large leafy squares and courtyards – known as 'airing courts' – where the inmates took their daily recreation. Spencer would spend much of his time in the hospital pushing trolleys and dragging loads the length of these never-ending corridors, often under the watchful eye of the non-commissioned officers who made much of his time so fearful.

Fig. 1
Ablutions (detail)
Sandham Memorial Chapel
(North Wall) See Cat. 3

Fig. 2
Beaufort War Hosptial exterior, *c.*1916
Glenside Museum, Bristol

Fig. 3
A group of RAMC non-commissioned officers, with RSM William Kench in the second row, third from the left, June 1916

Frequent attempts had been made to soften the appearance of the asylum: in 1902, 2,500 potted plants were supplied by the estate gardener to the wards; a further 4,000 plants were installed four years later and the grounds were planted with specimen trees including several unique grafts so favoured by late Victorian horticulturalists. In 1912 the asylum's Commissioners asked to see more pianos in the wards, and a year later central heating was extended to the male side. The building's design was equally enlightened: rather than install oppressive metal bars over the ground-floor windows, the architect Henry Crisp had designed windows with cast-iron glazing panes giving an outward impression of normality but with maximum security assured.[4]

Although the courtyard railings have long since been taken down and most of the metal-paned windows replaced, the old asylum can seem a grey and cheerless place. It must have appeared a chilling sight for the little-travelled and insular Spencer.

By the time he arrived in 1915, the asylum had undergone a major conversion.[5] Like many hospitals across the country it had been requisitioned by the War Office, which had demanded 15,000 beds to be supplied nationally for war wounded.

Forty-five asylum patients were retained to work the farm, the service departments and the kitchen garden, but the remaining 900 inmates were evacuated to rural asylums, some as far afield as Cornwall and Dorset.[6] Three months were spent converting the institution to house up to 1,460 wounded soldiers. Day rooms and night wards were converted into 24 medical and surgical wards. Corridors were made ready to take a further 180 emergency beds. Even the maximum-restraint cells – with their outward opening doors and steeply sloping window sills – were requisitioned for use. Throughout the asylum, rooms were adapted to act as operating theatres, radiography departments and pharmacy stations. Despite these significant alterations the hospital retained some of its pre-war character, and wartime photographs of the wards show them with large potted plants and ornate furnishings, though little could disguise the hard deal tables, the flagstone floors and the high windows with their cast-iron glazing bars. In one memorable photograph Spencer can be glimpsed – a diminutive, slightly dishevelled figure in an ill-fitting tunic – surrounded by long avenues of beds, each separated by large wooden lockers, those very same lockers that Spencer and his fellow orderlies had to spend so much time scrubbing.

Renamed 'The Beaufort War Hospital, for the general medical and surgical treatment of sick and wounded soldiers', many of the existing personnel were given new roles in the armed services. The Asylum Superintendent, Dr Blachford, became Lieutenant-Colonel RAMC, his horse-drawn cab replaced with a motor car. Physicians and surgeons arrived. A photograph shows the non-commissioned officers, including the heavily-built RSM Kench who quite terrified the diminutive Spencer (Fig. 3).

Spencer rarely encountered the officers. Orderlies, two to each ward, were at the very bottom of a complex nursing hierarchy – 'one-third housemaid, one-third waiter and one-third valet'.[7] They worked under the authoritarian – and unchallenged – command of ward sisters drawn from the Queen Alexandra's Imperial Military Nursing Service Reserve, supported by a cadre of nurses trained by the Red Cross. While no medical officer can be found on the walls of the Sandham Memorial Chapel at Burghclere, there are nurses in evidence: one appears in the canvas *Sorting the Laundry* (Cat. 6). She may be the former asylum matron, Miss Dunn, whom Spencer found to be less intimidating than many others. Perhaps because of this he associated the laundry – which was lit from above by roof lights – with a church-like atmosphere. Despite the bustle, the heat and the noise, Spencer enjoyed an unthreatened peace in the laundry, one of the few places where he could gain some personal composure in the teeming metropolis of the Beaufort.

Veterans of the Great War had little affection for the military hospitals: in letters and memoirs they complained of an inhumanity that seemed

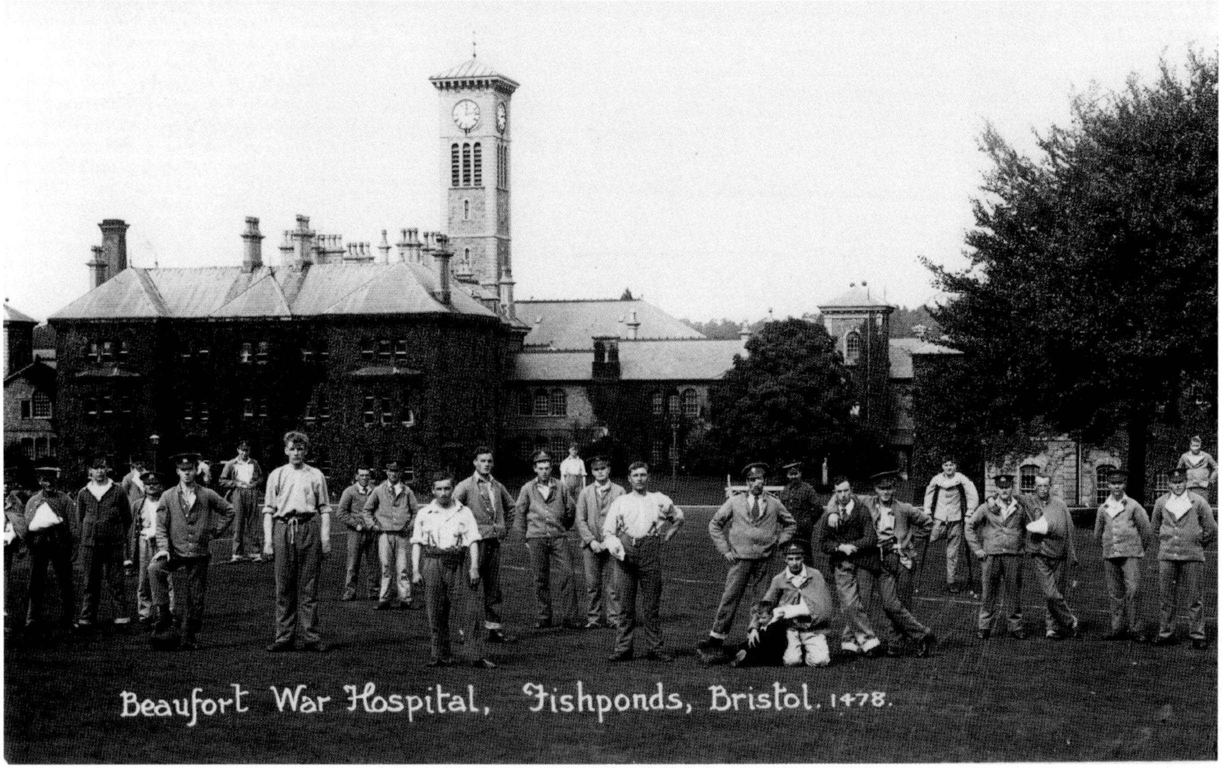
Beaufort War Hospital, Fishponds, Bristol. 1478.

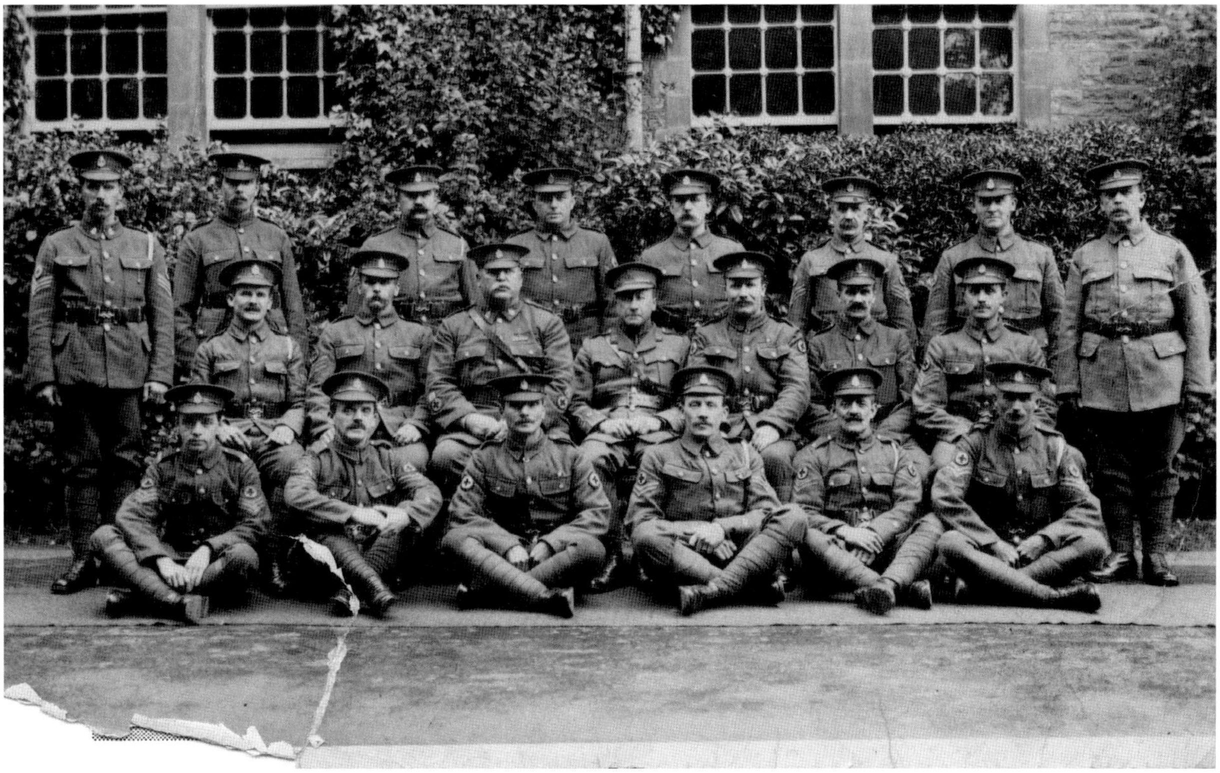

Fig. 4
Newly arrived wounded, Beaufort War Hospital, c.1916

to increase with distance from the battlefield. At the front, wounded soldiers were treated by fellow-combatants and by familiar regimental doctors. 'The wounded man,' recalled one soldier, 'is in a moment a little baby and all the rest become the tenderest of mothers. One holds his hand; another lights his cigarette. Before this, it is given to few to know the love of those who go together through the long valley of the shadow of death.'[8] All this changed in the rear of the battle zone and in the general hospitals back in 'Blighty'. Given the restrictions on wartime transport, their journey from the front might be surprisingly rapid. Spencer's brother, Gilbert, recalled his first terrifying moments as a medical orderly when he was confronted by a 'ward full of wounded Gallipoli soldiers, their skins sunburnt and their clothes bleached and the soil of Suvla Bay still on their boots' (Fig. 4).[9]

Of course, the military had no intention of making hospitals appear too comforting; the intention was to patch up the wounded and return them promptly to active duty. Convalescence was not to be enjoyed; for many it was sour recuperation in grim and loveless surroundings, remembered bitterly for 'Brutal injections ... People nearly crying with pain. Gloomy buildings with bathroom taps all loose and tied to the wall with string ... Meals never hot, worse than ordinary camp food and only served at strictly regulated times'.[10] There were a few diversions. Henry Williamson recollected: 'Months and months of pain and contentment: regular grub and fags, military band outside once a week, and sometimes a theatre, riding in a toff's car', though he also described '[t]he terrible silence of the white wards, the swish of felt slippers, the terrible white walls and crying, the strange white sheets and beds in a row'.[11]

In the paintings at Burghclere, Spencer suppressed the muffled agonies of the hospital. His letters, though, are testimony to the casual brutishness and the uneasy tension between the wounded and their non-combatant guardians, with their 'cushy' jobs and protected status. Duty back in the front line became something of a release from the petty regime, harsh treatment and frustrations of the military hospital.

Passing through the 'Gates of Hell' at Beaufort signalled a change in Spencer:

> *as soon as I had passed through that gate, and was walking down the drive, all my patriotic ardour, which I had struggled hard to retain, seemed again to leave me. A great clammy death seemed to be sitting or squatting on all my desires and hopes. Everything seemed so false. The day did not seem like day to me and the men did not belong to day. I felt that these beings, should they journey to where my home is, would evaporate into nothingness long before they got there.*[12]

Some 30 years later he recalled with characteristic clarity his initial miserable impressions of the hospital grounds:

> *Even the trees & laurel hedges were affected; they were so deadly ... had someone been around in the morning & dusted them with a duster? A cobweb had been missed here & there. The ground was hard and had a 'ring' of iron about it, the lamp-posts, sign-posts, railings & the trees seemed to be 'riveted' to the ground: a steel-like uniformity prevailed & naught could prevail against it.*[13]

Across a courtyard, along an interminable glazed veranda, through a wide corridor with very 'old-fashioned wall-paper', then into a ward decorated with reproductions from the Victorian *Pears' Annual*, more like a nursery than a military hospital, the weird incongruity persisted. Spencer encountered his new company: a merchant's handyman, an assistant from the booksellers, W.H. Smith, 'a great hulking man sprawling on the empty bed opposite me; a man who had come straight from a corn-merchant's yard, a man used to heavy outdoor work'.[14] Fascinated and appalled by his new circumstances, Spencer knew he was now trapped in a place for which he was utterly ill-prepared. Within weeks the Beaufort would shatter the stillness and unity of his pre-war enclosed 'Cookham' world, but in so

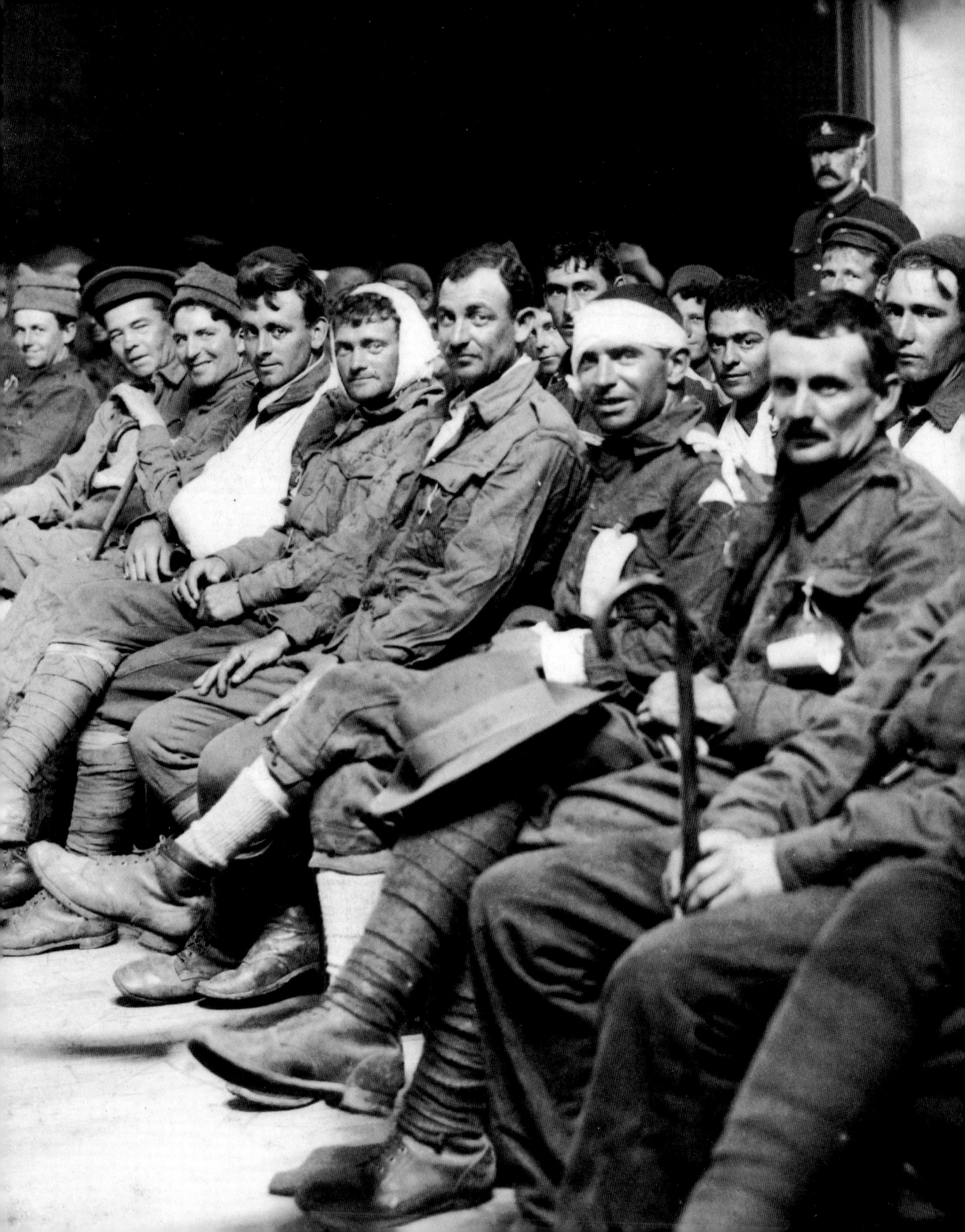

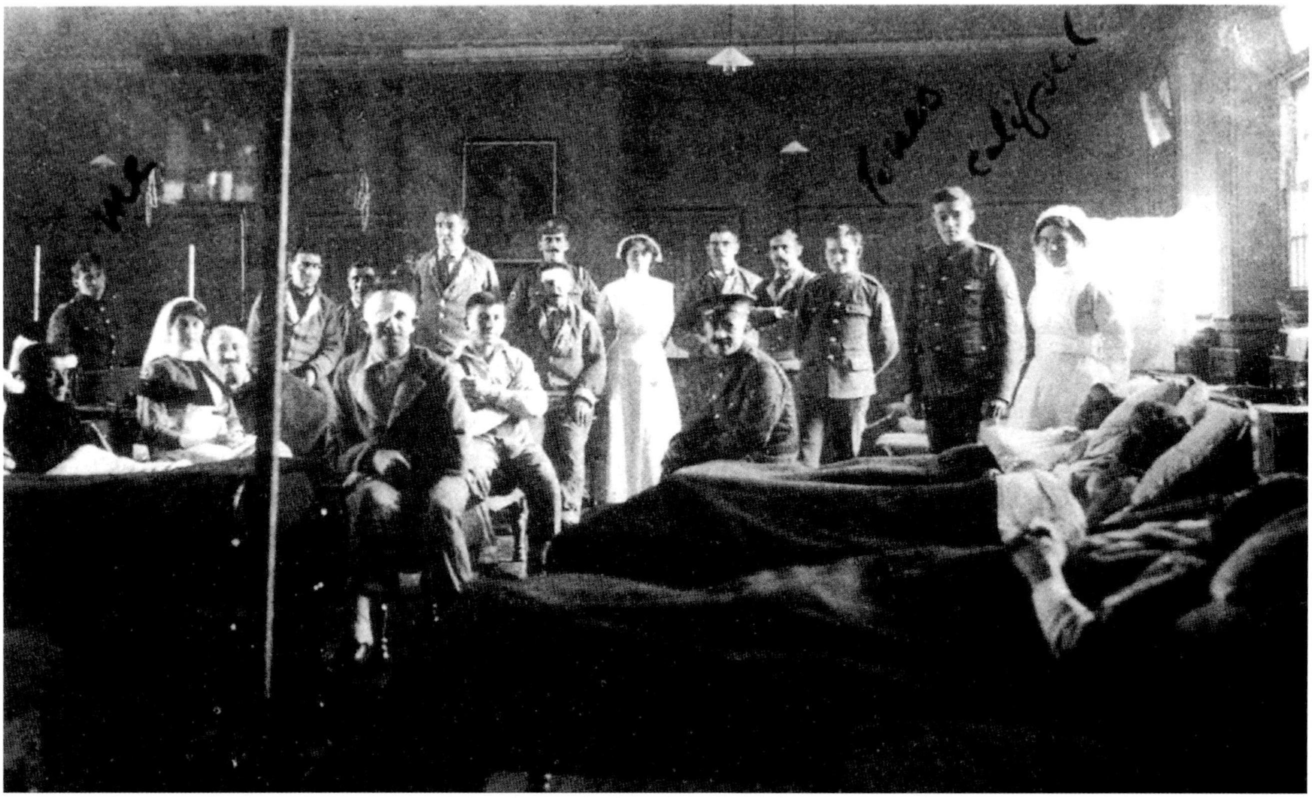

Fig. 5
Hospital Ward, Beaufort War Hospital, with Stanley Spencer on the extreme left, marked as 'me', *c.*1915
Glenside Museum, Bristol

doing would stimulate the enquiring and curious side of his mind that had remained dormant until that moment. With its 'innumerable unanalysable mental shocks'[15] it felt like a prison sentence:

> *It was a case of having discovered that we had each made some awful mistake and were in a trap, and the stupefied expression on each of our faces proclaimed this ... We had each to find our levels ... in our own way. It was a case of every man for himself, and this instinctive feeling produced an atmosphere at once of unfriendliness between us. We each became to each other a symbol of our own helplessness. This consciousness, as those minutes dragged on, of a growing estrangement, was terrible, and all this to be happening in a big room rather like in feeling to the coziness of one's own bedroom at home.*[16]

Despite this grim induction, the irrepressible and energetic Spencer soon found his feet. Drawing on his natural ebullience and his incorrigible interest in everything around him, his second day found him in better spirits:

> *I had to scrub out the Asylum Church. It was a splendid test of my feelings about this war. But I still feel the necessity of this war, & I have seen some sights, but not what one might expect. The lunatics are good workers & one persists in saluting us & always with the wrong hand. Another one thinks he is an electric battery.*[17]

Fetching and carrying, cleaning and scrubbing (always on his hands and knees, always with the brick-like blocks of 'Monkey Brand' soap) were the daily lot for Spencer. From reveille at 05:00 his long working day was spent in and around the Male Infirmary (M.I.) Wards 4A and 4B where once male inmates had been treated for physical illnesses. Each ward had a dayroom – the 'A' section, its walls covered in wallpaper and framed pictures – and a dormitory, the 'B' section. Throughout the asylum's long war service both sections were crammed with beds (Fig. 5):

Seeing the patients in beds that were nearly on a level with one's eyes when seen through the door from 4A ward gave M.I. ward a feeling of looking into a chancel (usually a little up from the nave) ... 4B was a bigger, darker & rather more convincing ward than M.I. ... 4A was a long corridor ward with innumerable cubicles opening into it ... I rather liked this 4B ward about 3.30 in the afternoon, which was the time when I usually took the dressing drums down to the polished steriliser somewhere at the end of a stone passage right over in the other wing of the hospital. When I started up this ward on this long journey I felt like some engine of a long train when starting to glide out of Paddington on a non-stop Irish Mail via Fishguard journey. Somehow I felt exhilarated that there would be no stops, & peace at each end.[18]

Spencer committed these sensations deep into his memory. Many years later, he was able to recall the asylum's minor details – the width of the stripes in the 'old-fashioned wallpaper', the sheen of an enamel bowl, the pattern on a counterpane, the fall of light on painted tiles – though he was never quite sure why he was able to do so. In his wartime diary he surmised that 'at the most important moments of my life I generally remember the least important facts'.[19] Under the pressure of personal survival, facts – the pictorial nouns of his art – had assumed a primacy over feeling. Allowed to marinate during the months and years of active service that followed, this ability to recollect the minutiae of the hospital would enrich the imaginary narrative of the Burghclere panels. In one of the predella panels, *Washing Lockers* (Cat. 17), Spencer recalled the vivid colours of the cavernous washroom – 'six baths, about twenty hand basins, and a huge acreage of floor'[20] – where 'the baths were a deep sort of magenta colour and shiny, and when you had a row of them end-view on, they looked marvellous'.[21] Spencer's recollection of surface and texture is quite astonishing, the passage of paint describing the coarse sacking of the aprons a tour de force, enriched by dense personal associations:

whenever I had been frequently in a particular place employed on some job, I would become so in harmony with the place and the job, it being regular, that at last I would discover happy, homely places in the most unlikely places. There, only to mentally place myself between these baths and be scrubbing the floor is at once to feel inspired.[22]

The washrooms, wards and corridors of the Beaufort furnished Spencer with an infinite taxonomy of pictorial forms. Invariably he had little problem dredging them from his wartime memory, despite the fact that he drew relatively little when based in the hospital. Effortlessly, he could recollect the enamel finish of the circular basins or the limp angles of the cold-water copper taps in the washrooms, the dull gleam of a floor under one of the verandas or the pliable surface of a hot-water bottle, but on occasion his recall failed him: 'I sat there, George, for half an hour trying to think what a sponge looked like, but it was no good. I had to go home and get mine.'[23] In the panel *Ablutions* (Cat. 3), the painted sponge is an extraordinary thing: beautifully described, it hovers in mid-air, seeming to float free of all physical attachment, except as an element in Spencer's memory. Possibly few other British painters of the last century have had such an understanding of the exact identity of inanimate objects. Peter Burra, one of the many visitors to the chapel as it was being painted, described Spencer's ability to bring out the uniqueness of things as like a lover's overpowering declaration of love for everything they saw in their partner or, in their absence, in their belongings. It was an intense, quite blinkered declaration that would brook no vagueness: it required (and invariably received) absolute clarity of visual expression. Indeed, Spencer himself believed that 'To see anything imaginatively is to see a thing for the first time'.[24]

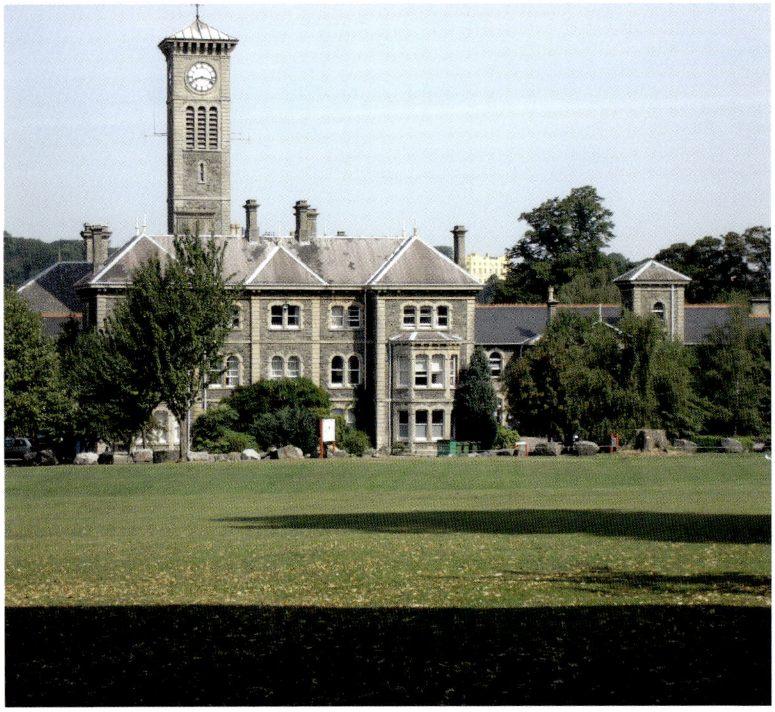

Fig. 6
The Beaufort War Hospital today, as UWE Bristol Faculty of Health and Applied Sciences, Glenside

Perhaps this explains the almost unique strangeness of Spencer's personal vision. He tried to capture objects in paint through the fullest absorption of every thing 'into' himself. This was coupled with the recognition that the absolute identity of things – sheets, sponge, towels, taps, iron gates – was paramount because in that self-identity they were revealed to him as the 'Forms chosen by God'.

A common eye would have missed, overlooked and neglected the everyday things that became the spiritual nouns – the 'burning bushes' – of Spencer's pictorial vocabulary. The Beaufort War Hospital teemed with such evocations, indeed it still does to this day (Fig. 6). Eric Newton expressed deep admiration for Spencer's ability to proclaim and reclaim the distinct value of objects – whether it be a sponge, chair, kitbag, watch-chain or length of barbed-wire. Yet it was not just the ability to copy or reproduce distant objects with unnerving clarity; it was Spencer's expression of them as 'authentic fragments of autobiography'.[25] Kitty Hauser understood how he was capable of absorbing the very being of an object, its physiognomy, or the essentials of a gesture or a sense of place, and capture its internal equivalence. It might lie dormant for decades waiting for Spencer to retrieve (indeed 'resurrect') its essence in a drawing or a painting.[26]

At the chapel at Burghclere, Spencer aimed to reconcile past and present through the act of pictorial reunification – a kitbag is reunited with its owner, an item of laundry with its wearer, a key for a gate, the quarter-master and his blankets, a resurrected soldier returning his cross. The murals are a hymn in paint to redemption and reconciliation, where the miraculous and commonplace are synergistic, the narrative 'a mixture of an ordinary circumstance with a spiritual happening'.[27]

Yet there was one final, and curious, element that Spencer left wholly unreconciled. Behind the altar-stone in the chapel, out of view to all but the most inquisitive visitor, Spencer painted a single beam of stone a yard long, lying on its side, a solitary rectilinear column of whiteness that rests somewhat forlornly at the foot of the great pile of crosses. Neither cruciform nor easily seen by the passing eye, what is it meant to represent? Is it – like the notch carved out of one of the larger crosses over the altar – an emblem of imperfection, a small piece of Spencer's heaven-on-earth that would never be realised? Could this single beam of stone be a reference to Stanley himself, whose own cross could not have been fully formed as he was one of the survivors? Or maybe it is a sad reflection of his own loss of vision, his exhaustion after a decade of working with the memory of the war, another memento mori sent to remind us that, although the soldiers may have gained their individual redemption, Spencer would carry the weight of the Beaufort, Bristol and the Balkans long after he had left Burghclere. [28]

Notes

Spencer first made a record of his war experience in 1919 (held in the Tate Archive as TGA 733.3.28). This draft formed the basis of a notebook written as he developed his ideas for the Oratory at Burghclere (TGA 733.3.84). The notebook was typed up in 1948 (TGA 733.3.85). A section was later added to this typescript (TGA 733.3.128).

1 Stanley Spencer to Florence Spencer, 27 June 1918, TGA 756.4 (the typescript of these letters is TGA 733.1.753).
2 See Donald Early, *'The Lunatic Pauper Palace': Glenside Hospital Bristol, 1861–1994: Its Birth, Development and Demise*, Friends of Glenside Hospital Museum, Bristol, 2003; see also Paul Gough, *Stanley Spencer: Journey to Burghclere*, Samson & Co., Bristol, 2006.
3 Stanley Spencer, 'Account', 1918, TGA 733.3.83.
4 Recreational activities at the asylum – and later while it was renamed the Beaufort War Hospital – included concerts, amateur dramatics and dances. The archive at the Glenside Hospital Museum, Bristol, contains several photographs of such events.
5 Initially, only 520 beds were required in Bristol for war wounded; 260 of these were to come from the Bristol Royal Infirmary; Southmead Hospital offered a similar number in its newly built wards. As casualties mounted these numbers had to increase, but the 1,460 beds provided at the Beaufort were the largest single contribution made by the city.
6 After the Armistice the vast number of the inmates returned from their evacuation to Bristol.
7 Lyn Macdonald, *The Roses of No Man's Land*, Michael Joseph, London, 1980, p.150. Spencer wrote in one letter, 'sweep wash & give bedpans 5 o'clock to 8 in the evening'. He added, 'I would give anything to belong to the Royal Berkshires' (TGA 8116.55).
8 Josiah Wedgwood, *Essays and Adventures of a Labour MP*, HMSO, London, 1924.
9 Gilbert Spencer, *Stanley Spencer by His Brother Gilbert*, Gollancz, London, 1961, p.137.
10 Arthur Graeme West, *The Diary of a Dead Officer*, Herald, London, 1918. Not for nothing were the RAMC sometimes known to front-line soldiers as 'Rob All My Comrades'. Denis Winter suggests that the tension was due largely to the unexpressed guilt felt by the orderlies. Denis Winter, *Death's Men: Soldiers of the Great War*, Penguin, Harmondsworth, 1987, p.202.
11 Henry Williamson, *The Patriot's Progress*, Geoffrey Blies, London, 1930, pp.189–91.
12 Stanley Spencer, 'Reminiscences', Glasgow, 1944, TGA 733.3.86, in Richard Carline, *Stanley Spencer at War*, Faber and Faber, London, 1978, pp.50–51.
13 'Reminiscences', TGA 733.3.86.
14 Notebook/diary, 1915–18, TGA 733.3.83.
15 Notebook, 1944–5, TGA 733.3.85.
16 'Reminiscences', TGA 733.3.86.
17 Stanley Spencer to Jacques and Gwen Raverat, July/August 1915, TGA 8116.54.
18 'Reminiscences', TGA 733.3.86.
19 Notebook/diary, 1915–18, 733.3.83.
20 Gilbert Spencer 1961, p.139.
21 Stanley Spencer to Richard Carline, ?1928, in Carline 1978, p.182.
22 Stanley Spencer to Richard Carline, 1929, in Carline 1978, p.182.
23 George Behrend, *Stanley Spencer at Burghclere*, Macdonald, London, 1965, p.8.
24 TGA 733.2.3. Peter James Salkeld Burra left a short typescript that relates his experience of the chapel as it neared completion in the early 1930s. Given the title 'Spencer's Oratory' by Richard Thompson of the Burra-Moody Archive, a copy is held at the Sandham Memorial Chapel. Though Burra writes with great beauty and insight, Spencer's voice is also clear throughout.
25 Eric Newton, *Stanley Spencer* (Penguin Modern Painters), Penguin, Harmondsworth, 1947, p.9.
26 For a fuller exposition on the phenomenology of equivalence see Kitty Hauser, *Stanley Spencer*, exh. cat., Tate, London, 2001, pp.73–4.
27 Stanley Spencer to Richard Carline, 1928, in Carline 1978, p.184.
28 So exacting was Spencer about the architectural detail of the chapel that as late as 1933 he was still fussing about small aspects of the design, writing to Mary Behrend in January 1933 that he still wanted a painted line to be added to the surface of the dado rail in lieu of a groove that could not now be cut into the plaster: 'The grooves or lines divide the six feet widths of the predella picture into seven spaces.' Stanley Spencer to Mary Behrend, 16 January 1933, TGA 882.8. See 'The Holy Box' in Gough 2006, p.196.

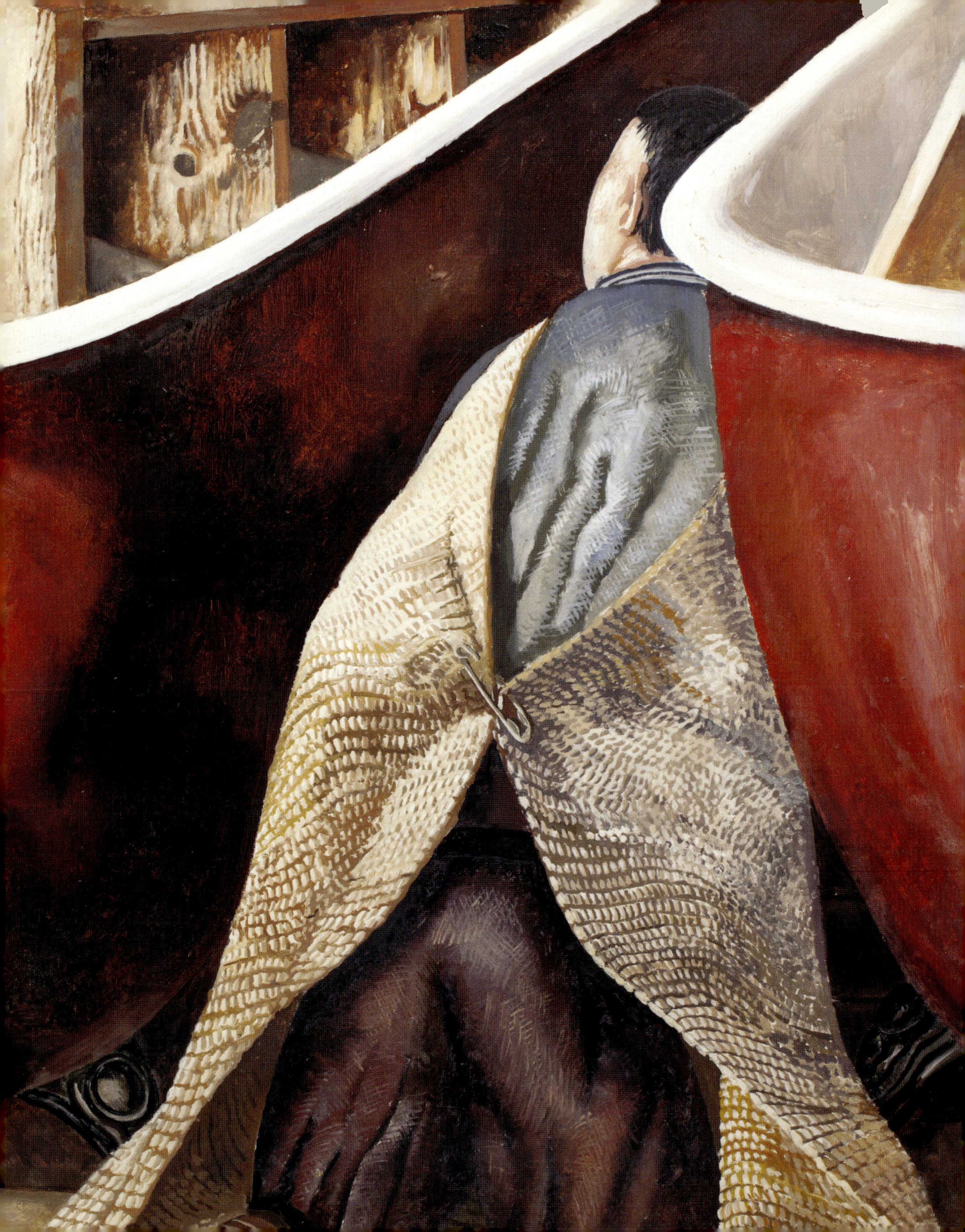

The Reluctant Maecenases: John Louis and Mary Behrend

Amanda Bradley

England has been described – provocatively and not wholly accurately – as a nation that is 'mingy' in recognising the value of its own artists.[1] There is some truth, however, that during Stanley Spencer's *fleurissement*, and that of his contemporaries – Paul Nash, C.R.W. Nevinson and Mark Gertler, amongst others – new English artists were encouraged to look abroad, namely to Paul Cézanne and his disciples, for their inspiration and lead. In the second *Post Impressionist Exhibition* of 1912, the 18-year-old Spencer's *John Donne Arriving in Heaven* was hung alongside Henri Matisse and Pablo Picasso. It was an extraordinary coup and a privilege, but Spencer later fell out with Roger Fry and Clive Bell, the exhibition organisers and the main proponents of 'significant form'. Spencer himself was riled that 'lovers of French art were such philistines about mine', and was furious that the Earl of Sandwich should chatter about his recent acquisition of a Post-Impressionist picture in front of the Sandham Memorial Chapel *Resurrection* (Cat. 9).[2]

The Behrends – John Louis (1881–1972) and Mary (1883–1977) – were resolute in their support of British artists (Figs 2 and 3). They were part of – and yet, as we shall see, distinct from – a group of usually non-Establishment figures who were seminal in the cultivation of inter-war artists. They were charming, hospitable, generous to a fault and highly attuned to the needs and foibles of the artist at work. In the introduction to the sale of some 63 pictures from their collection at the Leicester Galleries, London, in 1962, the critic Eric Newton wrote a paean to their taste and singularity as collectors.[3] He argued that they were neither patrons (for they were not 'self-conscious benefactors') nor collectors (for they were not conscious of their possessions), but simply bought 'what they liked. And liking, for them, was hardly distinguishable from loving ... their instinct for quality and excellence was and still is, unerring.'[4] Newton cites the Sandham Memorial Chapel, at the Behrends home at Burghclere, as 'one of the bravest and most enlightened acts of patronage that ever happened

Fig 1.
Washing Lockers (detail)
Sandham Memorial Chapel
(South Wall) See Cat. 17

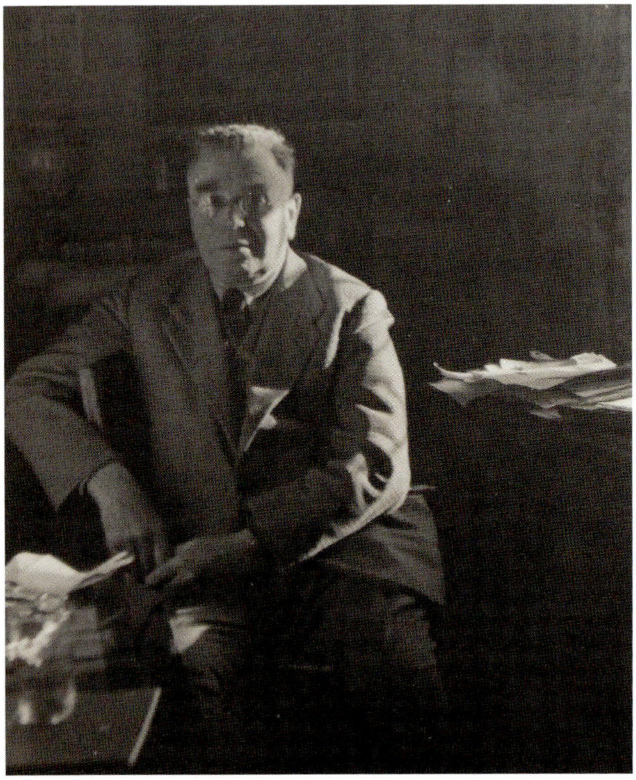

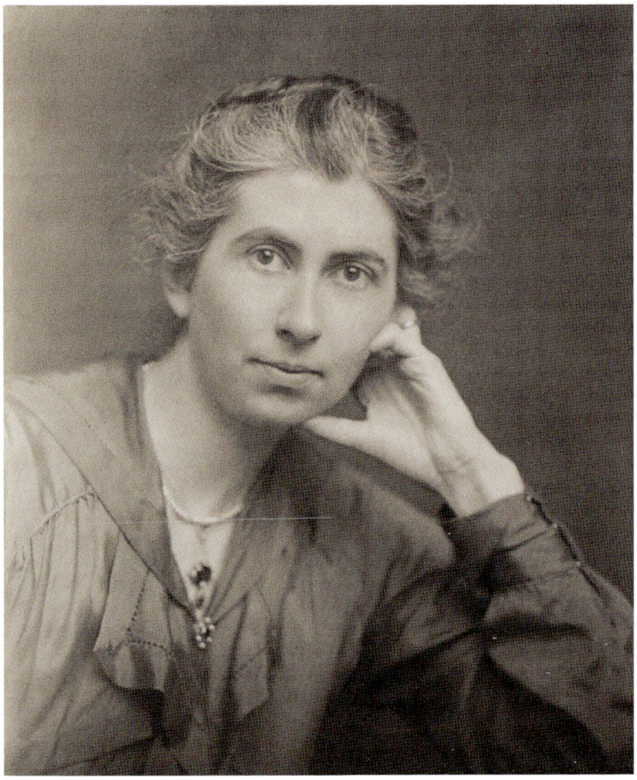

Fig. 2
Photograph of J.L. Behrend, date unknown
The Behrend Collection, National Trust archive

Fig. 3
Photograph of Mary Behrend, date unknown
The Behrend Collection, National Trust archive

to an artist', and yet the Behrends have been largely forgotten, in favour of some of the more self-publicising and ebullient patrons of the time.[5] Eardley Knollys, one-time regional representative of the National Trust (recruited by James Lees-Milne), an artist himself and instrumental in the Trust's acquisition of the chapel, was furious at the lack of recognition when Mary Behrend died at the age of 94. 'Both had been ignored all their lives', he stormed.[6] An article about them had been published in *Country Life* in 1978,[7] but this was after both their deaths; and although Knollys had opined that neither had been given an obituary, they both had indeed appeared in the obituaries section of *The Times* (Mary's written by Peter Pears).[8] Moreover, the Courtauld Institute, during the directorship of Anthony Blunt, had wanted to give a reception in their honour in 1970, but due to their age and frailty, this proposal had lapsed. Nevertheless, they have never quite been granted the credit they are due (something they neither courted, nor probably wanted). Their obituaries appeared against the expressed wishes of their son, George, who did not want to have to deal with letters of condolence. This complicated and rather bitter man further clouded their legacy in his autobiography, which continually accuses them of disliking children (notably their own) and blames his own impoverishment on their cultivation of the arts, and, in particular, Stanley Spencer. 'My pram was probably the most expensive ... possible to buy in 1922, being pre-Stanley Spencer Chapel (which took all the money)' is a characteristic, self-pitying lament.[9] He was, however, acutely sensitive to contemporary criticism of Spencer's work and, in particular, his familial association with the chapel. When Kenneth Clark gave a lecture at the Aldeburgh Festival, with which George Behrend helped, some of his slides were burnt by the heat of the projector. Such was Behrend's paranoia that he felt Clark blamed him, purely because 'he disliked Spencer and everyone to do with him'.[10] George Behrend's inept and selectively truthful autobiography is, however, useful in providing biographical information on his family – information that needs to be read with a critical eye, but is otherwise scarce. Behrend money was made primarily from dealing in cotton seed in Egypt, chartering ships on the Baltic Exchange in London and milling rice. The company had been founded as B. & D. Behrend by John Louis' father and uncle, who hadn't been born wealthy, but had been driven, in particular, by John's Uncle Bernard, who was a talented trader and dealer. The family were Orthodox Jews, John Louis' mother having been born into a wealthy Portuguese Jewish family; originally from Hanover, they arrived in England in 1855.

John Louis was something of a bon viveur, whose enjoyment of the arts led to his introduction to Mary Sandham at a party given by the patron and hostess Lady Ottoline Morrell.[11] Mary was not well-off and came from a family of devout High Church Anglicans, who had served in the British Army for generations. She had been christened Phyllis Mary, but detested her name almost as much as her future husband detested the name Louis, to the extent that he changed his name to John by deed poll in around 1909. John Louis was promptly packed off to Egypt by his uncle in order to learn the family trade, such was his concern that his nephew might fall in love with a gentile. When he was allowed back home in 1910 he was 28, and promptly married Mary in a registry office, witnessed by their friends Henry and Annie Game, who hosted a small party at their house afterwards. The bridal couple then returned to their respective homes and spent their wedding night apart. This religious intermarriage was less of a concern to Mary's family since John converted to Christianity and, perhaps more pertinently, was rather wealthy.

By 1915 John Louis had joined the Mounted Infantry to escape from the London office of the family firm and Uncle Bernard. On the death of his father and uncle, he inherited only a fraction of the family business. The Behrends were smarting from his defection; half the business went to his mother, the other half being split between his two sisters and himself. In 1918, they bought Grey House in Burghclere, which became the family home for 36 years and a gathering point for their many artistically minded friends, of diverse disciplines, that they had made. Set against a backdrop of walls densely packed with paintings, they hosted the likes of Benjamin Britten, Peter Pears, Henry Lamb, the playwright St John Irvine, Marie Rambert, Eric Newton, Jean Inglis, as well as, of course, Stanley Spencer. The Behrends were a source of friendship and support – both financial and moral – to numerous artists throughout their lives. The highly acclaimed embroiderer, and Walter Sickert pupil, Madeleine Clifton was a long-term friend, who created the embroidered altar frontal for the chapel. Embellished with words from *The Tempest* and the New Testament (John 2:25), it is a deceptively modest piece with powerful spirituality. When Marie Rambert was faced with the closure of her theatre at the outbreak of the Second World War, rehearsals were immediately accommodated on the terrace at Grey House.

The Behrends were also supporters of Henry Lamb (see David Taylor's essay in this catalogue). He wrote of them to Ottoline Morrell: 'they are faithful generous, undemonstrative ... They are very nice. She is dark and pleasantly featured, lively, naive and sincere, but not striking in any way. The man is thick and curly haired also dark but reserved and rather intelligent and very nice. Both very young.'[12] Mary had commissioned from Lamb a portrait of Benjamin Britten, which their son, George, later sold to the composer. Britten was a close friend of the family, who acknowledged their generosity in his diaries, noting that they were 'cultured people who have done a tremendous amount to help artists'.[13] They had met him in the late 1920s, and again Grey House was offered to him as a quiet refuge for composing – a period which was seminal to his development. Mary Behrend had a particularly close relationship with Britten, almost akin to a 'sympathetic and civilised surrogate mother'.[14] Like Spencer, Britten corresponded principally with her, rather than with John Louis. Mary commissioned one piece of music from Britten, the Second String Quartet, Op.36, the manuscript of which he gave to her in 1945. Tragically, she destroyed this – along with much other material – later in her life.

It must have been refreshing for Spencer to have such musically minded benefactors. He had a strong musical background; his father was a music teacher and played the organ in Cookham church – an ability he passed on not only to Stanley, but also to one of his brothers, who was regarded a prodigy. Stanley was very accomplished at the piano and was passionate about Bach in particular. When he played on the nursery piano at the Martineaus' home (see below) he would linger over a chord saying, 'you hear that? ... and that?', spoken with such conviction that the children had thought he had composed the music himself.[15] He was even a member of the 143rd Ambulance Glee Club during the First World War.[16] His friendships were often born of a mutual love of music: Desmond Chute and Lionel Budden (later a world authority on Serbian folk songs), whom he met at the Beaufort War Hospital, were such men. It can be no coincidence that the chapel itself has been viewed in musical terms. Spencer's daughter, Shirin, commented on her father's innate understanding of music 'from the inside', and considered Burghclere 'fugal, with the cross being a fugal theme'.[17] Indeed, even to the musically illiterate, the rhythms of paint and form resonate throughout the space.

Undoubtedly the Behrends found creative genius exciting and alluring. They also had vision. After seeing Spencer's wash drawings pinned to the wall in Henry Lamb's house in Poole in 1923 they 'had a regular fret to get them realised', recognising the bold originality that was Spencer's own.[18] For the Behrends the artistic impetus was Spencer's, and it was very much his project: 'It infuriates us to see it [the chapel] as having been commissioned ... he had this thing complete in his head for so many years ... the whole thing was his idea.'[19] Such selflessness and such passion for the artistic process must surely be rare in any patron; they were as indulgent and as nurturing as any loving parent.

The Behrends were also generous to a fault. They tried to involve others in the building of the chapel (purpose-built on Stanley's insistence), even calling upon – unsuccessfully – the former Liberal Prime Minister, Herbert Asquith. When they finally committed in September 1923 (although Spencer was not able to start painting the walls for another four years), they were on their own, funding a project that cost them some £8,000.[20] They were not so wealthy as they had been in 1918 and Stanley realised that they were only comfortably off.[21] When one day a formidable woman looking round the chapel said to him, 'It smells of money here, doesn't it?', he answered, 'No, only courage.'[22] However, by the 1930s, feeling hard-up, he was already complaining that Mary wouldn't buy one of his portraits.[23] In a more flush moment, in 1955, he wrote to Mary suggesting that the proceeds of his BBC programme could go towards the upkeep of the chapel; he fulfilled this a year later, when he sent a 'rather small donation' to John Louis, in the hope that he would be able to send another (he adds, in typical Spencer-esque humour, that he looks 'pretty ghastly' in the film and that it is a bit 'crematorium-ish').[24]

It was, therefore, a relationship founded on mutual understanding and give-and-take. Certainly, this wavered at times; Spencer could be self-obsessed, and although supported by his family and the family help, Elsie Munday, it was an overwhelming project, with the added pressure, later on, of personal traumas. The smallest slight would smart; John Louis playfully called him a 'stick-in-the-mud' for wanting to return to Cookham – a comment that not only smarted, but mocked the sanctity of Cookham.[25] There were also moments of ingratitude: 'It is odd the way that neither the Behrends nor any of my London supporters, my usual patrons, never believed in the way of loving my own wishes regarding myself.'[26] This self-projection manifested itself in his hijacking of the entire chapel project, which the Behrends bore with astounding good grace. There exists a draft letter from Spencer, intended for John Louis Behrend, but probably never sent.[27] Although not specifically stated, Spencer refers to the heraldic plaque in the chapel, erected by the Behrends in memory of Henry Willoughby Sandham (known as Harry or Hal), Mary's brother who had died in 1920 from an illness contracted whilst on active service in Macedonia. Spencer had obviously not been consulted, and although the Behrends were quite justified in doing whatever they wished with the chapel, the baroque modelling and gilt embellishment of the shield admittedly jars with both the architecture and the painted interior. Spencer wrote: 'If you had been intending or had previously told me you were going to erect a huge equestrian statue of the Duke of Wellington in the centre of the room do you suppose that in thinking out the scheme I would not have had to take that into consideration?' He laments that the character of the shield is aggressive, compared to the 'essentially pacific' nature of his pictures.

Moreover, Spencer's involvement extended beyond the painted decoration of the chapel, and into the architectural planning. The Behrends' close friend, the architect George Kennedy (also a close friend of Henry Lamb), was soon ousted in favour of Lionel Pearson at Spencer's behest. Kennedy's plan, which included a narthex, was deemed too fussy – Spencer wanted a 'Holy Box'. The Behrends owned a portrait of Kennedy and his family by Lamb, which hung in the smoking room at Grey House, but after the chapel debacle they never spoke to Kennedy again. Pearson, architect of the monumental memorial to the Royal Artillery in Hyde Park, also fell foul of Spencer's architectural aspirations.[28] His artistic visualisation of space did not always translate architecturally, resulting in numerous uneasy compromises. The dado and the form of barrel vaulting became a notable source of contention, resulting in scores of illustrated letters (including that owned by the National Trust, dated 23 November 1925; Fig. 5). 'I suppose however that we had better give way to Stanley – though it pulls both ways to do so', wrote Mary Behrend in 1930 – it was a philosophy that had informed their relationship throughout the chapel project.[29]

The Behrends suppressed any private doubts ultimately because 'he believed in us and we believed in him'.[30] They were proud that there was no contract, written or otherwise; the whole project – the cost of which soared beyond their means – was based on trust.

The respect was mutual, and in the 1920s Spencer worked on a series of separate scenes for the chapel acknowledging the Behrends. One of them shows Stanley's wife Hilda looking at a cardboard model of the chapel (Fig. 4). One suspects that Mary was the driving force of the couple, and perhaps the more approachable, evidenced by the many letters from Spencer to her. He even sent her a cutting of a cartoon from the *Evening Standard* with a send-up of his *Saint Francis and the Birds*.[31] Mary acknowledged that '46 years is a long time to have stayed friendly', and it is true that Spencer tended to form strong relationships with nurturing figures such as the Raverats and the Martineaus. He seemed to look for, and need, this quasi-parental nourishment, and his intense friendships (with the likes of Henry Lamb and Desmond Chute) that did not contain or sustain this element tended to fade.

However close Spencer may have been to the Behrends, he probably failed to grasp the complexity of their religious background. He was creating an Anglican chapel, but the familial, religious and financial implications of this were significant for John Louis, and were undoubtedly a source of tension; George Behrend described their Jewish heritage as 'the No.1 skeleton in the cupboard'.[32] None of the Behrend side of the family was at the dedication – John Louis's mother, Rachael (always known as 'Bamma'), would have been particularly appalled. However, neither was Spencer, whose own brand of religion was deemed sufficiently idiosyncratic to offend the Bishop of Guildford, who officiated. He believed in God and was an ardent Bible-reader, but it was a shock to him to find 'how little my Faith has stood in my stead to help me' during the war.[33] Paul Gough has argued that war had made the concept of a personal God difficult for Spencer and indeed, for him, the joy of religion and God was found in biblical narrative and the everyday things that he loved.[34] His confused religious identity was, therefore, perhaps singularly appropriate for a converted Jew.

At a late stage in the project it was decided that the chapel should be dedicated to Harry Sandham.[35] He died of a ruptured spleen,

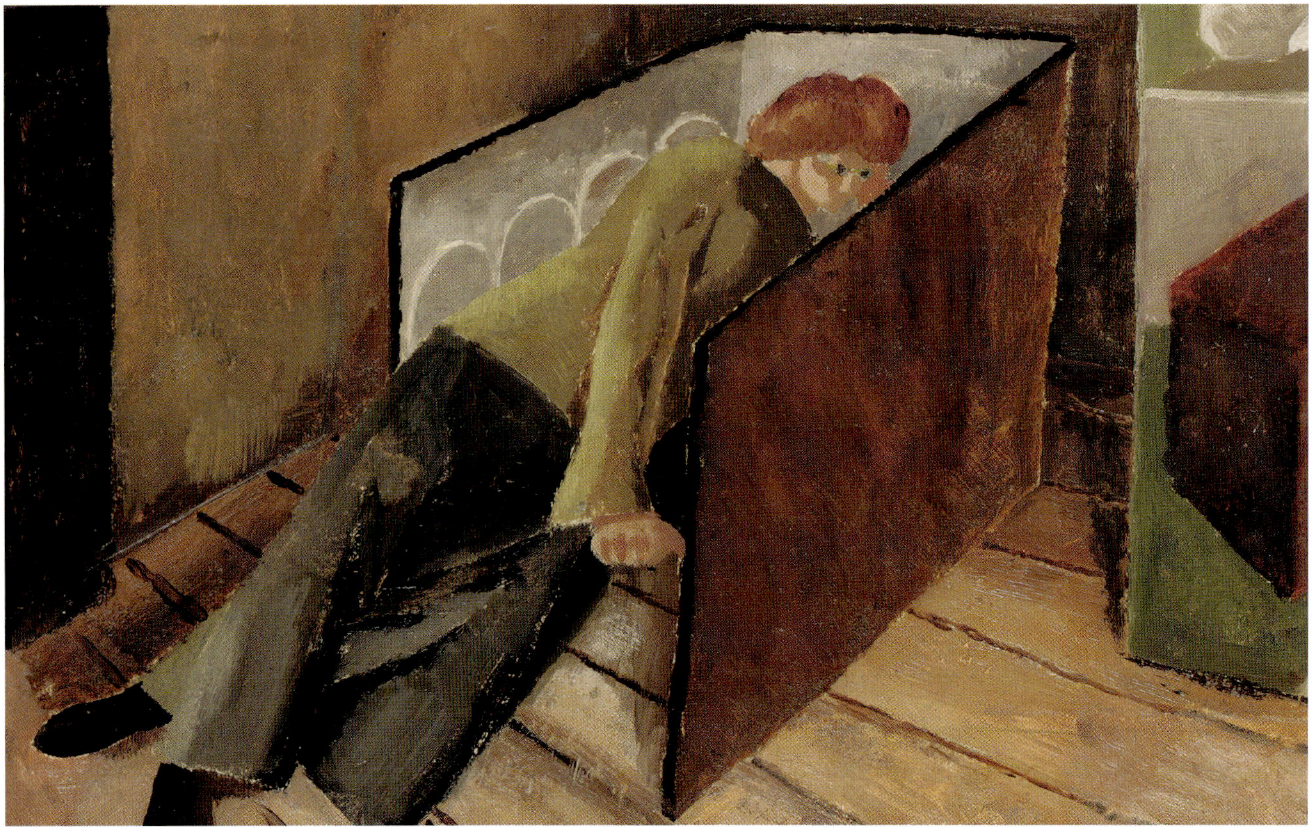

Fig. 4
Hilda Studying a Model for Burghclere, c.1930
Oil on paper
Collection of Catherine and William MacDougall

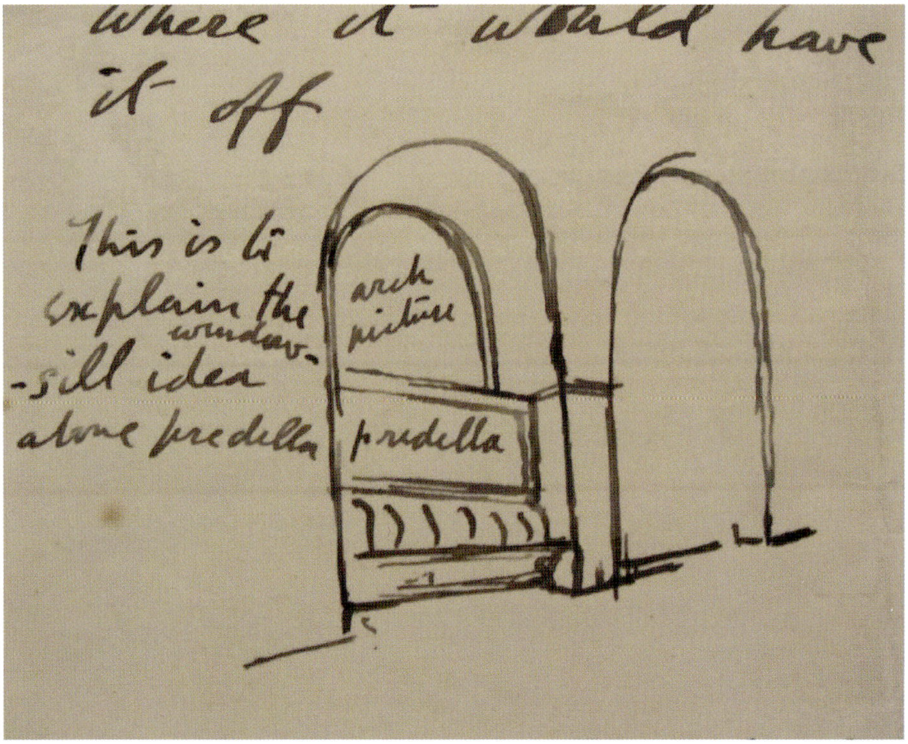

Fig. 5
Detail of a letter from Stanley Spencer showing barrel vaults, 23 November 1925
The Behrend Collection, National Trust archive

probably caused by malaria, and for many years thereafter, Hal was seldom mentioned by the family, probably because Mary Behrend had allegedly, and tragically, administered a fatal dose of brandy to him. His name does not appear on any local war memorials, probably because he died at home, and he was buried in a churchyard in Stoke D'Abernon, Surrey. This delayed decision to dedicate the chapel to him underscores the fact that the Behrends had initially financed the chapel purely out of a love of artistic endeavour. Indeed, save for the inflammatory plaque commemorating Hal's life (arguably overwhelmed by that commemorating Spencer), there are few, if any, references to Hal in the scheme. The mosquitoes buzzing over the tops of the nets in *Reveille* (Cat. 10) are perhaps the only direct reference to Hal's experiences serving in Eastern Europe; although Spencer – along with many other soldiers – had suffered from malaria whilst on the Macedonian front. In this way, the chapel is as much a memorial to all the soldiers who died on this forgotten front as to any individual. The 1920s saw a period of prolific monument building in Britain, accompanied by intense debate over the nature of memorials and the precarious balance between commemorating the dead and supporting the impoverished living.[36] Many had been left homeless after the war, so the almshouses either side of the chapel were a philanthropic addition; the residents also served a useful purpose, stoking the boiler which stopped the pictures getting damp. Again mindful of the prevailing mood, the Behrends chose to call the chapel the Oratory of All Souls (the name was changed when it passed to the National Trust). Spencer did not like the term 'Oratory' (because as a place dedicated to private prayer it suggested a certain inaccessibility) but the dedication to 'All Souls' was an important nod to the prevailing economic climate, when it would have been deemed inappropriate to have spent money on an elaborate private memorial.

That the Behrends were 'non-Establishment' perhaps gave them the freedom to develop such an inspired, individual and exacting taste (Eric Newton categorised the scope of their collection as 'English, with a sub-category that could be described as "affectionate"').[43] George Behrend commented that his 'parents had an unconventional way in which they went about being thoroughly conventional'. In his memoirs, Kenneth Clark noted that:

> *The great collections were not formed by bargain-hunters. In our youth, it was customary for Christian collectors to boast of how little they had paid for their prizes. 'Picked it up for a few coppers' was the usual phrase. Jewish collectors on the other hand, were proud to tell one what sacrifices they had made to obtain their treasures ... There can be no doubt which of these two standpoints denotes the greater love of art.*[37]

It can be of no doubt that John Louis' Jewish ancestry informed their artistic generosity and taste. Their taste was indeed considered avant-garde, except by the Bloomsbury set'[38] – although they did own a portrait of Vanessa Bell by Duncan Grant (bought for £20 in 1920). The Behrends owned many works by Spencer (Fig. 6) of diverse subject matter and style, including *Mending Cowls, Cookham* (now Tate), *The Ministers, Ming Tombs, Peking* (Government Art Collection) and *Swan Upping at Cookham* (Tate). Many of these were sold at Christie's and at the Leicester Gallery, along with works by Lamb (Fig. 7), Sickert, Gertler, Victor Pasmore, Gilbert Spencer, Max Beerbohm, Wilson Steer, Edward Burra and Augustus John, amongst other notable artists. To the uninitiated in the 1920s Stanley Spencer was shocking, but the chapel pictures were mild compared to some other pictures by Spencer owned by the Behrends. They owned *Love Among the Nations* (see Katy Norris' essay, Fig. 8; originally titled *Humanity*, and now in the Fitzwilliam, Cambridge), which is of brave and startling content. Some young Jesuit priests could barely take their eyes off it when being shown around Grey House; George Behrend noted how their 'eyes were glued to all those tits in the right hand top corner', and goaded his mother by proffering *Nude — Portrait*

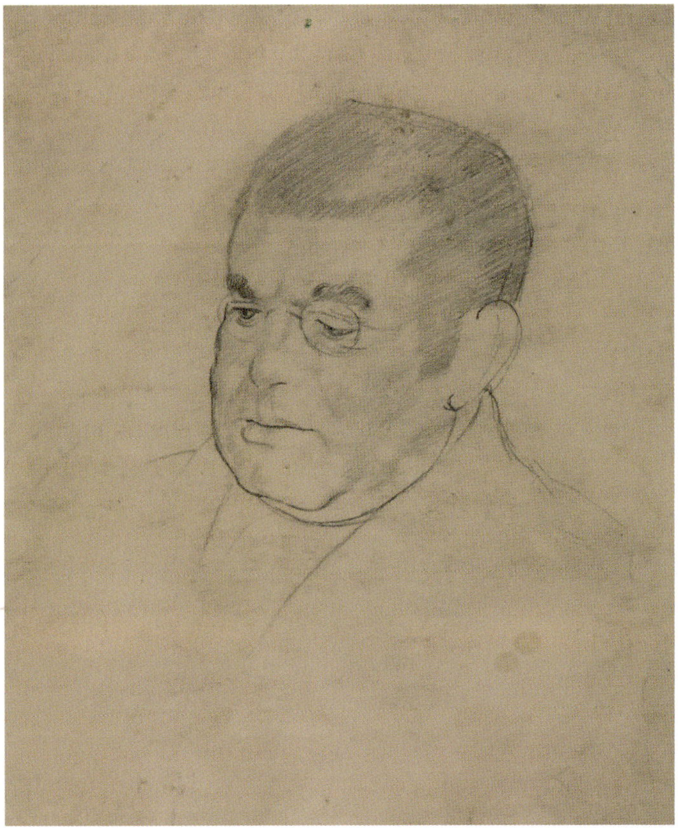

Fig. 6
Portrait of Louis Behrend, date not known
Graphite on paper
Tate: presented by Mrs Nancy Carline in memory of her husband, Richard Carline, 1982

of Patricia Preece (now in the Ferens Art Gallery, Hull), which was kept wrapped up in brown paper – she had only bought it in the hope that Stanley wouldn't do any more of Preece.[39] Mary Behrend could not stand her, which became a source of contention between her and Spencer; ' Mary has "rumbled" her alright', announced Spencer in his diary.[40] Stanley's relationship with Patricia also meant that he was forever itching to get back to Cookham to see her, whilst he was meant to be finishing off the chapel. The final canvas – *Washing Lockers* (Cat. 17) – had remained blank for more than a year until the family had retrieved it themselves, sticking it over the back seat of their open-top Daimler.

The Behrends' collection was appreciated by a diverse circle of friends and acquaintances — usually liberal (if not downright left-wing) and artistically minded. They were anything but socialites and guarded their privacy intently. They did not want any publicity surrounding the chapel and instead preferred to invite guests individually. In a letter of around 1928 Spencer notes that a number of the Behrends' friends had visited the chapel, adding that 'it would be rather dreadful if the Behrends had sent on to us all their thousand visitors like forwarding letters'.[41] This was probably unfair on two accounts: the Behrends were quite entitled to send whomever they wished; and moreover, those that were invited (the Slessers and the Japps) were part of an intimate circle. George Behrend accused Dudley Tooth or Patricia Preece of tipping off the press about its existence, at which point the Behrends were forced to hold a press day, given the number of inaccuracies being reported. In their own inimitable way, the Behrends treated the press royally, with a generous lunch at Grey House. Many years later, when the Pevsner Series and the accompanying BBC programmes caused the art world to discover that the Behrends were now living in Jersey, the BBC clamoured to get them to do an interview, using deceptive means to gain entry to the house.[42] However, their refusal to comply was resolute. They compensated for this by allowing George to publish his own book on the chapel, on the – very Wildean – condition that the images were in black and white.[43] Their view of social interlopers is perhaps summed up by a visit from the historian Hugh Trevor-Roper later in their lives, during which they felt as though they were 'rare exhibits' being inspected in a zoo.[44]

In this way they were quite different from Sir Edward Beddington-Behrens, another Anglo-Jew and Spencer patron, who moved in more elevated circles and took advantage of the similarity of their last names, sometimes taking credit for the chapel. Spencer wrote of Edward and John Louis:

> *Behrens and Behrend are two pretty men*
> *They both buy my pictures again & again*
> *They both like my works very much, so they say*
> *And make my life happy as a morning in May.*[45]

Spencer thought Beddington-Behrens a 'handful' who needed 'squashing', but he nevertheless rather delighted in the similarity of his patrons' names; he wrote to Mary: 'It looks as if names

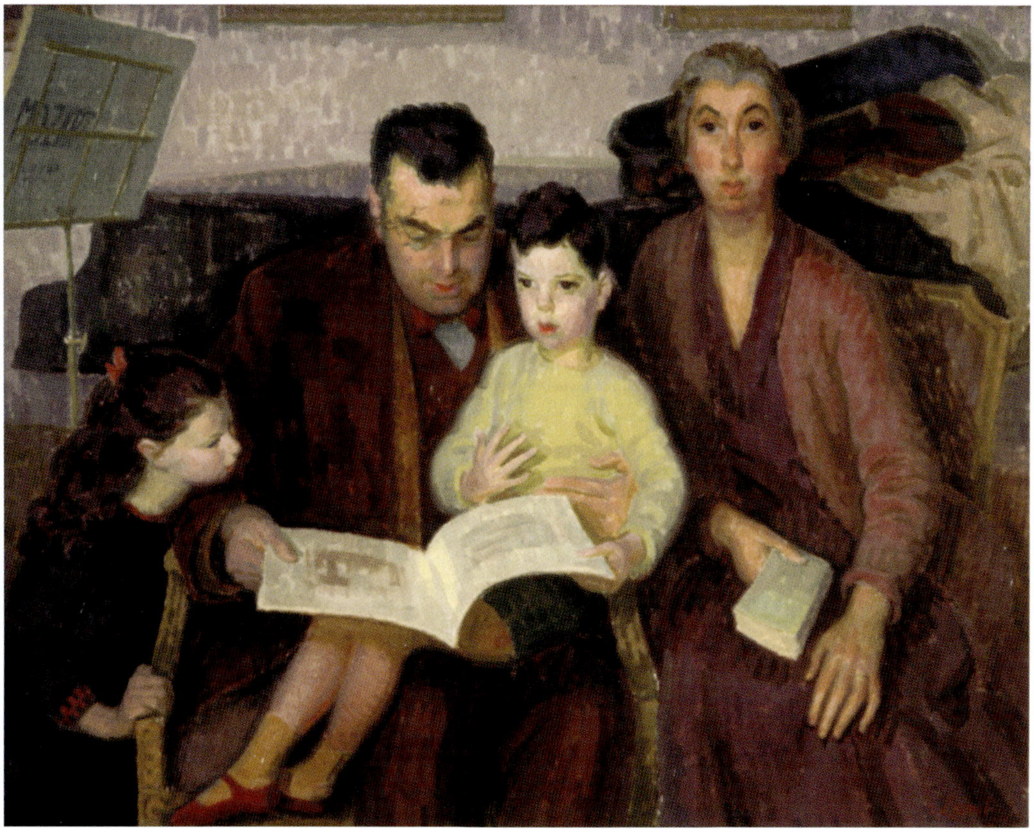

Fig. 7
Henry Lamb
Portrait of the Behrend Family, 1927
Oil on canvas
Brighton and Hove Museums

beginning with "Beh" or "Behren" will be doomed to buy some thing of mine, you will have to change yours or be ruined, but I expect you are already. First Behren(d) ruined/ Second Behren(s) at present sings French songs & things out of Operas very nicely.'[46]

Beddington-Behrens' uncle, Sydney Schiff (another enlightened patron of art, music and literature), had seen the chapel some four times and had been profoundly moved by it. He had also bought an early Spencer, *Two Girls and a Beehive* (1910; Private Collection).[47] Inspired by his uncle, Beddington-Behrens took Spencer to Saas-Fee in the Swiss Alps, in the hope that Spencer would be moved by the landscape there.[48] Typically Spencer avoided painting on the spot, and, as with the Sandham canvases, preferred to work from memory: 'It is much better than if I painted it on the spot because if I feel it sufficiently intensely to paint it from memory it has got to live.'[49]

Sir Henry Slesser, conversely, was a close friend of the Behrends, whom he had met at the Fabian Society. In November 1919, the Behrends had taken Stanley and his brother, Gilbert, to tea at the Slessers at Cornerways, Bourne End, Buckinghamshire – a convening place for the liberal intelligentsia. A few months later, in April 1920, Stanley moved in and painted some 20 pictures during this period, including *The Money Changers* triptych for their private chapel above the boathouse. They had a similar nurturing influence on Spencer as the Behrends, and later donated the silver altar cross for the chapel (they were devout Catholics). However, he was never as close to the Slessers as he was to the Behrends, noting that he felt like a 'lodger' in their company.[50]

Through the chapel, Spencer met the Martineaus, who were to become important patrons in his later years, and became *in loco parentis* to him, inviting him to nursery tea most days, securing his childhood home and supporting him in sickness.[51] Catherine (Cash) Martineau had met Spencer in 1942 when he had 'bowled me over taking me to Burghclere'.[52] He painted many family portraits, including one of Jack Martineau, who was Master of the Brewers Company (Private Collection). His regalia gave Spencer the chance to paint fur, something which gave him great pleasure. As he was finishing off the portrait he told Cash that he had 'popped up to the National Gallery' and had noted that 'my fur is as good as Tintoretto's! Better I think.'[53] This echoes a letter written by Spencer during the painting of the chapel in which he boasts that one of the lunettes had passages of paint that might rival the best of Titian.[54]

Financially the Martineaus (along with the Astors) were in a position to support Spencer in his later years in a way that the Behrends were simply unable to do.[55] Financial constraints in the post-war years left the Behrends in straitened circumstances with no servants and partially reliant on a farmstead, which supplemented rations. Their Egyptian rice mills were sold, and the proceeds were reduced by Sir Stafford Cripps' Capital Levy. Maintaining the chapel became an expensive exercise, mainly due to conservation issues resulting from the change in flow of hot and cold air between the double walls. The chapel was consequently given to the National Trust, with an endowment, in 1947 – singular in its form and content amongst existing Trust properties. Typically of the donors it was an enlightened and extraordinarily generous gift.

The rest of their collection was gradually sold off, a very few items being kept for the family. They moved from Burghclere, firstly to Llanwrin (another Grey House) in Wales and then to Jersey ('that bloody little island').[56] They both died peacefully in their sleep, Mary some years after her husband in a nursing home. There was no money left, their legacy instead residing on the walls of national galleries, and above all in the brave, outlandish and beautiful Holy Box that is Sandham.

Notes

I am grateful to Paul Gough, Oliver Garnett and Jane Martineau for reading early drafts of this essay. Paul Gough has, moreover, been unreservedly generous with his time, knowledge and enthusiasm. I am also indebted to Jane Martineau for imparting personal anecdotes and for giving her time and support.

1 Robert Hughes, 'English Art in the Twentieth Century', first published in *Time*, 1987, and reprinted in Robert Hughes, *Nothing if Not Critical*, Penguin, Harmondsworth, 1990, p.178.
2 Spencer had first met the Earl in 1925; the incident is recounted in Kenneth Pople, *Stanley Spencer: A Biography*, Collins, London, 1991, p.274.
3 John Louis had sold some items a year earlier at Christie's (10 March 1961), including works by David Bomberg, Charles Ginner, Henry Lamb and Spencer. George Behrend, Mary and John Louis' son, sold a considerable number of items from the collection at Christie's on 3 March 1978 and sporadically thereafter. My thanks to Jeff Pilkington, archive researcher at Christie's, for looking at Behrend sales for me.
4 Eric Newton, *Catalogue of an Exhibition of Paintings and Drawings from the Collection of J.L. Behrend*, exh. cat., Leicester Galleries, London, May 1962, p.3.
5 Newton 1962.
6 Cited in George Behrend, *An Unexpected Life*, Jersey Artists, St Martin, 2007, p.643; for more on Knollys see V. Light, *Circles and Tangents: Art in the Shadow of Cranbourne Chase*, Canterton Books, Morcombelake, 2011, pp.115–16.
7 I.M. Rawson, 'Patrons of Talent: The Behrends of Burghclere', *Country Life*, 26 October 1978, pp.1347–8. It is a charming, melodic piece, but hardly does them justice.
8 John Louis's obituary was published on 25 February 1972 and Mary's on 30 July 1977. I am grateful to Sarah Rutherford for bringing Mary Behrend's obituary to my attention.
9 George Behrend 2007, p.11.
10 George Behrend 2007, p.480.
11 Spencer was not wildly keen on Morrell: 'She calls me "nipper" which shows she does not know how to behave'. Stanley Spencer to Mary Behrend, not dated, Tate Archive TGA 882.17. She introduced the Behrends to Spencer at one of her parties in 1914.
12 Cited in Keith Clements, *Henry Lamb: The Artist and His Friends*, Redcliffe Press, Bristol, 1985, p.240.
13 Benjamin Britten, diary entry, March 1937, cited in Neil Powell, *Benjamin Britten: A Life for Music*, Hutchinson, London, 2013, p.129.
14 Powell 2013, p.135.
15 I am grateful to Jane Martineau for recounting this vignette.
16 Noted in correspondence between Kenneth Pople and Keith Clements, 30 June 1984, Cookham Gallery Archive (19.03).
17 Interview in the *Daily Telegraph*, 20 March 2001.
18 Mary Behrend to Richard Carline, 20 December 1959, TGA 825.2.
19 Mary Behrend to Richard Carline, 20 December 1959, TGA, 825.2.
20 The convoluted and complex negotiations surrounding the process of building and decorating the chapel are to be published by Paul Gough in his forthcoming publication on the building of the chapel, in which he has referenced numerous documents hitherto not studied by Spencer scholars.
21 George Behrend suggests that they never paid more than £200 for a picture, or £300 between the wars. George Behrend 2007, p.7.
22 Mary Behrend to Richard Carline, 20 December 1959, TGA 825.2.
23 Stanley Spencer to Mary Behrend, 11 October 1933, TGA 882.20.
24 Stanley Spencer to Mary Behrend, 29 December 1955, TGA 882.66; Stanley Spencer to John Louis Behrend, 3 April 1956, TGA 882.67. In the letter Spencer writes: 'creamatoriamish' – I have revised the spelling in the main text for clarity. My thanks to Adrian Glew for clarifying this.
25 Stanley Spencer to Unity Spencer, private archive, cited in Pople 1991, p.280.

26 Stanley Spencer to Unity Spencer, private archive, cited in Pople 1991, p.280.

27 TGA 825 (W15 and W16) (accompanied by a note from Richard Carline pointing out as much). My thanks to Ann Danks for bringing this note to my attention.

28 Paul Gough talks about the lost opportunity of allowing Pearson more imaginative space, contrasting the drama of the Jagger War Memorial with the temerity of the chapel. Paul Gough, *Stanley Spencer: Journey to Burghclere*, Samson & Co., Bristol, 2006, p.104 ff.

29 Mary Behrend, 25 November 1930, TGA 825.2.

30 Mary Behrend to Richard Carline, 20 December 1959, TGA 825.2.

31 Paper dated Monday 29 April 1935, enclosed with an undated letter. It was a send-up of David Lloyd George 'with thanks to Spencer's "St. Francis"'. TGA 882.35.

32 George Behrend 2007, p.19. He also notes 'the profound feeling of desertion that Jews have, when a Jew converts to marry a non Jew'.

33 Stanley Spencer to Desmond Chute, 1918, reprinted in Paul Gough (ed.), *Your Loving Friend, Stanley: The Great War Correspondence Between Stanley Spencer and Desmond Chute*, Samson & Co., Bristol, 2011, p.70.

34 Gough 2011, p.52.

35 There is no reference to malaria in his medical records, but it is likely that he had suffered recurrent bouts. He had been unable to return straight home after the war and his plea for discharge was only granted when the family called upon the intervention of Winston Churchill, then Secretary of State for War and Air (see notes made by Nick Batten, February 2010, Stanley Spencer Gallery Archive, Cookham).

36 Gough 2006, p.100.

37 Kenneth Clark, *Another Part of the Wood: A Self-Portrait*, John Murray, London, 1974, pp.193–4; cited in James Stourton and Charles Sebag-Montefiore, *The British as Art Collectors: From the Tudors to the Present*, Scala, London, 2012, p.21. I am grateful to Oliver Garnett for pointing out this reference.

38 George Behrend 2007, p.11.

39 George Behrend 2007, p.174. Father d'Arcy from Oxford had been invited to lunch in the hope that Stanley would be commissioned to decorate Campion Hall, Oxford. He had brought some younger priests with him.

40 Diary, 27 July 1934, cited in Adrian Glew, *Stanley Spencer: Letters and Writings*, Tate, London, 2001, p.166.

41 Stanley Spencer to Richard Carline, ?1928, cited in Glew 2001, p.140.

42 George Behrend 2007, p.625.

43 George Behrend, *Stanley Spencer at Burghclere*, Macdonald, London, 1965.

44 George Behrend 2007, p.627.

45 Stanley Spencer to Gwen Raverat, 8 September 1933, cited in Glew 2001, p.158.

46 Stanley Spencer to Mary Behrend, TGA 882.10.

47 It is tempting to recall Spencer being labelled 'the Proust of painting' (Pople 1991, p.200) in light of Schiff's close friendship with the French author.

48 The trip is recounted in Beddington-Behrens' autobiography, *Look Back, Look Forward*, Macmillan, London, 1963, p.92 ff.

49 Beddington-Behrens 1963, p.95.

50 Patrick Wright, 'Purposeful Art in a Climate of Cultural Reaction: Stanley Spencer in the 1920s', in Timothy Hyman and Patrick Wright (eds), *Stanley Spencer*, exh. cat., Tate, London, 2001, p.61.

51 In conversation with Jane Martineau.

52 Cash Martineau to Kenneth Pople, 4 February 1991, Cookham Gallery Archive (16.09).

53 Cash Martineau to Kenneth Pople, 18 March 1991, Cookham Gallery Archive (16.11).

54 Gilbert Spencer 1961, p.147, cited in Gough 2006, p.121.

55 Viscount Astor was bewildered that Spencer loved coming to stay with the Martineaus, in their chaotic house, full of children, rather than in stately Cliveden. My thanks to Jane Martineau for this information.

56 According to George, John Louis found the island claustrophobic; George Behrend 2007, p.628.

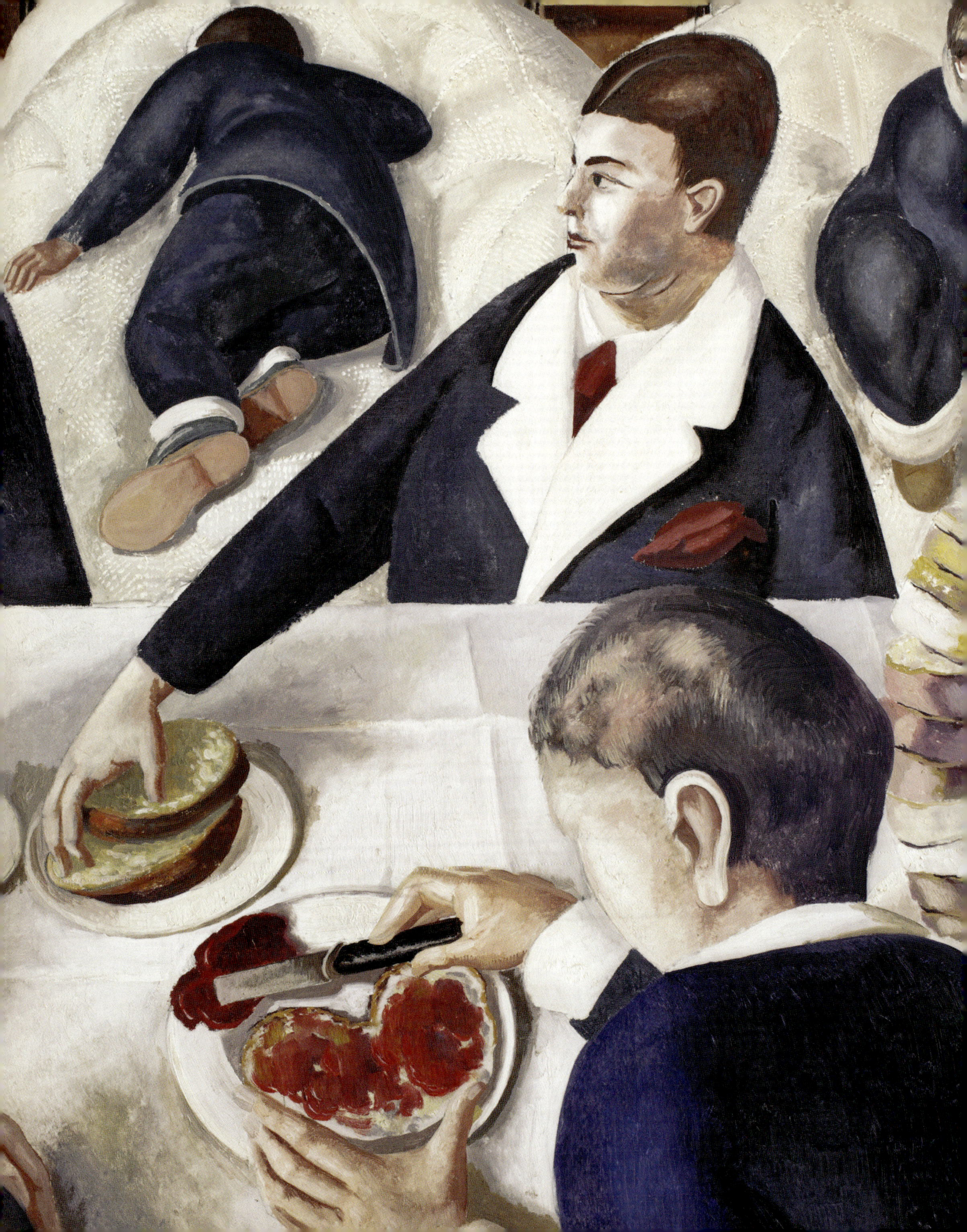

The Sun to Spencer's Planet: Henry Lamb and Stanley Spencer

David Taylor

> *Do not be unhappy about the war.*
> *The best way we can help is to paint.*
> Mark Gertler[1]

The Australian-born painter Henry Lamb (1883–1960) played an instrumental role in Stanley Spencer being commissioned by John Louis and Mary Behrend to produce the paintings for the Sandham Memorial Chapel. When Spencer first met Lamb, a fellow alumnus of the Slade School of Art, in November 1913, there was little to suggest their future friendship ('one of the most terrible days of my life', according to Lamb) let alone the significant, influential relationship they would have on each other's artistic output. Things had improved by the following year, when Lamb wrote to Lytton Strachey, 'I understood his origin & genre much better this time and he was much less nervous and trying; so that I really got to like him tremendously.'[2] As Paul Gough has described, 'Spencer sought out and attracted a succession of mentors and patrons. The painter Henry Lamb was one such individual who would play an important part in Spencer's war. Eight years older than Spencer, Lamb assumed the role of worldly patron to Spencer's "provincial innocent", the sun to Spencer's planet'.[3]

Raised in Manchester, Lamb studied medicine at Owens College in that city, before deciding to move to London to pursue a career as a painter. In 1906 he enrolled in the Chelsea Art School, run by Augustus John and William Orpen, and the following year he studied at L'Ecole de la Palette in Paris. Lamb was a founder member of the Camden Town Group in 1911, a group of like-minded English Post-Impressionist painters that centred their social world at the Camden studio of Walter Sickert, and whose members included Spencer Gore, Harold Gilman and Charles Ginner. They held three exhibitions between 1911 and 1912. Two years later Lamb also became a founder member of the London Group, although he did not exhibit with them.

A handsome, bohemian figure, described as an Adonis with hypnotic eyes, Lamb entranced men and women alike. Lytton Strachey, the subject of

Fig. 1
Tea in the Hospital Ward
(detail) Sandham Memorial
Chapel (South Wall)
See Cat. 13

perhaps his best-known portrait (commissioned by the Behrends in 1914, now at the Tate), was in love with him, and Ottoline Morrell, with whom he had an affair, described him as 'a figure who seemed to come from a vision of Blake'.[4] Lamb's first meeting with Spencer came about because of an interest that he had in Spencer's enigmatic *Apple Gatherers* (Tate Britain), painted in 1912–13, and on show in Contemporary Art Society's summer exhibition at the Goupil Gallery in London. Spencer wrote to him after he was told of how impressed he was by the picture:

> *Dear Mr Lamb ... Your friend Mr Japp told me that you like my picture at the Contemporary. It gives me great pleasure to enclose herewith a photo of it. I think it looks better in this photo than it does in the original. I hope to see you some day – I don't go to London now so I hardly ever see any body or any works of art.*[5]

Lamb bought the picture for £30 in October 1913, apparently with the intention to sell it on, both for a profit and as a means of giving some of the proceeds to Spencer.[6] It was after a nervous Spencer brought the canvas to him at his then studio in the Vale of Health Hotel in Hampstead that Lamb, who was suffering from a bad cold, commented on it being the worst day of his life, and Spencer, writing to his friends, the Raverats, said, 'I like him & do not feel him to be a low worm. I do not think his work is interesting, except sometimes.'[7] Lamb sold the picture and gave the profit to Spencer, as he intended, who sent in return a receipt, saying it was 'right to be businesslike'.[8] The association between the two artists grew – a year later, in 1914, Lamb was staying with Spencer at Fernlea, the Spencer family house in Cookham, and they soon became close friends.

Following the declaration of war in August 1914, Lamb sensed 'a certain return of military feelings occasioned by the bad news', and enlisted at the recruitment office in Putney, although he decided to withdraw.[9] However, mindful of his medical training, Lamb volunteered for work at Guy's Hospital, London, where he was taken on as an outpatient dresser, and the next year he recruited to the Hôpital Anglais du Casino in Fécamp in Normandy, as a medical assistant. After training with the Royal Army Medical Corps he became a Lieutenant in the Special Reserve of Officers and was posted to Salonika in Macedonia the next year, with the 2/3rd Northampton Field Ambulance. Lamb had two further postings, in Palestine and France, before the end of the war, and in 1918 he was awarded the Military Cross. He returned to the Vale studio in Hampstead and started work on his two greatest war paintings, *Irish Troops in the Judean Hills Surprised by a Turkish Bombardment* (Fig. 2) and *Advanced Dressing Station on the Struma, 1916* (Fig. 5).

In March 1918, Lord Beaverbrook, along with the Ministry of Information, formed the British War Memorial Foundation, which was charged with taking responsibility for the future programming plans of the War Artists Advisory Committee. This began the process of a number of younger artists being commissioned to produce war paintings as part of a large, national campaign of commemoration, and Lamb and Spencer were part of a group of Slade painters, including David Bomberg, Darsie Japp, Augustus John and Wyndham Lewis, who were approached.

Over the winter of 1919–20 many of the paintings commissioned (potentially for a Hall of Remembrance that was never realised) were displayed in the exhibition *The Nation's War Paintings*, held at the Royal Academy. Amongst these works were some of the most powerful and moving images that commemorated war in painted form, including John Singer Sargent's *Gassed*, Paul Nash's *The Menin Road*, Spencer's *Travoys Arriving with Wounded at a Dressing-Station at Smol, Macedonia, September 1916* and Lamb's *Irish Troops in the Judean Hills Surprised by a Turkish Bombardment* (all in the Imperial War Museums collection). Favourable reviews of the exhibition exemplified that 'Whereas only a few years before modern art had been derided and dismissed, now it was seen as being amongst the finest and most forceful official images of the conflict', showing how contemporary figurative painting evolved

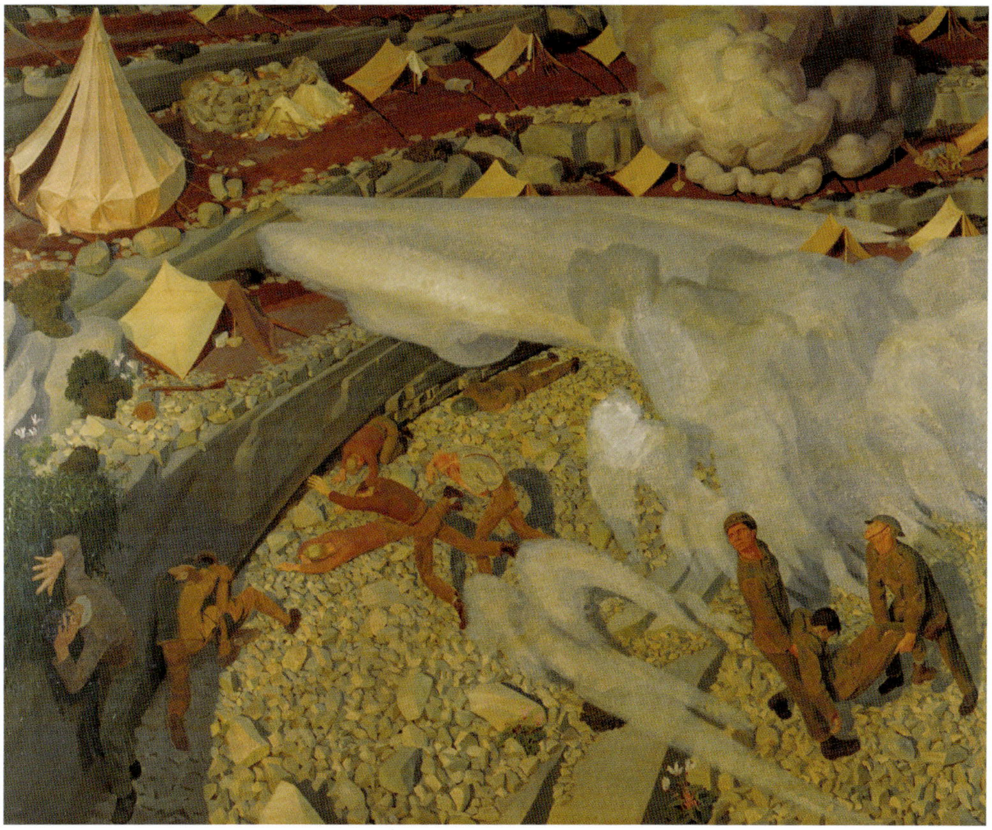

Fig. 2
Henry Lamb
Irish Troops in the Judean Hills Surprised by a Turkish Bombardment, 1919
Oil on canvas
Imperial War Museums

to become accepted and established, as well as representative of the recent war.[10]

After the war Lamb had been commissioned by the government's War Artists Advisory Committee to paint a picture to be part of a series of large war canvases, and in September 1919 Lamb began working on his best-known war painting, *Irish Troops in the Judean Hills Surprised by a Turkish Bombardment* (Fig. 2). The composition, based on Lamb's experiences in Palestine, uses a high viewpoint to emphasise a sense of the artillery shells dropping on the Irish troops:

> *The scene is laid in a natural amphitheatre in a fold of the Judæan* [sic] *hills, and towards the close of day the ordinary routine has been suddenly interrupted by a bombardment. It is probably not an incident of much importance; merely the sort of spasmodic visitation to which, like a dust storm, even a quiet part of the line would be liable. Two of the shells have already landed and burst, and a rush for shelter is still going on.*[11]

The canvas shows how Lamb was influenced by Spencer, especially in the experimentation with scale and the slight distortion of the soldiers' limbs, and how Lamb 'obtained inspiration from Spencer's stylisation of forms with their flattened simplifications and often awkward but arresting compositions'.[12]

Lamb moved to Poole in Dorset following the war, and it was here that he painted Spencer's portrait in 1921 (Art Gallery of Western Australia). It was also in Poole, two years later, that Lamb played his most significant role in Spencer's career. Spencer had been staying with Muirhead Bone at Steep in Hampshire, until Bone had tired of his difficult nature had asked him to lodge elsewhere. Spencer enquired of Lamb if he could have a room with him at Poole, and moved in for a period during the summer of 1922 – over the next few years, Henry was to be a haven, a rescuer, a 'father confessor', as Richard Carline called him, to Stanley.[13]

Spencer had likewise been on the front line in Macedonia, and the following summer, during another stay, Lamb told the painter Richard Carline

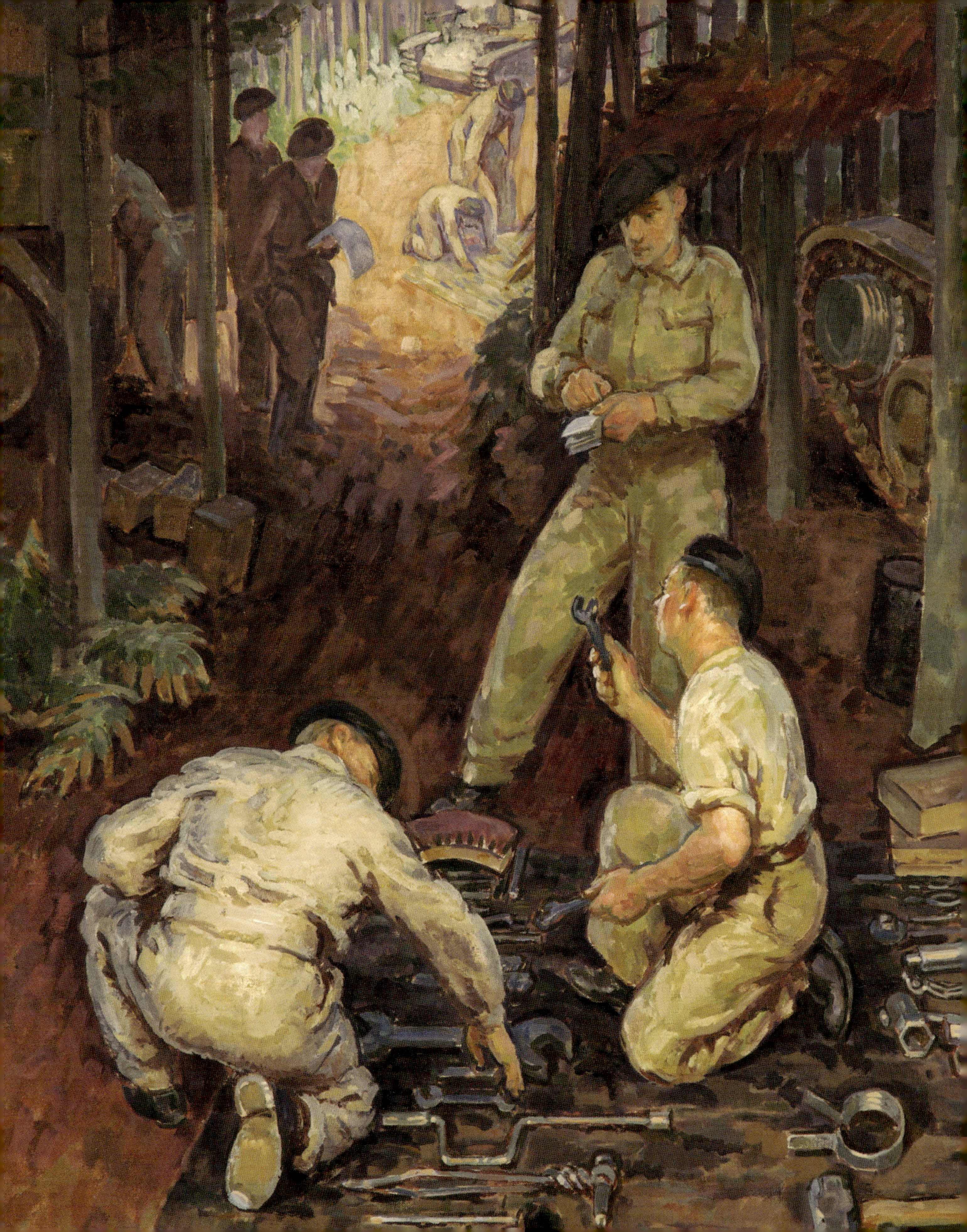

that Spencer was 'sitting all day evolving acres of Salonika and Bristol war compositions', drawings that Lamb's friends and patrons, John Louis and Mary Behrend, saw at Lamb's home in Hill Street.[14] Spencer had also, in his own words, in a letter that year to Hilda Carline, 'drawn a whole architectural scheme of the pictures'.[15] Lamb had already introduced Spencer, along with his brother Gilbert, to the Behrends at Burghclere (and they already owned Spencer's *Swan Upping at Cookham*) but after seeing the drawings in Poole the Behrends decided that Spencer should decorate the interior of the chapel that they were building to commemorate Mary Behrend's brother, Lieutenant Henry Willoughby Sandham, who, like Spencer and Lamb, served in Macedonia but who had died of a war-related illness in 1919 (see Amanda Bradley's essay in this catalogue). John Louis Behrend declared, 'We felt at once that we would like to do something about this castle in the air, partly because we had admired so many frescoes in various churches and chapels in Europe; but mainly because the designs struck us as bold, original and deserving of any encouragement we could give.'[16] However, it took four years after the Behrends had decided on Spencer as the artist they wanted to decorate the chapel for the commission to come to fruition: 'Stanley was exultant: "What Ho, Giotto!" he is said to have exclaimed.'[17] News of the commission led Spencer to write to Lamb, revealing his appreciation of the debt he owed to the older artist, 'Of course I expected to hear something nice when you said the Behrends were getting keen as the result of your efforts but I did not expect quite such glorious news as I received this morning.'[18]

Although Spencer's cycle of pictures for the chapel was painted on canvas, he originally wanted to paint it in fresco, a reminder of the series by Giotto in the Arena Chapel in Padua that he admired (see Simon Martin's essay). The Sandham Memorial Chapel paintings, apart from the ethereal altarpiece *The Resurrection of the Soldiers* (Cat. 9), show scenes of everyday life from Spencer's time with the Army, at the Beaufort War Hospital in Bristol (see Paul Gough's essay), at Tweseldown Camp near Aldershot and in Macedonia. Spencer painted the canvases at Burghclere between 1926 and 1932. The five years it took to complete the paintings for the chapel turned out to be a hugely cathartic experience for Spencer, following the traumatic journey he undertook in Bristol and Macedonia, as he described, 'The Burghclere memorial redeemed my experience from what it was, namely something alien to me. By this means I recover my lost self.'[19] As Eric Newton observed in 1947:

> *The one big 'event' in his life was his service as a Red Cross Orderly and, later, as a soldier in Macedonia in the war of 1914–18. During those years experiences of a new kind assailed him. Not the everyday experiences of village life so vividly reflected in most of his paintings, but a sudden set of temporary impacts in which close companionship with men his own age, suffering, movement, violent activity were forced upon him, snatching him away from a world in which he could be a spectator into a world of action.*[20]

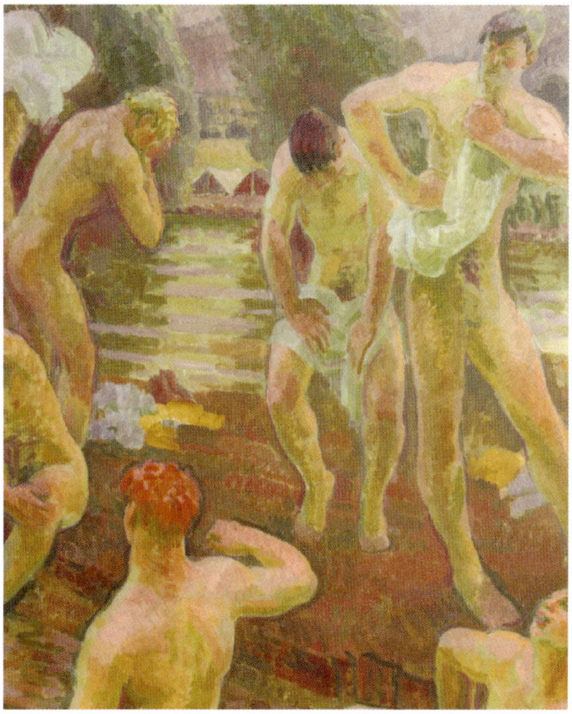

Fig. 3 (Opposite)
Henry Lamb
Tool Inspection, 1942
Oil on canvas
Salford Museum and Art Gallery

Fig. 4
Henry Lamb
Troops Bathing at Salonika (detail), 1917
Oil on canvas
On loan from a private collection to Southampton City Art Gallery

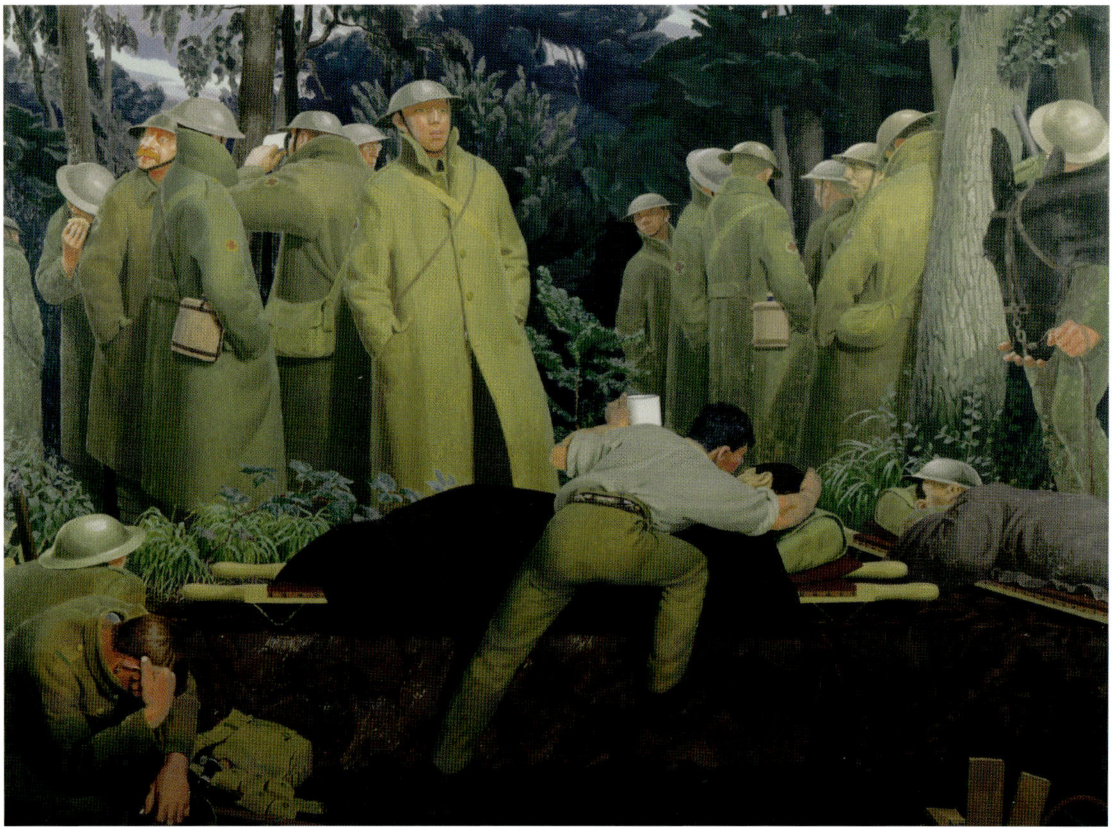

Fig. 5
Henry Lamb
Advance Dressing Station on the Struma, 1916, 1920
Oil on canvas
Manchester City Galleries

Fig. 6
Henry Lamb
Sir Stanley Spencer, 1928
Oil on canvas
National Portrait Gallery, London

The decorative scheme at Sandham afforded Spencer the opportunity to draw on his love for the Italian primitive painters. Lamb would similarly reveal his own interest in primitivism – he was especially influenced by the Tahitian work of Paul Gauguin and various painters of the Pont-Aven school in Brittany, which can be seen in some of the more symbolist pictures he produced in France in 1910 and 1911, and in Ireland in 1912 and 1913. Prior to enlisting in 1914, Spencer wrote to Lamb, 'If I go to war, I go on condition I can have Giotto, the Basilica of Assisi book, Fra Angelico in one pocket, and Masaccio, Masolino and Giorgione in the other' (he actually took some of his Gowans & Gray booklets on Italian Master painters and a copy of Ruskin's *Modern Masters*).[21]

Lamb's war paintings include images that show both the similarities and differences between his and Spencer's painting at the same time. His *Troops Bathing, Salonika*, painted in 1917 (Fig. 4), shows a scene of soldiers washing and drying themselves on a river bank in Macedonia, and is painted in a variety of assured brushstrokes, including green and pink flesh tones that mirror the same colours in the water and landscape. The composition, comprising multiple figures busied in various activities, and the slight distortion of some of the soldiers' limbs to emphasise their gestures, seem stylistically similar to some of Spencer's war pictures. The development of Lamb's style can be seen when a Second World War picture of his, such as his 1942 *Tool Inspection* (Fig. 3), is considered in comparison to a picture of a similar subject matter by Spencer, for example *Kit Inspection* (see Cat. 5) painted after the First World War.

The inspiration that Spencer took from his time in Salonika is revealed in a letter he wrote to Lamb in the summer of 1917, when he declared, 'I am a thousand times more determined to do something a thousand times greater than anything I have done before when I get home, & am storing up energy all the time.'[22] Alfred Yockney, the Secretary of the War Artists Advisory Committee, wrote to Spencer in May 1918 to enquire if he was willing to paint an

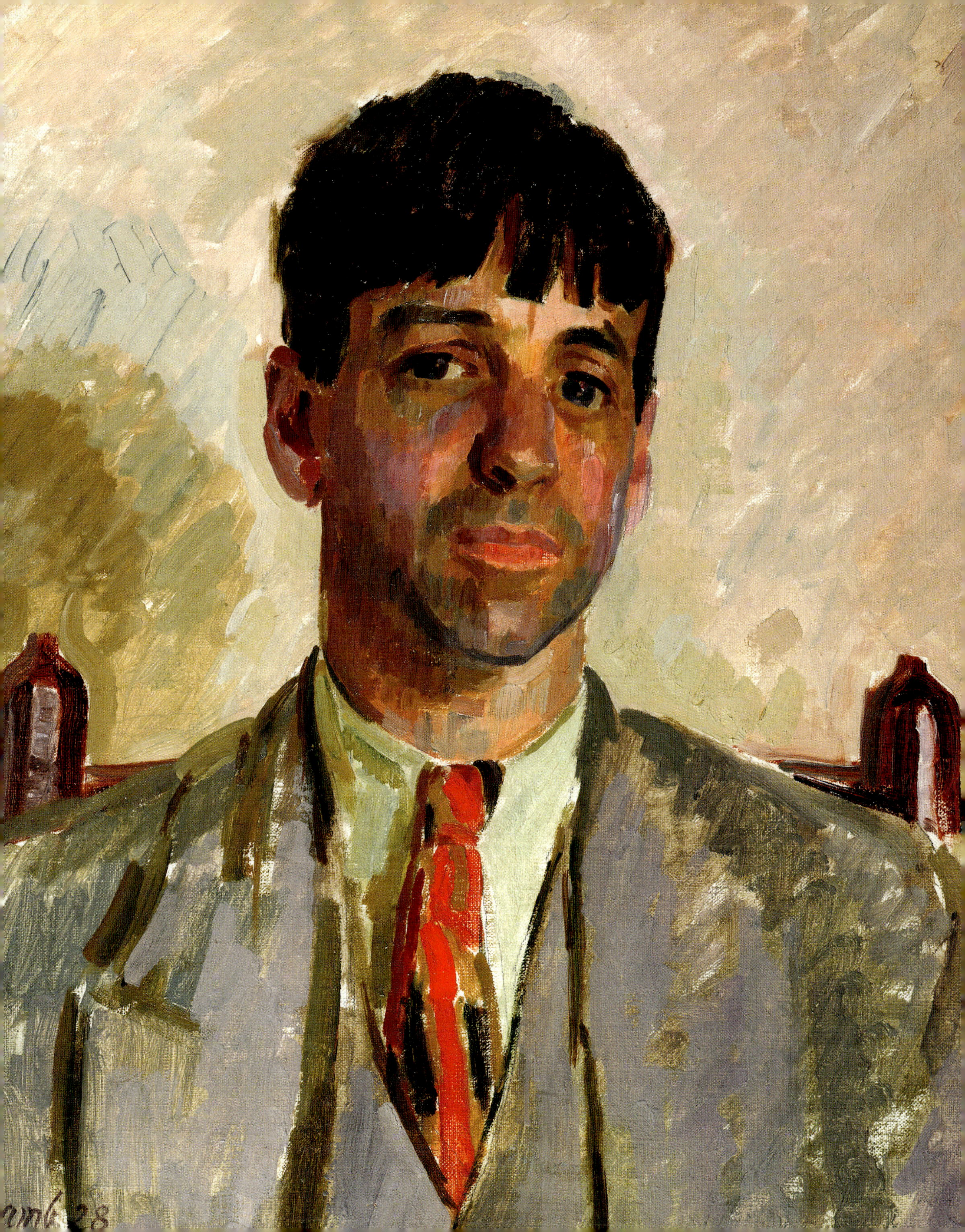
vmb 28

official war picture to be part of a potential series of large-scale paintings displayed in a specially designed Hall of Remembrance in London. Spencer was delighted by the letter, but he was still at the front in Salonika, and was unlikely to be released from his duties – as Yockney explained to Paul Nash, 'Unfortunately we have not been able to secure his services. The matter is hung up at the War Office.'[23] A frustrated Spencer waited in vain for the official commission to arrive from London, despite receiving letters from friends that referred to him being successfully commissioned as an official war artist, as he longed to realise the pictures he had been thinking of painting since being in the Balkans. Despite the dangers of his daily life and the fact that he appears to have been treated as an outsider by his fellow troops, he enthused to Lamb that he was 'as much influenced by this particular Sector as I was by Cookham in peace times'.[24]

In 1920 Lamb painted *Advanced Dressing Station on the Struma, 1916* (Fig. 5), commissioned by Manchester City Art Gallery, showing a forest clearing in which:

> *A group of stretcher-bearers stand by at the rendezvous, waiting to be despatched on their several tasks during the coming night. A sculpturesque tridimensional treatment of the group and the landscape background suggests the monotonous passage of the minutes of tense expectation which is the mood of the pictures and of the figures, to which the activity in the immediate foreground is the foil. The details are treated with the same minute realism. The footmarks in the mud are reproduced with an almost emotional fidelity.*[25]

After the war Lamb would paint Spencer on several occasions, including in a group portrait, showing him animatedly holding forth in *The Tea Party*, painted in Poole in 1926 (Private Collection), and in single portraits, painted in 1921 (Art Gallery of Western Australia) and in 1928 (National Portrait Gallery, London) respectively. The latter portrait (Fig. 6) is full of movement, ranging from the loose, thin brushstrokes that make up the sitter's clothes, to the colourful, vertical marks that describe his face, befitting Lamb's confession to Dora Carrington, that 'The portrait turned out better than I had expected, seeing that he never stopped his chatter.'[26]

Portraits also made up the majority of Lamb's commissions when he would later become an official war artist during the Second World War. By this stage in his career, Lamb's painting style had, understandably, evolved since he last depicted soldiers in wartime, and his portraits had become somewhat formulaic, although their draughtsmanship and use of colour could still impress and move the viewer. One such example is his wistful 1942 portrayal of *Gunner Paul March (Canadian Forces)* (Fig. 7) leaning on a table and holding a cigarette, one of a series of portraits of Canadian servicemen then in Britain, presented by the War Artists Advisory Committee to the Imperial War Museum (now in the Government Art Collection).

Spencer's multi-faceted relationship with Lamb changed over time and Lamb would sometimes become disillusioned with his younger friend – 'Lamb was a remarkably tolerant and enabling patron, offering money, advice, accommodation and professional support that was not always appreciated, if even acknowledged, by Spencer'.[27] When Lamb eventually became bored with Spencer, in the 1920s, he still lauded his paintings, describing the '"noble constancy" of the little gentleman's work ... together with the astounding novelty of such a personality stepping in at this time of day to restore narrative art to its primitive purity'.[28] Lamb has become a somewhat overlooked artist in the twenty-first century, but a significant element to the friendship he had with Spencer is the background to the commission of what would turn out to be Spencer's masterpiece. As Keith Clements wrote in 1985, 'The story of the Burghclere Memorial Chapel is well documented and well known but Henry has not always been given proper credit for his role in the initial stages of the scheme.'[29]

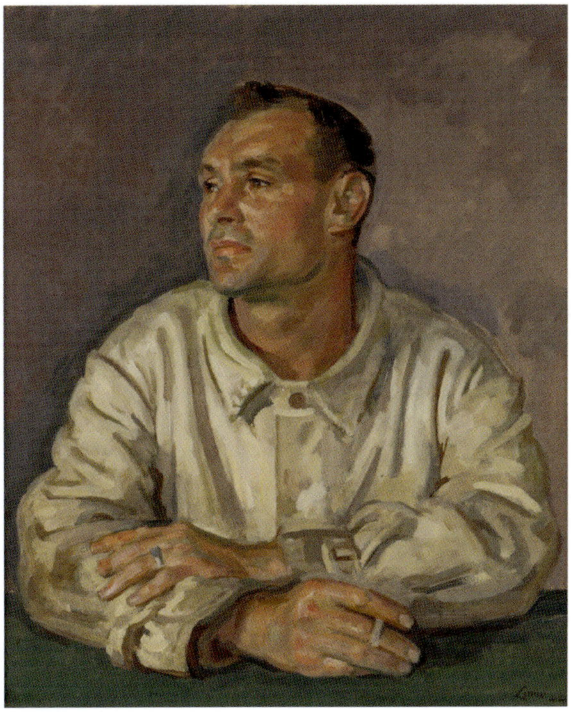

Fig. 7
Henry Lamb
Gunner Paul March (Canadian Forces), 1942
UK Government Art Collection

Notes

1 Mark Gertler to Dora Carrington, August 1914, quoted in David Boyd Haycock, 'A Crisis of Brilliance: The Slade and Six Young British Artists', in David Boyd Haycock, *Nash Nevinson Spencer Gertler Carrington Bomberg: A Crisis of Brilliance, 1908–1922*, exh. cat., Dulwich Picture Gallery, London, 2013, p.28.
2 Keith Clements, *Henry Lamb, The Artist and His Friends*, Redcliffe Press, Bristol, 1985, p.207.
3 Paul Gough, *A Terrible Beauty: British Artists in the First World War*, Samson & Co., Bristol, 2010, p.244
4 Clements 1985, p.141.
5 Clements 1985, p.207.
6 See David Boyd Haycock, *A Crisis of Brilliance: Five Young British Artists and the Great War*, Old Street, London, 2009, p.170.
7 15 December 1913, Tate Archive TGA 8116.32, quoted in Gough 2010, p.244, n.8.
8 Clements 1985, p.210.
9 Clements 1985, p.215.
10 Boyd Haycock 2009, p.305.
11 Albert Rutherston (ed.), *Henry Lamb*, Ernest Benn, London, 1924, p.19.
12 *Henry Lamb*, exh. cat., Manchester City Art Gallery, Manchester, 1984, p.7.
13 Clements 1985, p.239.
14 Duncan Robinson, 'Stanley Spencer in Retrospect', in Steven Parissien (ed.), *Stanley Spencer and the English Garden*, exh.cat., Compton Verney, London and Compton Verney, 2011, p.12.
15 Duncan Robinson, *Stanley Spencer*, Phaidon, Oxford, 1990, p.33.
16 George Behrend, *Stanley Spencer at Burghclere*, Macdonald, London, 1965, p.6.
17 Paul Gough, *Stanley Spencer: Journey to Burghclere*, Samson & Co., Bristol, 2006, p.102.
18 Clements 1985, p.242.
19 Timothy Hyman, 'A Note on Burghclere: The Sandham Memorial Chapel, 1927–32', in Timothy Hyman and Patrick Wright (eds), *Stanley Spencer*, exh. cat., Tate, London, 2001, p.240.
20 Eric Newton, *Stanley Spencer* (Penguin Modern Painters), Penguin, Harmondsworth, 1947, p.13.
21 James and Julie Lawson, 'Stanley Spencer's Vision at Port Glasgow', in Keith Bell, Martin Hammer, James and Julie Lawson, Andrew Patrizio and Duncan Thomson, *Men of the Clyde: Stanley Spencer's Vision at Port Glasgow*, exh. cat., Scottish National Portrait Gallery, Edinburgh, 2000, p.34.
22 Adrian Glew, *Stanley Spencer: Letters and Writings*, Tate, London, 2001, p.89.
23 Alfred Yockney to Paul Nash, 2 October 1918, Imperial War Museum 267A/6, f.139, quoted in Boyd Haycock 2009, p.294, n.7.
24 Glew 2001, p.92, quoted in Boyd Haycock 2009, p.294.
25 Rutherston 1924, p.24.
26 *Henry Lamb* 1984, p.49.
27 Gough 2010, p.244.
28 Clements 1985, p.245.
29 Clements 1985, p.242.

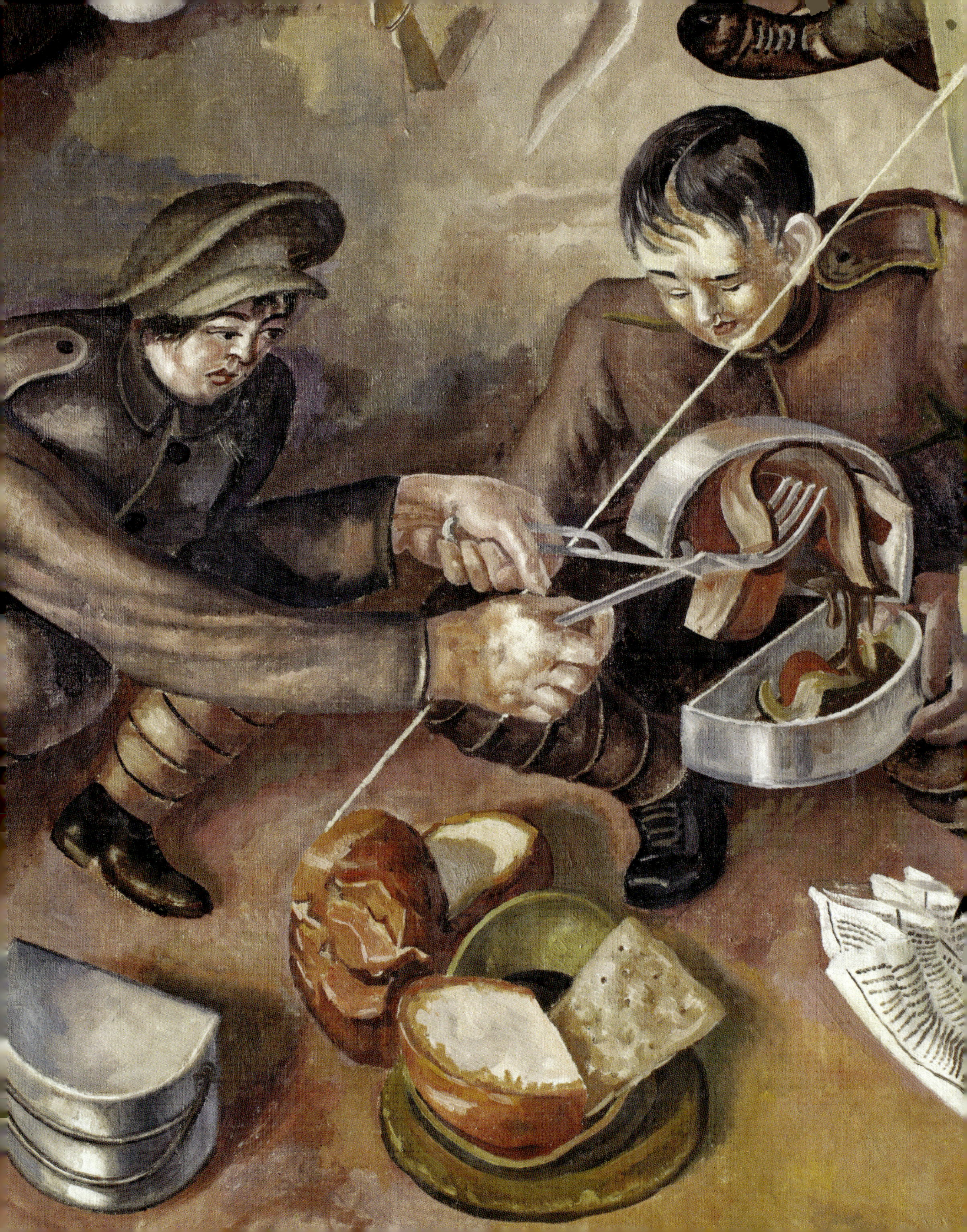

Between Men: Masculinity and Fraternity in Stanley Spencer's Vision of War

Katy Norris

The First World War has been recognised as an irreversible historical rupture, a shattering of the previously established political, social and economic order. It was the first conflict in which modern weaponry was trialled and tested, resulting in the deaths of over eight million allied and enemy forces, as well as unprecedented causalities on both sides.[1] This trauma was none more apparent than in the damage wrought on the male body itself, which was not only laid vulnerable to the protracted annihilation of mechanised warfare, but first systematically conditioned and regulated by the military authorities. In the years after the First World War the question of masculine disempowerment became the focus for artists and writers, many of whom attempted to articulate their personal accounts of bloodshed and catastrophic loss. Meanwhile, as if in answer to this anti-war rhetoric, a counter-culture of honour and remembrance instigated by the Imperial War Graves Commission emerged in Britain giving rise to public memorials such as the Cenotaph in London's Whitehall. These monuments concentrated on collective rather than individual experience, ultimately repositioning military death as a necessary sacrifice for the nation.[2]

The Sandham Memorial Chapel in Burghclere holds an ambiguous position in this trajectory. A monument to a single person, it was originally conceived purely as an outlet for Spencer's unique vision of war and neither overtly glorifies nor condemns military combat. Across the cycle of arched paintings and predellas that line the chapel's walls, acts of violence or heroism are deliberately avoided in favour of commonplace events, described by the artist as 'a general reflection of the attitude of men during the war'.[3] The works are also resoundingly autobiographical, based upon the specific roles of medical orderly, soldier and patient that were each fulfilled by Spencer. Given that the pictures portray the artist's own experiences one might consider the cycle within the context of neutral reportage. A deeper reading has typically relied upon the final picture painted directly upon the

Fig. 1
Camp at Karasuli (detail)
Sandham Memorial Chapel
(North Wall)

vast end wall of the chapel where Spencer's unique interpretation of the Resurrection (Cat. 9) is transplanted on to a Macedonian battlefield. At first glance this chaotic landscape filled with uprooted crosses and twisted, fragmented bodies emerging from a barren stretch of no man's land perhaps comes closest to depicting the devastation caused by war. But the painting is actually concerned with redemption through Christ, a scene of deliverance that offers spiritual if not physical salvation to the fallen men. Described by the artist as a 'conglomeration of happenings & then release in the Resurrection', the pictures have previously been interpreted as a cycle of crisis and resolution, in which peace and masculine authority are seemingly restored.[4]

In her analysis, Sue Malvern has argued that such a reading is to oversimplify Spencer's meaning, rendering his experience as 'unnegotiable and closed rather than fractured, contradictory and unresolved'.[5] In terms of masculine identity the assumption here hinges upon the reinstatement of conventional gender codes and the shared belief in the male duty of dying for one's country. However, Spencer's version of war promotes a much more fluid interpretation of masculinity than has previously been acknowledged. In addition to the relationships of friendship, mentorship and fraternal love upon which military camaraderie was based, Spencer places men in domestic, nurturing and emotionally supportive roles that were traditionally perceived to be the domain of women. When we consider the strict and limiting parameters that have typically surrounded masculine identity in the First World War, these pictures are surprisingly open in their portrayal of the ways men could act and behave.

Spencer's conception of gender difference is deeply tied to his intriguing personal history, the impact of growing up in the parish village of Cookham where he spent much his existence but also his relationships with his first wife Hilda Carline and his second wife Patricia Preece, with whom he had already embarked on a courtship by the time he completed the chapel in 1932.[6] The details of Spencer and Preece's complicated affair and ultimately unconsummated marriage are already well documented; however, it is worth recognising here that Preece's dominance over Spencer, her manipulation of his misplaced affections and urges, represents an inversion of the normative roles assigned to men and women. Spencer's explicit self-portraits with Preece dating from the late 1930s, such as *Leg of Mutton Nude* (Tate; also known as *Double Nude Portrait: The Artist and His Second Wife*), introduce adult themes of sexual desire and carnal knowledge into his work, although overwhelmingly they are a reflection that such physical gratification remained largely unfulfilled. In these compositions control is emphatically given over to the woman, leaving Spencer powerlessly deliberating the security of his own manhood.

For Spencer the First World War can be similarly characterised as a period of personal development from childish innocence to knowledge and experience. Much like his relationship with Preece, it was a time when he evolved an acute sense of his physical self, a realisation of his body's capabilities and limitations, both of which were brought into sharp focus by the brutality of war. Spencer was only too aware that his small stature did not match up to the military ideal promoted by the War Office. Given that he was initially ruled out of participating in active service, it was only after his transfer to Salonika on the Macedonian front in August 1916 that he experienced battle first-hand, albeit in an auxiliary role as stretcher-bearer for the Field Ambulance unit. His involvement in military manoeuvres such as the evacuation of casualties during the failed attack on Machine Gun Hill were a proof of strength, but Spencer had to wait for regulations around enrolment to be relaxed before he could be considered fit for active duty. Finally, he was accepted as an infantryman for his county regiment, the Royal Berkshires, in spring 1917, and yet Spencer's war was further interrupted by hospitalisation due to reoccurring bouts of malaria. At every turn, physical weakness continued to thwart his progress, at times becoming a source of great frustration. These emotions eventually surfaced in his paintings for the chapel, specifically in his representations of the Beaufort War Hospital, in which women, though almost entirely absent, again have an emasculating influence.

Immediately before his posting to the Beaufort in 1915, Spencer wrote despairingly to the painter Henry Lamb, exclaiming, 'I expect my duties will be cleaning out the lavatories and taking the "Pan" around the ward. It seems such rotten luck that Gil [Spencer's brother Gilbert] and I had to do this instead of being "tummies" [tommies].'[7] On the whole, this prediction proved to be accurate. For Royal Army Medical Corps (RAMC) volunteers such as Spencer, day-to-day existence was filled by gruelling domestic chores centring on the care and upkeep of wounded soldiers. As Paul Gough has previously noted, the new demands that were placed upon the hospital in wartime required a thorough reordering of men and women's responsibilities. In this environment male orderlies were the lowest in a rigid hierarchy, officially presided over by the Lieutenant-Colonel but which in reality was enforced by the ward sisters from the Queen Alexandra's Imperial Military Nursing Service Reserve. Described by Spencer as 'ill-natured, cattish and conceited', these women were a source of great malcontent for him, and yet it was their strict standards of hygiene, cleanliness and grooming that ultimately dictated life at the Beaufort.[8] Although they are underrepresented in terms of their physical appearances in the hospital scenes they can be recognised as an inhibiting presence and a disciplining force that is mapped upon the bodies of the orderlies. In a reversal of conventional gender roles, men can typically be seen stooping, crouching or kneeling close to the ground as a symbol of their subordination to their female counterparts.

The issues surrounding gender difference are addressed by Spencer in *Sorting the Laundry* (Cat. 6), the only example from the cycle explicitly to feature both male and female hospital staff. The scene centres on three orderlies separating patients' personal clothing from linen and is presided over by the former asylum matron, Miss Dunn, shown at the bottom-right corner checking items against a logbook. In many respects these people are sidelined by the multiple layers of fabric under which the male body in particular is overpowered and fragmented. To the right of the painting one figure is almost totally effaced by a large towel, his legs protruding awkwardly from beneath the tasselled fringing, whilst on the other side another man battles furiously against a colossal wall of starched sheets. His exertions are utterly futile, seemingly culminating in the impenetrable heap of spotted handkerchiefs piled at his feet. Blocks of pattern such as this are repeated elsewhere in Spencer's depictions of the Beaufort, most notably in the flowered wallpaper and carpets of *Frostbite* (Cat. 11) as well as the busy bedspreads in *Bedmaking* (Fig. 2 and Cat. 15). The latter is perhaps the best illustration of the highly decorated billet rooms that the orderlies were expected to inhabit but the space is actually fictitious, formed from a conflation of different memories deriving from Spencer's experiences

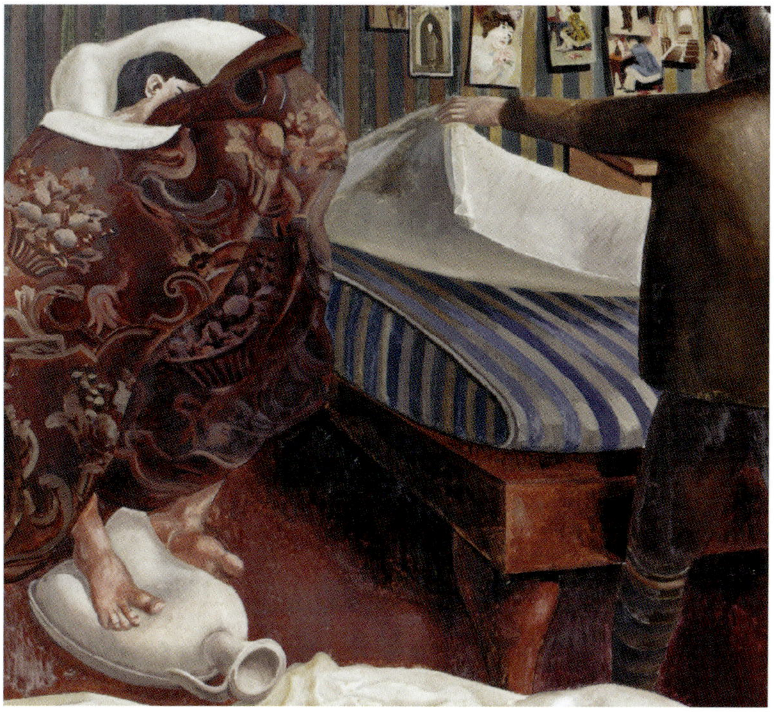

Fig. 2
Bedmaking (detail)
Sandham Memorial Chapel (South Wall) See Cat. 15

Fig. 3
Ablutions
Sandham Memorial Chapel (North Wall) See Cat. 3

during the war.[9] Reimagined as claustrophobic and suffocating environments, it is in these feminised, domestic and essentially invented interiors that much of the action takes place.

Appropriately, Spencer's representations of routine chores at the Beaufort are predominantly confined to the limited rectangular format of the lower predellas in the chapel. An exception is *Ablutions* (Fig. 3 and Cat. 3), where the chaos of the hospital washroom fills every inch of the arched canvas. A place of sanctuary away from the interference of the ward sisters, the washroom appears as an all-male environment apparently untouched by the women's ordered regime. Here the men's physical presence is asserted, emphasised by the lean, taught muscularity of their bodies and the sheer expanse of pale skin. Essentially a protective covering to be preserved and looked after, skin has a special significance in the painting and gives rise to the various processes of shaving, washing, drying and anointing that take place throughout the picture. It determines the relationships between the men, distinguishing the position of the orderlies as care-givers and the patients as the subjects of their nurturing actions.

The fraternal dynamic in the masculine realm of the washroom can be better understood in terms of 'homo-social desire', described by Eve Sedgwick as a continuum of relations between people of the same sex. Importantly in her analysis, 'desire' is not necessarily used to infer erotic feelings, but more broadly describes the powerful social force or 'glue' that holds relationships together, whether involving male friendship, mentorship or love.[10] In *Ablutions* these bonds are forged specifically around the male body where a network of connections between the men is established, based upon the sensation of touch. Points of contact are created by the overlapping torsos and limbs that navigate our eye around the canvas, starting from the soapy head on the top right-hand side and arching round anti-clockwise to the bottom corner where another man stoops down to rinse his face. Amongst this activity certain areas are particularly charged. Just to the left of the picture's centre, our attention is drawn to the process of painting a fine film of brown iodine upon a patient's chest, a delicate action that is countered by the orderly's firm grip on the man's arm. Below this, one man can be seen rubbing a patient with a towel, momentarily laying his head upon his back. The tactility of their brief exchange is described in detail, evoking the coarse texture of the towelling against the palm of the orderly's hand and face, as well as the feel of the hot, damp skin underneath. The passivity of the patient together with our heightened awareness of his tender skin act as a reminder of the fundamental susceptibility of the male body – its liability to damage or attack – whilst the actions of the orderly demonstrate the ability for men to nurture and heal. In every respect it is an affectionate, feminised representation of manhood that complicates the ideal of dominance, strength and emotional constraint that has typically been promoted.

Across the cycle, masculine identity is changeable according to the social and cultural circumstances of the men's surroundings, which in turn are framed by the temporal and geographical shifts from the Beaufort hospital to the front line in Salonika. Painted across the spandrels above the chapel's arched canvases, the vast panoramas of the Army settlement at Kalinova and the riverbed at Todorovo offer an astonishingly comprehensive account of military life. Featuring over 70 infantrymen of different ranks, including privates, sergeants and officers, the lack of women is perhaps the most notable aspect, but even more significant is the way that the men bond and interact over domestic tasks from cooking rashers of bacon (Fig. 1) and tidying their camps to washing shirts and scrubbing their summer shorts. In the absence of women Spencer's soldiers adhere to a new patriarchal order that is decidedly more harmonious and cohesive than the regime at the Beaufort.

The extent to which this resulted from social conditioning can be seen in the arched painting, *Kit Inspection* (Cat. 5), set in

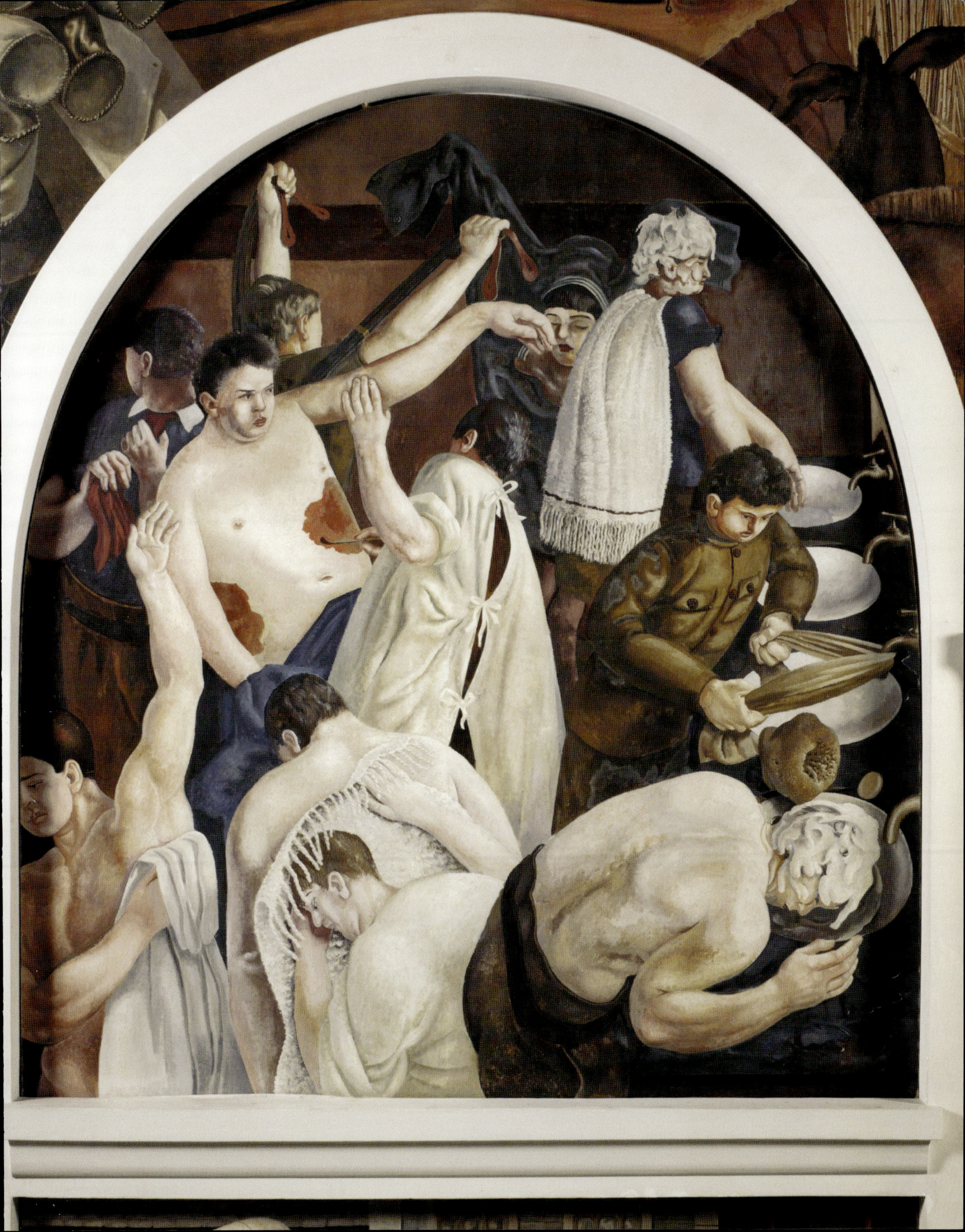

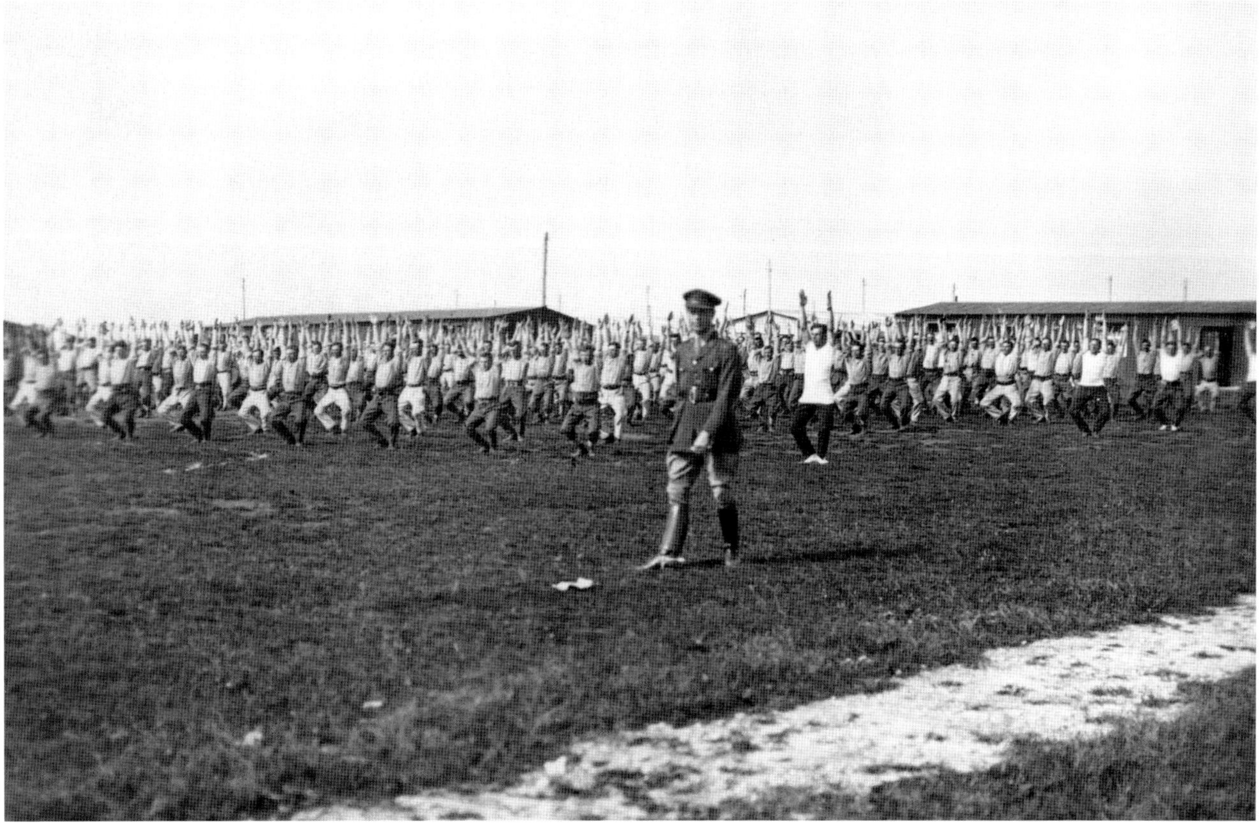

Fig. 4
Scene at an artillery training camp in England, 1917
Imperial War Museums

Tweseldown Camp near Aldershot where Spencer trained before his transfer to Salonika in 1916. Here RAMC volunteers are shown practising laying out their groundsheets and items of kit with meticulous attention to detail. The position of the three servicemen in the foreground of the composition mirrors the triangular formation of orderlies in the lower predella, *Sorting the Laundry* (Cat. 6), but the focus here is, by contrast, on productive action rather than futile movement. Even in the all-male environment of the training camp it is noticeable in *Kit Inspection* that domestic upkeep and personal grooming are performed without direction from a higher authority. It represents an evolution from the supervised activity at the hospital, where disciplinary power is assimilated by the male soldiers to the point that it operates through their own self-regulating actions.

In his influential publication, *Discipline and Punish: The Birth of the Prison*, the social theorist Michel Foucault explains how power functions in hierarchical institutions to ensure that individuals assimilate and conform to authority. Using the example of the prison system where inmates are subjected to a rigid programme of timetabling and surveillance, he asserts that disciplinary control is first internalised by prisoners before being enacted and ultimately reinforced through repeated actions.[11] Although the results of disciplinary force can therefore be seen in people's physical behaviour, in Foucault's analysis power ultimately works from within to change the way we want to be and do for ourselves. The same disciplinary model can be found in the infantry training that was received by soldiers and which Spencer himself experienced at Tweseldown. For the war authorities, the main purpose of this was to bring individual soldiers into line with the rest of their battalion by fostering a sense of group solidarity, generally known as '*esprit de corps*'.[12] A number of positive reinforcements around male comradeship and the military body were introduced to support this, including the use of standardised uniforms to inspire pride in the aesthetic qualities of the group, as well as coordinated physical exercise to bind men together in their quest for a muscular body (Fig. 4). Rooted in the tradition of men's organisations, most notably the Boy Scouts but also the lesser known League of Health and Strength, these strategies were the product of the same transformative power described by Foucault which, rather than having a constrictive or prohibitive effect, opened up new ways of being and doing.[13]

Correspondence between Spencer and his friend Desmond Chute during his summer at Tweseldown supports the idea that military training had a life-enhancing effect on civilian recruits.[14] For Spencer, arriving from the stifling domestic drudgery of the Beaufort, the experience was especially rejuvenating. In one letter dating from the beginning of his ten-week stay he gives an account of a typical morning:

> *First thing this morning we were out on the parade in our shirt sleeves and slippers doing Swedish Drill ... After breakfast cleaned up for parade at 8.30, paraded & then told off to several wagons which we began to shove and shawl along. It was perfect. I felt as if my soul would burst for joy. It is extraordinary how these experiences quicken my whole being ... Yesterday we went for ten mile route march. A whole company ('W' Coy) in one confounded lump, moving; in front one man (captain) like those egg laying insects with a little head and a tremendous body ... over sandy bumpy ground and then gorse and fir trees. It all seemed just right.*[15]

Almost akin to a religious experience, the immersive pleasure of group exercise instilled in Spencer a positive feeling and generosity of spirit. It transferred to the rest of his battalion and even extended to the company's sergeant. Spencer enthused, 'He is so naturally virile & keen, intent, & yet extraordinarily expansive. His boyish energy intelligence & interest is beautiful.' Though the artist later complained of the threatening and bullish behaviour of the officers and sergeants, his first encounter with military authority was one of adoration, which followed a pattern of identification and emulation generated by the shared experience of moving together.[16] Keen to progress to the next stage of his journey in Macedonia, Spencer became impatient with the training regime, but the importance of 'muscular bonding' in cultivating emotional and physical attachments with his fellow men cannot be overstated.[17]

Some 12 years later the impact of synchronised drill spilt out into his depictions of Army encampments in Salonika made for the chapel, in which coordinated movement seems to emerge instinctively during periods of calm and recuperation. Away from the strains of battle a sense of harmony prevails, as in the painting *Filling Water-bottles* (Cat. 12) where a convoy of wounded soldiers is shown drinking and replenishing their water supplies from a natural spring. The vision of a trio of soldiers simultaneously swigging from their bottles recalls an earlier memory from Spencer's training at Tweseldown when he witnessed a large detachment of soldiers leaving for the Macedonian front. His admiration for these men dressed in their 'sun helmets & ... lovely cool "drill" suits' is expressed by his vivid recollection of their tropical uniform, in particular the way he lovingly recorded the shimmer of golden light upon their distinctive helmets (Fig. 5).[18]

Spencer's peaceful depiction of the soldiers in Salonika differed from those of his contemporaries, particularly those associated with the Vorticist movement who responded to the harsh reality of active service by adopting the 'strong, virile and unsentimental' style of the machine age.[19] The angular delineation of the machine-gunners in Christopher Nevinson's painting *La Mitrailleuse* (Fig. 6) ruthlessly aligns their bodies with the terrible weapon, reducing them to little more than a component in the ensuing catastrophe. Completed whilst

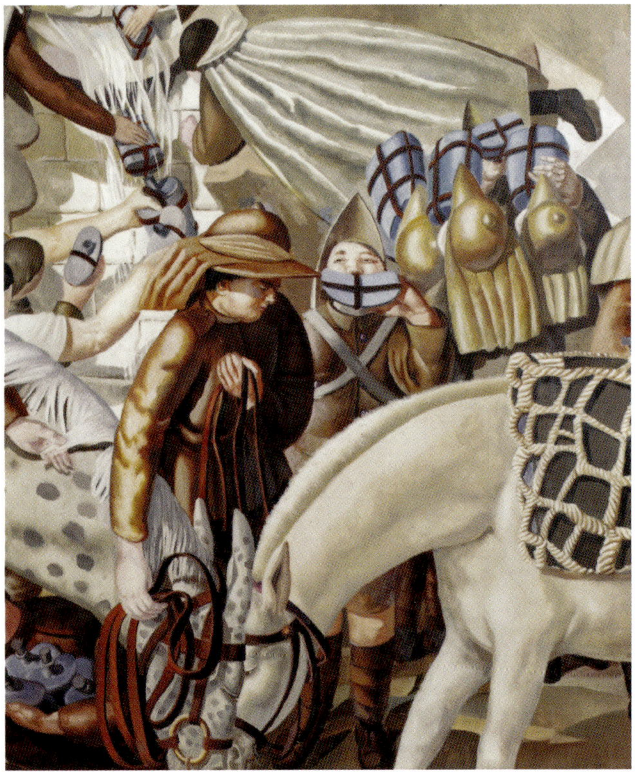

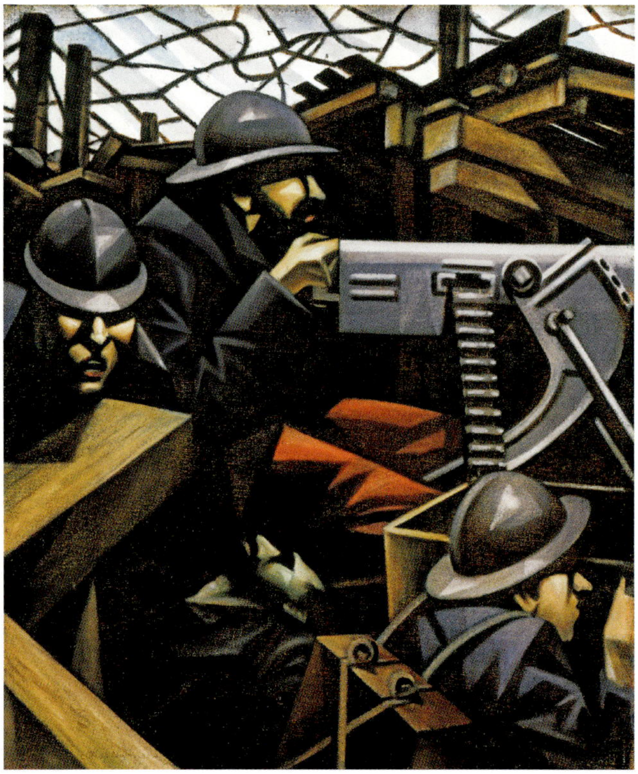

Fig. 5
Filling Water-bottles (detail)
Sandham Memorial Chapel
(South Wall) See Cat. 12

Fig. 6
Christopher Richard
Wynne Nevinson
La Mitrailleuse, 1915
Oil on canvas
Tate, presented by the
Contemporary Art Society, 1917

Nevinson was on leave in 1915, barely a year after war was declared, this representation of trench warfare is perhaps the most powerful visualisation of how extensively the male body could be integrated with the military ethos of *esprit de corps*.

Meanwhile, other artists more readily acknowledged the human devastation caused by the conflict. William Roberts, who served as a gunner in the Royal Field Artillery and endured some of the most violent action, drew upon the relationship between man and the machine to convey a sense of the brutality experienced at the front. In *The First German Gas Attack at Ypres* (1918, National Gallery of Canada), he represents the traumatic death of soldiers due to chlorine poisoning, their writhing and convulsed bodies accentuated by the painting's cruel geometry, whilst others can be seen bravely holding the line with mechanical efficiency. Roberts' next composition, *A Shell Dump, France* (Fig. 7), made for the British War Memorial Committee in 1918, again makes reference to the affiliation between the soldiers' bodies and their weaponry but the composition lacks the impact of the earlier painting, representing the rather laborious task of counting and itemising artillery shells. As Paul Gough has recognised, Roberts' handling of the subject is overly stylised to the point that the hard-edged Vorticist aesthetic becomes emotionless and formulaic.[20]

Although a similar theme is explored by Spencer in his painting *Dug-out (or Stand-to)* (Cat. 7), a markedly more human portrayal of soldierly experience is conveyed. Positioned adjacent to the final Resurrection scene, it is last in the series of paintings on one side of the chapel and recounts the ceremonial stand-to-arms that took place every morning and evening in the trenches. The robotic movement of the soldier's bodies is linked to the rhythmic pattern of military belts running across the top of the shelter suggesting to us that the men are drilled and prepared for enemy attack. Yet their gestures are ambiguous, making it unclear whether they are reaching for their harnesses or

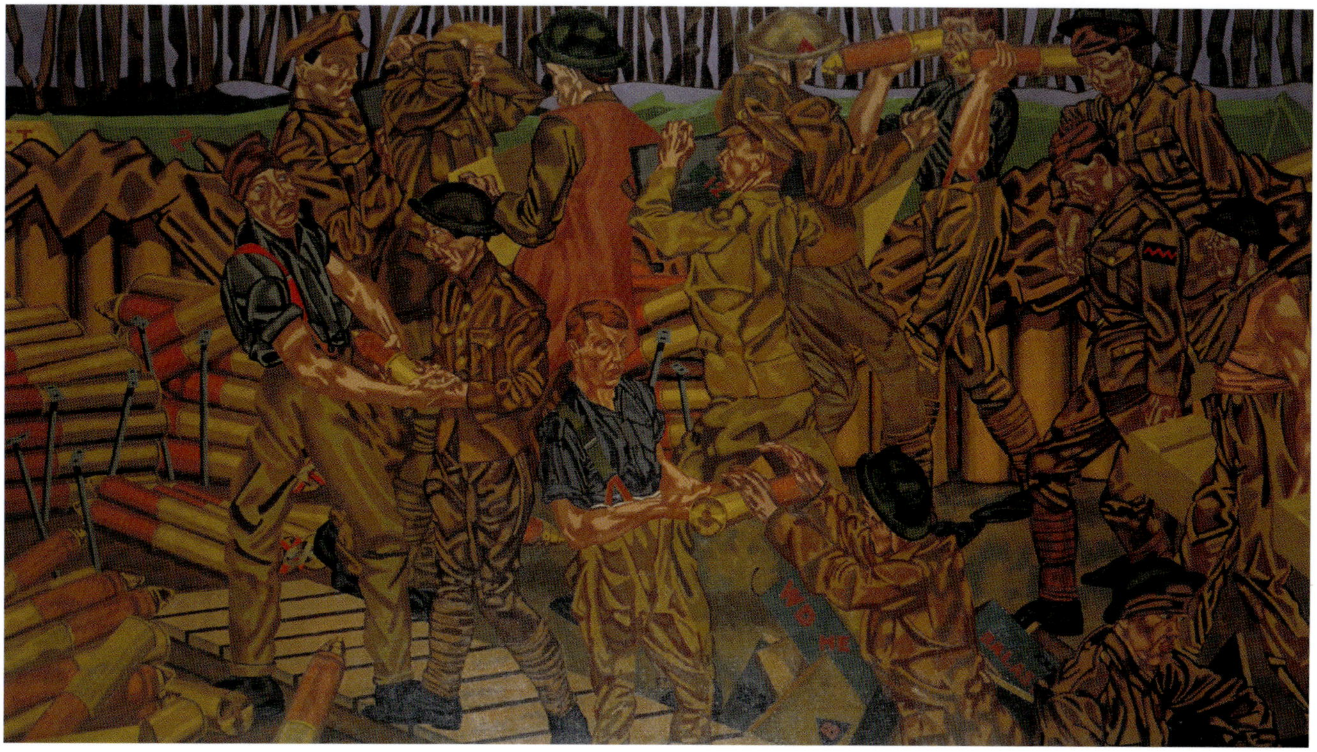

resting them back down. The latter may be the case as Spencer spoke of how *Stand-to* arose from 'thinking of how marvellous it would be if one morning, when we came out of our dug-outs, we found that somehow everything was at peace and that war was no more'.[21]

His animated portrayal of Sergeant Challonor in this scene, a soldier Spencer remembered for his incredible courage who died in action in Macedonia, reflects the immense power of the artist's imagination to reverse the tragic order of war. Depicted in camouflage and strung with grenades in the bottom left of the picture, Challonor emphatically responds to and impacts on his surroundings, demonstrating a physical agency that stands in contrast to the inert and lifeless bodies represented by Nevinson and Roberts. It is this sense of corporeality that is ultimately manifested in *The Resurrection of the Soldiers* (Cat. 9), a spiritual jouissance of intuitive and visceral sensations in which the fallen soldiers erupt into action and rise from their graves.

The representation of feeling, sensing bodies is channelled elsewhere in the chapel paintings through subtle references to personal gestures and physical inflections, such as the way an infantryman might carry his kitbag or rest his head whilst sleeping. This humanising portrayal ultimately serves to reassert a sense of the soldiers' individuality and was the result of Spencer's singular attitude towards masculinity that was unconstrained by the military ideal. For him, the usual distinctions between male and female behaviours were frequently blurred. This subversion was heightened during periods of extreme physical experience and, in his representations of the Beaufort and Salonika, reflected the personal disruption endured by Spencer due to the war. Across the cycle, fear, anxiety and desire are positively embraced as part of the natural continuum of masculinity, whilst the capacity for men to nurture, support and look after one another ultimately establishes them as agents for peace and reconciliation rather than destruction.

Fig. 7
William Roberts
A Shell Dump, France, 1918
Oil on canvas
Imperial War Museums

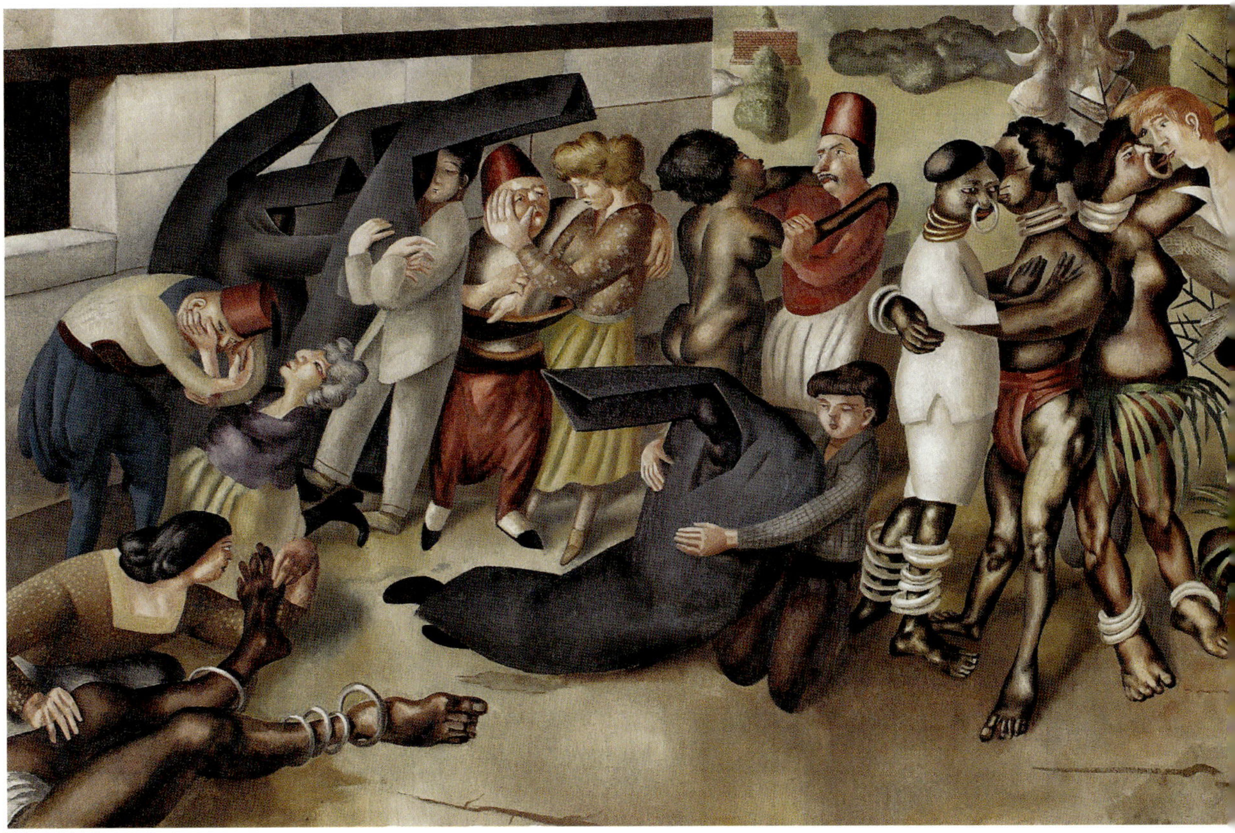

Fig. 8
Love Among the Nations, 1935–6
Oil on canvas
The Fitzwilliam Museum, Cambridge

Spencer's treatment of masculinity led to his most personal and erotically charged works created during the mid-1930s, including the composition *Love Among the Nations* (Fig. 8), where the barriers of gender, age and race are broken down through a series of erogenous sexual unions. The painting confirms Spencer's strongly held belief in 'salvation through the flesh', that the horror of war could be overcome through the reassertion of bodily sensations and pleasures. As he was to reflect in 1935:

> *During the war when I contemplated the horror of my life and the lives of those with me, I felt the only way to end the ghastly experience would be if everyone suddenly decided to indulge in every degree and form of sexual love, carnal, bestiality, anything you like to call it. These are the joyful inheritances of mankind.*[22]

Notes

1 David Cannadine, 'War and Death, Grief and Mourning in Modern Britain', in Joachim Whaley (ed.), *Mirrors of Mortality Studies in the Social History of Death*, Europa, London, 1981, p.197.
2 Paul Gough, *Stanley Spencer: Journey to Burghclere*, Sansom & Co., Bristol, 2006, pp.156–60; Sue Malvern, 'Memorizing the Great War: Stanley Spencer at Burghclere', *Art History*, no. 2, June 2000, pp.182–204.
3 Exert from Stanley Spencer's Notebook, 6 December 1946, published in Adrian Glew (ed.), *Stanley Spencer: Letters and Writings*, Tate, London, 2001, p.142.
4 Stanley Spencer's Notebook, 6 December 1946, in Glew 2001, p.142.
5 Malvern 2000, p.182.
6 Kenneth Pople, *Stanley Spencer: A Biography*, Collins, London, 1991, p.277, pp.356–65. Spencer first met Preece during an extended break from Burghclere in 1929 when he returned to Cookham. Between 1932 and 1933 his friendship with Preece grew and she encouraged his interests. The couple were married in 1937 although the union was not consummated.
7 Stanley Spencer to Henry Lamb, 19 July 1915, Tate Archive TGA 945.27, quoted in Gough 2006, p.26.
8 Stanley Spencer to Gwen and Jacques Raverat, undated *c.*1915, quoted in Gough 2006, p.45.
9 Gough 2006, p.30. As Gough has noted there is some confusion as to whether the room actually resembles a requisitioned house in Salonika although he asserts that the origins for the painting lay in the billets at the Beaufort.
10 E.K. Sedgwick, *Between Men: English Literature and Male Homosocial Desire*, Columbia University Press, New York, 1985, pp.1–2.
11 Michel Foucault, *Discipline and Punish: The Birth of the Prison*, 2nd edition, Vintage, New York, 1995, originally published in French in 1975.

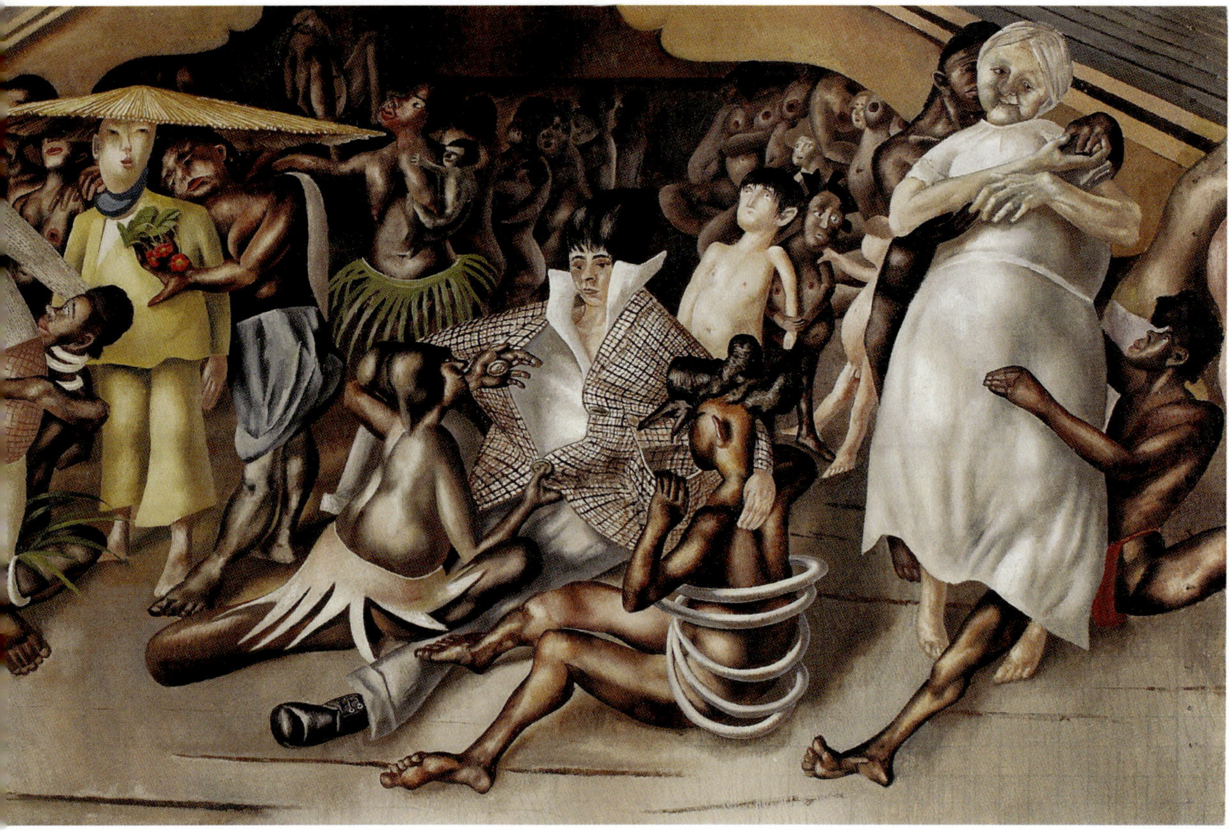

12 Joanna Bourke, *Dismembering the Male: Men's Bodies, Britain and the Great War*, Reaktion Press, London, 1996, pp.128–37.
13 Bourke 1996, pp.137–44.
14 Bourke 1996, p.76.
15 Stanley Spencer to Desmond Chute, dated May 12 1916, quoted in Richard Carline, *Stanley Spencer at War*, Faber and Faber, London, 1978, p.61; quoted in full in Paul Gough (ed.), *Your Loving Friend Stanley: The Great War Correspondence between Stanley Spencer and Desmond Chute*, Samson & Co., Bristol, 2011, p.76 (Letter 3).
16 Stanley Spencer to Desmond Chute, Summer 1916, quoted in Gough 2011, p.36 (Letter 10). Spencer wrote, 'I shall never be able to stand the bullying of the sergeants. At least I shall stand it but it will always hurt me, always shock me.'
17 Bourke 1996, pp.144–70; W.H. McNeil, *Keeping Together in Time: Dance and Drill in Human History*, Harvard University Press, Cambridge, MA, 1995, p.2.
18 Stanley Spencer to Desmond Chute, Summer 1916, quoted in Gough 2011, p.90 (Letter 9).
19 'Vital English Art: A Futurist Manifesto', *Observer*, 7 June 1914, quoted in Paul Gough, *A Terrible Beauty: British Artists in the First World War*, Sansom & Co., Bristol, 2010, p.97.
20 For a detailed discussion of the two paintings see Gough 2010, pp.287–90.
21 Stanley Spencer to Richard Carline, 1928, quoted in Richard Cork, *A Bitter Truth: Avant Garde Art and the Great War*, Yale University Press, New Haven and London, 1984, p.297.
22 Carline 1978, p.166.

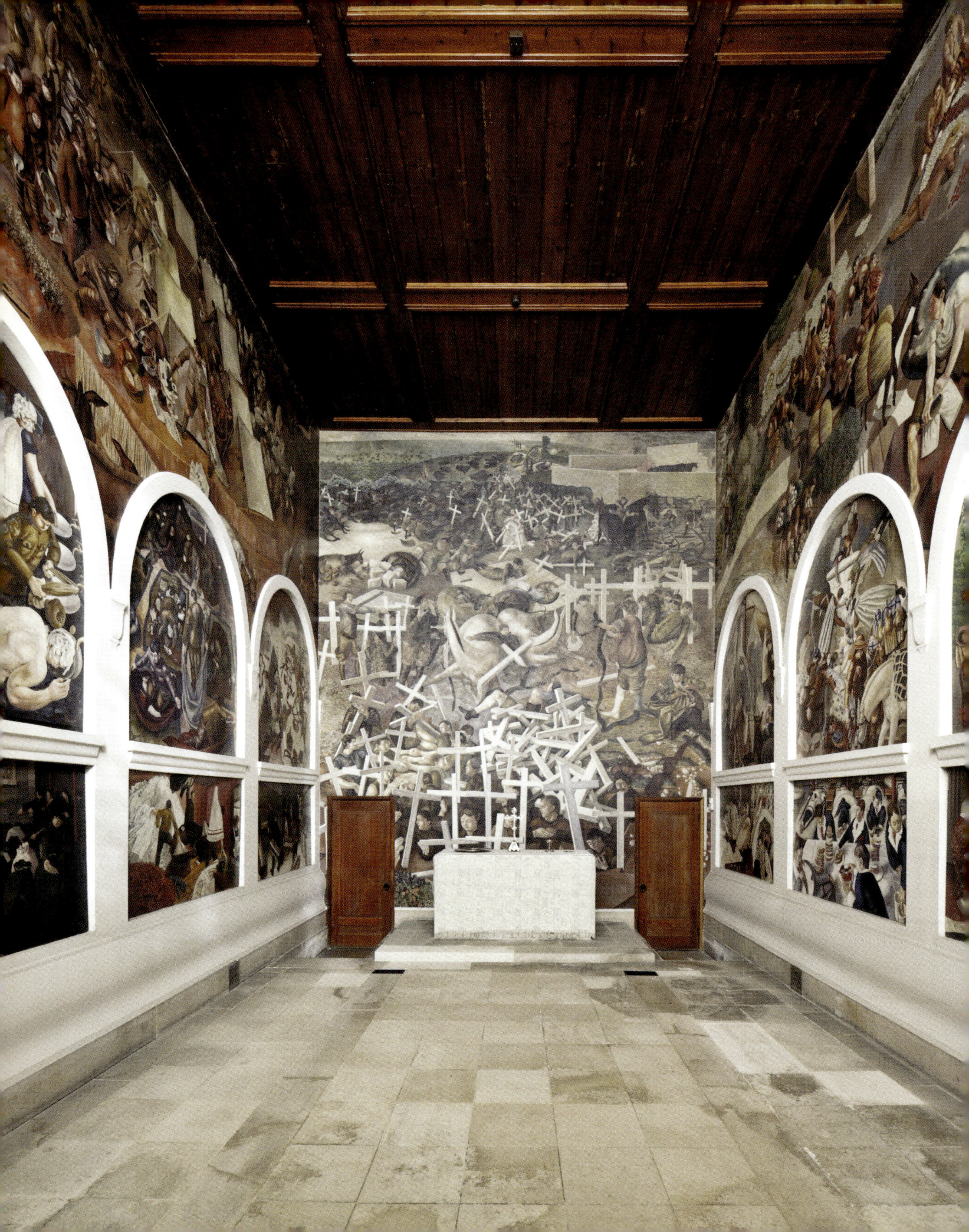

'What Ho, Giotto!': Stanley Spencer's Holy Box and the Influence of the Italian Primitives

Simon Martin

In the decade following the First World War, nearly every town and village in Britain erected monuments to the fallen from their community as an outward expression of their loss. Such memorials oscillate between honouring the sacrifice of a 'lost generation' and the naming of the individual soldier – reflecting the personal nature of each family's grief and wish to mourn the death of a loved one buried in a distant, often unknown grave. At the same time that Sir Edwin Lutyens' vast and iconic *Memorial to the Missing of the Somme* was being constructed at Thiepval in France, between 1927 and 1932 the artist Stanley Spencer (1891–1959) was working on his own highly idiosyncratic war memorial in the Hampshire village of Burghclere. Whilst the Thiepval Memorial can overwhelm the visitor with the engraved names of over 72,000 men who died between July 1916 and March 1918, affirming the notion of a sacrifice to a greater national good, a visit to Burghclere is an intimate, comforting and uplifting experience that bears no such message.

Although technically the monument to an individual soldier, Lieutenant Henry Willoughby Sandham, and dedicated as an Oratory to All Souls, the Sandham Memorial Chapel is more than anything else an artist's deeply personal response to his own experience of the war. Housed within a modest, modern red-brick building that has been likened to a municipal crematorium or water board pumping station,[1] Spencer's cycle of murals has been described by the historian Simon Schama as 'the most powerful art to emerge from the carnage of the Great War'.[2] As a commemoration of the First World War, the chapel has no parallel. Spencer's scheme is a total work of art, an installation that employs the language of the early Italian Renaissance to reflect on a twentieth-century war. Unlike the imagery of many war memorials, Spencer's murals do not depict acts of great bravery or sacrifice, nor do they depict the battlefields of the Western Front which was to be the focus of the work of so many other war artists. Instead, Spencer focused on the

Fig. 1
Interior of Sandham Memorial Chapel, view towards the altar and East Wall

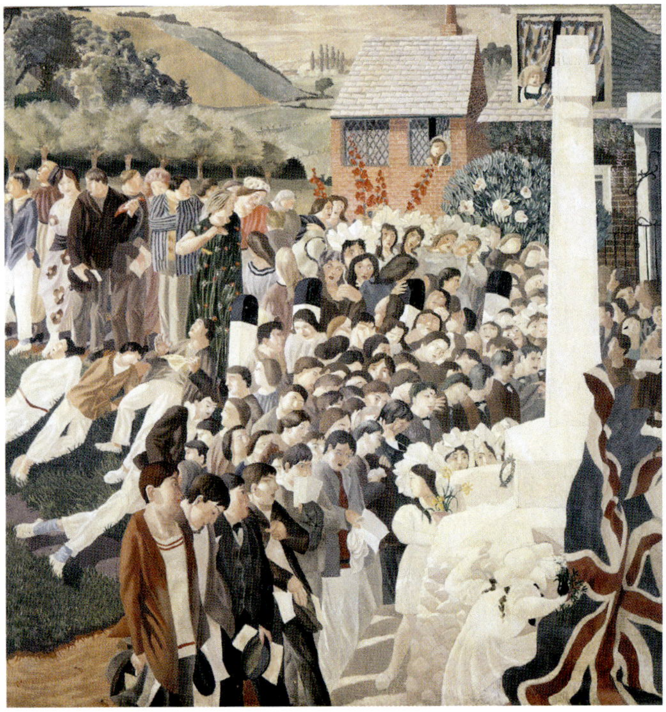

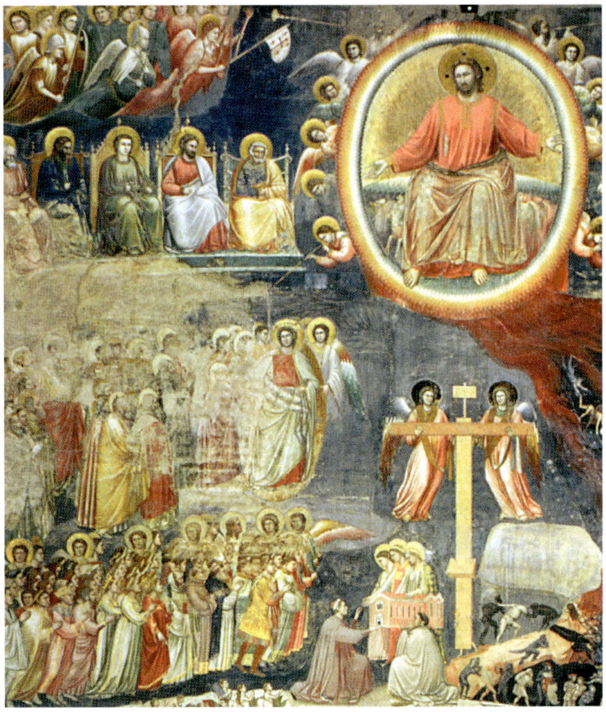

Fig. 2
Unveiling a War Memorial at Cookham, 1921
Oil on canvas
Private Collection

Fig. 3
Giotto di Bondone
The Last Judgement, c.1305
Fresco
Scrovegni (Arena) Chapel, Padua, Italy

un-heroic, everyday aspects of military service, drawing on his own experiences in the war. It amounts to a subversive memorial that is ultimately a depiction of the Resurrection in which hierarchies of rank and social status are collapsed in a way that is akin to medieval doom paintings (see *The Resurrection of the Soldiers*, Cat. 9). As with other paintings of Spencer's early career, such as *The Resurrection, Cookham* (1924–6, Tate), the chapel frames incidents, individuals and locations from the artist's life within a loosely biblical narrative so that the scenes depicted are simultaneously modern and yet rooted in archetypes from religion and art history. As such it challenges our conventional notions of history and memorialisation.

The unveiling and dedication of war memorials was an almost daily occurrence throughout the 1920s, a decade that was shaped by the process of commemoration and recovery. In 1921 Stanley Spencer recorded such a scene in his own village of Cookham in Berkshire. The subject of *Unveiling a War Memorial at Cookham* (Fig. 2) had particular resonance for the artist; not only was it based on a familiar place that was to be the setting of so many of his paintings, but also the memorial was inscribed with the names of members of his community, not least his elder brother Sidney Spencer, who had been killed in combat.

The picture's presentation of the ritual of personal grief and public mourning has a timeless quality, which transcends the particular moment that is depicted, in part because it is based on an archetypal scene: figures at the base of the Cross. The composition of the painting closely follows part of the fresco of *The Last Judgement*, from *The Life of Christ*, in the Scrovegni Chapel in Padua (Figs 3 and 4), Italy, also known as the Arena Chapel, which was to be Spencer's main point of reference in the Sandham Memorial Chapel. Completed in 1305–6, the Scrovegni Chapel was painted by the Italian early-Renaissance artist Giotto di Bondone (1267–1337). In Spencer's painting, the form of the faithful souls assembled beneath the cross in Giotto's fresco is translated into the shape of the

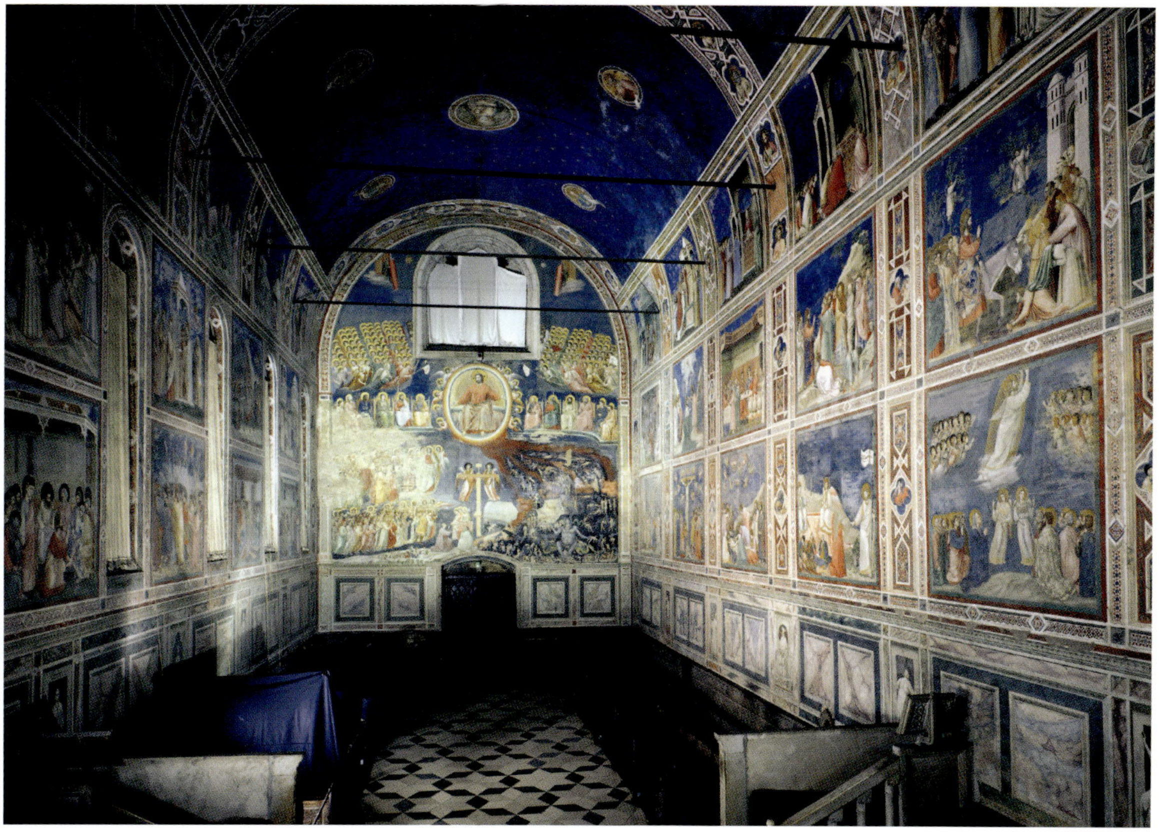

Fig. 4
Giotto di Bondone
View of the chapel looking towards *The Last Judgement*, c.1305
Scrovegni (Arena) Chapel, Padua, Italy

crowd at the war memorial. A tier of angels in the fresco becomes a line of Cookham residents standing on a grassy verge, whilst frilly bonnets worn by several of the women are suggestive of the halos that surround the heads of Giotto's host of angels. The Union Jack, draped over the base of the monument, recalls the folds of the robe of Enrico Scrovegni, the donor of the eponymous chapel, who kneels next to those being resurrected and, assisted by a priest, offers his church to the three Marys.

If *Unveiling of a War Memorial at Cookham* were to be a diptych it would correspond to the descent into hell on the other side of the cross in Giotto's fresco (Fig. 4). Yet, whereas other war artists such as Paul Nash and C.R.W. Nevinson depicted visceral scenes of devastation on the Western Front that were suggestive of a hell on earth, Spencer's vision of war was always with an eye to peace. He wrote that the painting 'was intended to express the absence of hurry ... and to express the peaceful life that I visualised people could live if there was no war'.[3] It had been commissioned, but later rejected, by the collector Sir Michael Sadler, and had its roots in an idea for a painting of 'a religious service at the front' which had been suggested as the subject for a commission from the Ministry of Information (MOI) whilst Spencer was on active service in Macedonia from August 1916.[4] Spencer had been unable to paint this subject due to the MOI's failure to release him from his regiment, and instead he later painted another work based on his wartime experiences, *Travoys with Wounded Soldiers Arriving at a Dressing Station at Smol, Macedonia* (1919, Imperial War Museum London). Spencer recalled:

> *I had wanted this religious significance in all I did to be realised, & this seemed the chance to express this link or fusion. And now, besides doing that (as I tried to do in the big Travoys picture) I felt a wish to join that war-experience-hope felt in midst of war & war experience, to my Cookham love & home feeling & the religious feeling as well. This*

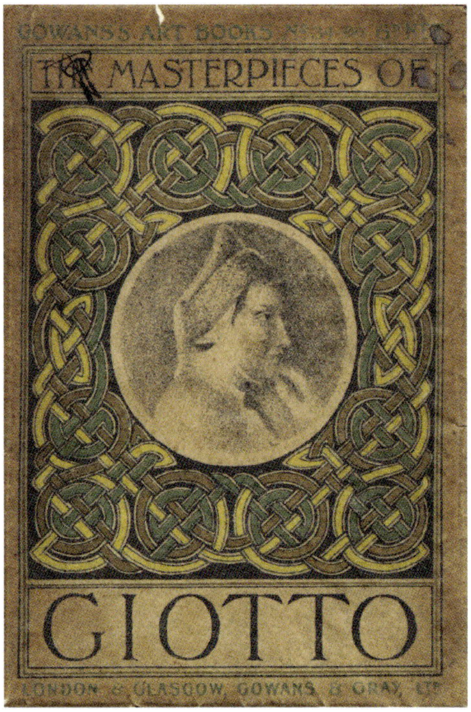

Fig. 5
The Masterpieces of Giotto
Published by Gowans & Gray, 1909

wish found for me considerable fulfilment in the 'Unveiling a War Memorial' painting. The service was not at the front, but in Cookham.[5]

As with his fellow British artists Edward Burra and William Roberts, Spencer's figurative paintings of modern life that reference stylistic motifs from the Old Masters can be seen as part of the wider *rappel à l'ordre* (or 'return to order') in modern European art following the First World War, characterised in the work of the German Neue Sachlichkeit (New Objectivity) artists such as Christian Schad, Otto Dix and Georg Scholz, the Valori Plastici artists in Italy such as Gino Severini, Mario Sironi and Giorgio de Chirico, and Jean Cocteau, Pablo Picasso and Fernand Léger in France. For Spencer it was not so much a rejection of abstraction as the continuation of a figurative path on which he had set out before the war.

His enthusiasm for the paintings of Giotto and other Italian early Renaissance masters had begun whilst he was a student at the Slade School of Art from 1908–12. At the Slade he had been part of an extraordinary generation including Adrian Allinson, David Bomberg, Dora Carrington, Mark Gertler, Paul Nash, C.R.W. Nevinson, William Roberts and Edward Wadsworth, which was described by the drawing master Henry Tonks as the school's last 'crisis of brilliance'.[6] Tonks had fostered an appreciation of the art of the Renaissance, giving the students assignments with set titles that were drawn from themes from the Old Masters.

Spencer acquired numerous Gowans & Gray sixpence pocket editions about the Florentine and Sienese Masters (Fig. 5), and in 1911 was given a copy of John Ruskin's book *Giotto and His Works at Padua* (1854) by his Slade friends, the artists Jacques and Gwen Raverat. At this time Spencer was developing his own idiosyncratic and deeply held Christian beliefs, and he later recalled: 'my becoming conscious of the rich religious significance of the place I lived in. My feelings for things being holy was very strong at this time.'[7] Spencer's depiction of Cookham as a 'holy suburb of Heaven' in subsequent works concurred with Ruskin's view of Giotto that, 'apart from all reference to the legends, there is something peculiarly beautiful in the simplicity of conception ... as though believing that angels might appear anywhere, and any day, and to all men, as a matter of course, if we could ask them'.[8]

At the Slade, Spencer had painted numerous religious subjects, including *The Nativity* (1912, University College London), which won the Summer Composition Competition, and *John Donne Arriving in Heaven* (1911, Private Collection), which was shown in the *Second Post-Impressionism Exhibition* organised by Clive Bell and Roger Fry at the Grafton Galleries, London, in the autumn of 1912, alongside the work of Cézanne, Matisse, Picasso and the British artists Vanessa Bell, Eric Gill and Duncan Grant.[9] Fry's advocacy of continental Post-Impressionist artists was grounded in his admiration for early Italian art, and in the pre-war years he located the force of Gothic and Primitive Italian art in its formal values of colour and design, rather than its literal and religious content.[10] His fellow Bloomsbury critic Clive Bell declared of the art that 'moved' people that, 'the greater part is what is called "primitive"

... In primitive art you will find no accurate representation, you will find only significant form. Yet no other art moves us so profoundly.'[11] Together with his fellow Slade students Allinson, Bomberg, John Currie, Gertler, Nevinson and Wadsworth, Spencer was part of a loose and temporary grouping dubbed the 'Neo-Primitives' who synthesised the influence of the early Italians with the Post-Impressionist colours of artists such as Paul Gauguin. Their interest in the Italian Primitives was informed by several important exhibitions in London in the pre-war years, which included Botticelli, Mantegna and Giorgione at the Royal Academy in 1908, 1910 and 1912, the Umbrian School (Gozzoli, Piero della Francesca, and Signorelli) at the Burlington Fine Arts Club in 1910, and the Grafton Gallery's *Exhibition of Old Masters* including works by Giotto, Duccio, Masolino, Gozzoli, Signorelli and Giorgione in 1911.[12] In addition, Spencer regularly visited the National Gallery where he would have seen the significant collection of fourteenth-century Italian paintings, which had been acquired in the nineteenth-century by Sir Charles Eastlake. 'I wish the National Gallery was in Cookham', he was to write to the artist Henry Lamb in October 1913, 'but I have many reproductions of fine pictures of Old Masters, lent me by the Raverats. They stimulate me; they quicken me. Do they not do so to you?'[13] The following spring Spencer wrote to Henry Lamb asking him to send him 'anything by Lorenzetti', explaining how: 'I am getting a good collection of postcards. I do not put them into a book; because I like to look at them separately. I take one out, according to how I feel, and put it somewhere in the room, so that I can look at it if I feel inclined. It sort of keeps me company and makes me work ... P.S. Do not forget the Lorenzetti.'[14]

In his influential book *Art*, published in 1914, Clive Bell had urged his readers to 'go to Santa Croce or the Arena Chapel and admit that if the greatest name in European painting is not Cézanne, it is Giotto'.[15] Yet, if Spencer had been so inclined to leave Cookham to travel to Padua to see for himself, it was not possible due to the outbreak of the First World War in the summer of 1914. Even when writing to Henry Lamb of his thoughts of enlisting in the military, Spencer was to refer to the Old Masters: 'It is intolerable to be out of it; I cannot think. ... If I go to war, I go on condition I can have Giotto, the Basilica of Assisi book, Fra Angelico in one pocket, and Masaccio, Masolino and Giorgione in the other.'[16]

Spencer did not enlist immediately, instead volunteering for military training in the Maidenhead Civic Guard and attending St John Ambulance classes at Bray, whilst continuing to paint works such as *The Centurion's Servant* (completed September 1914, Tate), *Mending Cowls, Cookham* (1915, Tate) and the diptych *The Resurrection of the Good and the Bad* (1915). The asymmetric shapes of the latter canvases were due to Spencer's unsuccessful plan for them to be positioned above the chancel arch in Cookham church. They signalled the start of Spencer's interest in depicting the subject of the Resurrection, which was to be the theme of so many of his post-war pictures, but also his desire to create site-specific installations of his paintings. It was an ambition that he was not able to realise for several years, but throughout his war service Spencer was to speak of his desire to paint frescoes based on his experiences. Whilst posted to the Beaufort War Hospital near Bristol after enlisting with the Royal Army Medical Corps in July 1915, Spencer wrote to the artist and poet Desmond Chute of how: 'I should love to do a fresco of an operation ... How mysterious the hands look – wonderfully intense. There was something very classical about the whole operation',[17] and to Jas Wood: 'I am still thinking about the hospital, which the more I think about, the more it inspires me. I am determined that when I get a chance, I am going to do some wonderful things – a whole lot of big frescoes.'[18]

Just as he had promised to Lamb at the outbreak of war, Spencer carried his art books with him during his military service. In May 1916, he wrote to Chute from Tweseldown Camp in Surrey of how he had books on Giotto and the Church of St Francis of Assisi, 'So that even Giotto is dragged into this drill' and that 'the camps and tents make me want to do a

Fig. 6
Study for the North Wall of Sandam Memorial Chapel, c.1923
Wash on paper
Stanley Spencer Gallery
(Presented by J.L. Behrend through the Friends of the Stanley Spencer Gallery, 1972)

Fig. 7
Study for the South Wall of Sandam Memorial Chapel, c.1923
Wash on paper
Stanley Spencer Gallery
(Presented by J.L. Behrend through the Friends of the Stanley Spencer Gallery, 1972)

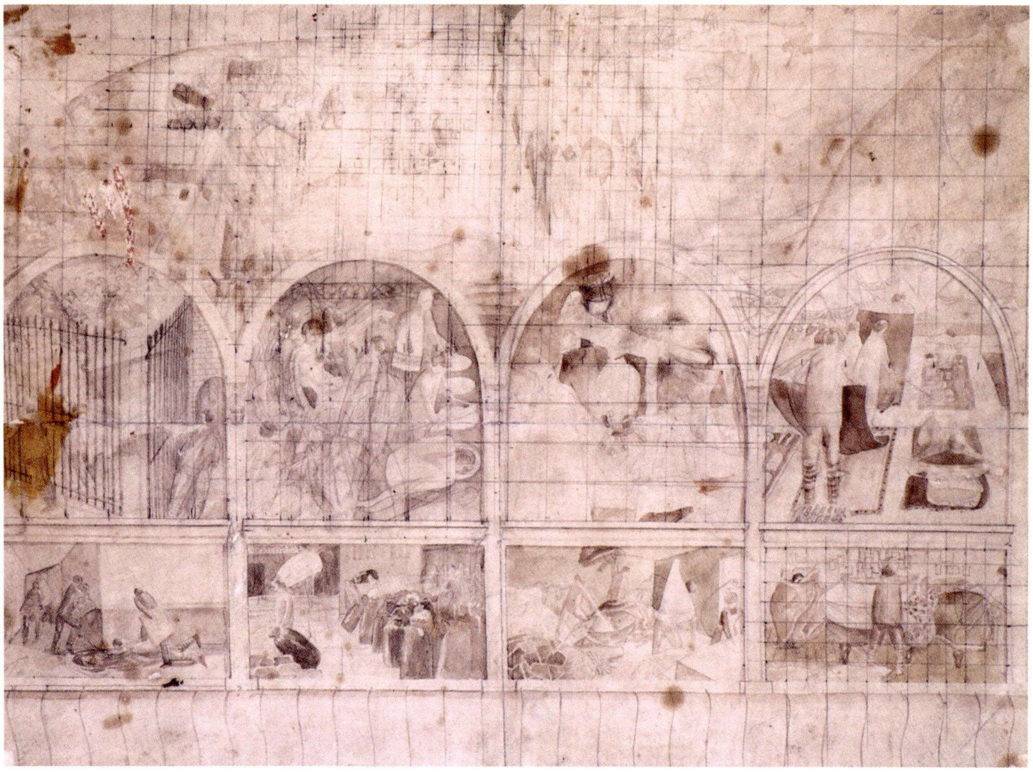

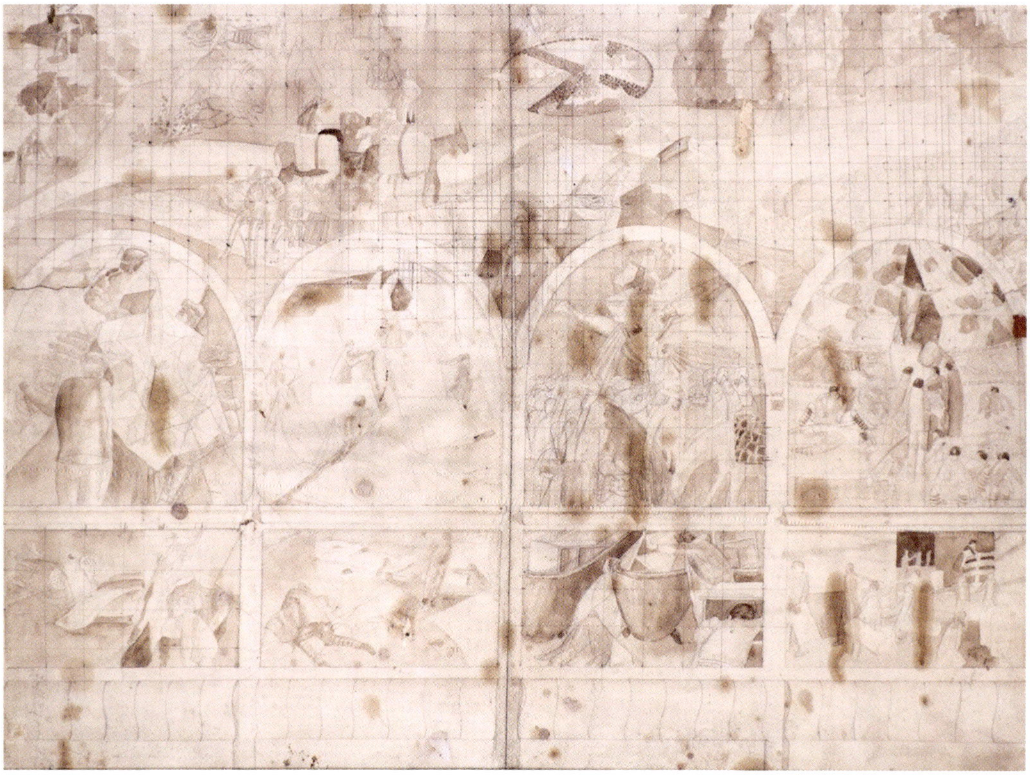

big fresco painting'.[19] After he was assigned as an orderly to the 68th Field Ambulance in Macedonia in August 1916 his resolve to make paintings of his war experience was deepened and took form in a plan to create paintings for a church. Recovering from malaria at the 49th General Hospital in Salonika in October 1918, Spencer wrote to his sister Florence, 'When I come home I am going to learn fresco painting and then, if Jacques Raverat's project holds good, we are going to build a church and the walls will have on them all about Christ. If I don't do this on earth, I will do it in Heaven.'[20]

Spencer's ambitions for painting site-specific schemes were repeatedly frustrated in the years following the war. In 1920, Spencer was one of several artists chosen by Sir Michael Sadler to produce decorations for Leeds Town Hall, but his preliminary design was found unsuitable by William Rothenstein, and the following year he had another unfulfilled commissioned from Muirhead Bone to paint a mural for the Memorial Hall in the village of Steep, for which he prepared drawings of *Scrubbing the Floor* and *Soldiers Washing*, based on his experiences at Beaufort, elements of which were later realised in the panels for Burghclere (Cat. 2 and 3). He was at least able to work with a particular space in mind when creating a series of religious pictures set in Cookham, such as *The Last Supper* (1920, Stanley Spencer Gallery) and a triptych of *The Money Changers* (1921, Stanley Spencer Gallery), for the private oratory of his patron Sir Henry Slesser, an Anglo-Catholic. 'You see when I do a big picture I like to feel that it is for some special wall or building', he wrote to Lady Ottoline Morrell. 'I like the architectural feeling I sometimes get in some of my pictures but this kind of thing can't develop without having some definite *scheme* of pictures. It is so difficult to get people to see that I want to do big pictures to appear bang next to each other cheek to cheek, & *nothing* in between.'[21]

Following a painting expedition to Yugoslavia with the Carline family in 1922, which brought Spencer relatively close to where he had been posted during the war, Spencer began to make detailed drawings for a scheme of war paintings based on his experiences. 'Stanley sits at a table all day evolving acres of Salonica and Bristol war compositions', wrote Lamb to Richard Carline whilst Spencer was staying with him in Poole in June 1923. Spencer went so far as to produce plans of an architectural scheme featuring sidewalls in two registers with a series of arched upper panels with predellas below and an unbroken end wall behind the altar, loosely echoing Ruskin's drawings of the Scrovegni Chapel. Whilst teaching at the Ruskin School in Oxford in November 1922, Spencer explained his interest in the predella format:

> *It is rather interesting to think of pictures in the way musicians think of music. The early Italians would sometimes do a series of pictures related one to the other ... You have people ... who are interested in having pictures that go together, but that is not quite what I mean. I mean the dramatic integral relation, such as one has in a sonata in music, between the first, second and third movements, in relation to painting each movement being a picture ... A Predella is rather like a Prelude to a fugue in music, or a prelude and codetta with a fugue in between. I feel there is a fine architectural element in this.*[22]

When the collectors John Louis and Mary Behrend saw and admired the drawings whilst visiting Henry Lamb, Spencer had found his own Scrovegni to be patrons for the building of his chapel. Reportedly he exclaimed, 'What ho, Giotto!' when he eventually heard that the decision to build the chapel had been reached (Figs 6 and 7). The artist was later to observe that it was 'built in the air ... that is to say not commissioned'.[23] It is significant that the starting point of the project was the result of the Behrends wishing to realise Spencer's vision, rather than it originating as a memorial to Lieutenant Sandham. As John Louis Behrend was later to write: 'it is true that when the building was up we had the idea of dedicating it to the memory of my wife's brother, H.W. Sandham, who served also on the Salonika front; and this has led to some confusion. But it is certain that, without Stanley, poor Hal would have had no memorial.'[24] Regardless of original intention, the Sandham Memorial Chapel is

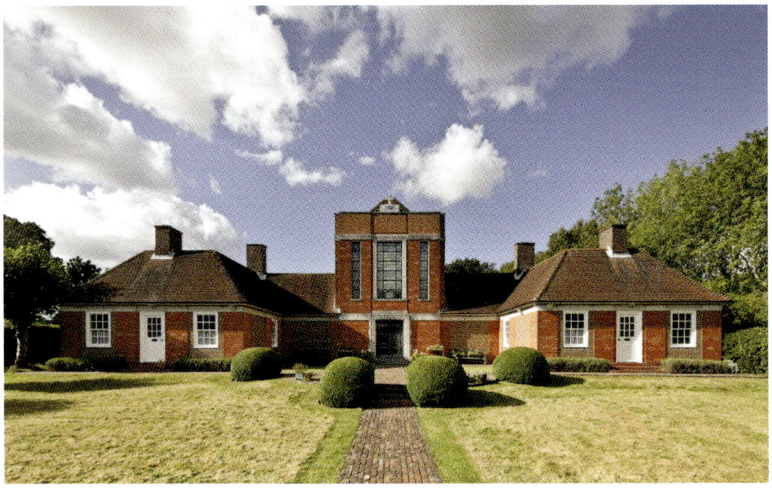

Fig. 8
Exterior of Sandham Memorial Chapel, Burghclere, Hampshire

like the Scrovegni Chapel in Padua in that it takes the notional form of the medieval chantry chapel, built for the benefit of the departed soul of a deceased person to help speed it to heaven, hence the symbolic importance of Spencer's *Resurrection of the Soldiers* (Cat. 9) on the East Wall. Yet the Behrends' complicated religious background (John Louis Behrend was a convert from Judaism; see Amanda Bradley's essay in this catalogue) underpins the fact that the chapel format was a convention that met Spencer's desire to create a 'Holy Box' for his cycle of paintings. Now in the custodianship of the National Trust (Fig. 1), the chapel occupies a fluid position between being a memorial, a place of devotion, an art museum, a heritage attraction or simply a place of reflection. In this respect, Spencer's paintings at Burghclere may look back to wall-based Renaissance precedents such as Giotto in the Scrovegni Chapel and Basilica of San Francesco in Assisi, Ambrogio Lorenzetti in the Palazzo Pubblico of Siena and Michelangelo in the Sistene Chapel in Rome. However, the chapel also sets its own precedents for modern art, whether the creation of modern religious artworks for sacred spaces, such as Reverend Walter Hussey commissioning artists such as Henry Moore and Graham Sutherland at St Matthew's Northampton and Chichester Cathedral; the Rothko Chapel in Houston, USA; or the now ubiquitous notion of site-specific installations in contemporary art galleries and non-conventional spaces.

Although the architect Lionel Pearson designed the exterior of the building, after an aborted first design by the Behrends' preferred choice, George Kennedy, the interior was a *Gesamtkunstwerk*, a total work of art created to Spencer's single-minded and detailed plan. 'I have decided the proportions of everything', Spencer wrote to his sister Florence: 'Length of building, height of roof, kind of tiles, height of dado and cornice, projection of moulding of arches, size and place of window and door, so that the architect only has to make a builder's drawing from my measurements.'[25] In another letter to Lamb indicating Giotto's continued presence as a point of reference, Spencer wrote of his belief that 'my own ideas about the building are the best; that it ought to be plain outside, just like a box, and that there ought to be no ... architectural ornament or features outside whatever. Richard Carline said that the Padua Chapel was just a plain block sticking straight out of the ground' (Fig. 8).[26] Although he initially hoped to have an arched east wall for his *Resurrection*, as at Padua, it was not to be possible and so instead the building follows a rectangular format.

Spencer also initially wished to work in fresco and had experimented with the medium using Vitruvius' recipe, but ultimately it was not practical in the English climate and the paintings were realised in oil on canvas. Spencer's project to paint his own equivalent to the Italian frescoed churches came at a time when mural painting as a modern art form for post-war society was the subject of great interest, as exemplified by the socially engaged Mexican muralists Diego Rivera, José Clemente Orozco and David Alfaro Siqueiros, and Italians such as Carlo Carrà, whose monograph on Giotto was published in English in 1925. It also coincided with a revival of interest in the native English tradition of wall painting following the publication of the monumental tome, *English Medieval Painting* (1929), by the conservator Professor E.W. Tristram and Tancred Borenius, who also began work at this time on the restoration of the doom (Last Judgement) painting on the chancel arch at Stratford-upon-Avon. Like many doom paintings, Spencer's scheme of soldiers at the Beaufort War Hospital and in Salonika features anecdotal details and pastoral motifs, and ultimately promises redemption.

Spencer's project at Burghclere is loosely mirrored in the plot of the Booker Prize-nominated novella, *A Month in the Country* by J.L. Carr, in which the protagonist Tom Birkin returns from the war and is hired to uncover the fourteenth-century painting on the wall of a country church. The experience is a healing process, during which Birkin feels close to the long-dead and unknown wall-painter, 'a nameless painter reaching from the dark to show me what he could do, saying to me as clear as any words, "If any part of me survives from time's corruption, let it be this. For this was the sort of man I was."'[27] Whilst Spencer was in the village of Burghclere creating his own wall paintings, like Birkin he was reaching back to artists from the distant past in order to understand and create a frame for the troubling events of his recent present.

Writing of Spencer's extraordinary ability to see the modern world through the lens of artists such as Giotto, Masaccio and Lorenzetti, Henry Lamb wondered at 'the astounding novelty of such a personality stepping in at this time of day to restore narrative art to its primitive purity, lost in history since Fra Angelico and in every child after the age of 12 or 13'.[28] Like Giotto's Scrovegni Chapel, Spencer's Sandham Memorial Chapel is a masterpiece of its age, and yet it is also timeless. It is a memorial that is not about death or violence, but the experience of *living* in wartime, and about the promise of life beyond death through memorialisation, and the existence of the past in the present. As Spencer later claimed: 'I wanted when I had finished the Burghclere work to do not a chapel to do with war but to do with the more vital meaning of peace.'[29]

Notes

1 See Patrick Wright, 'Purposeful Art in a Climate of Cultural Reaction: Stanley Spencer in the 1920s', in Timothy Hyman and Patrick Wright (eds), *Stanley Spencer*, exh. cat., Tate, London, 2001, p.43.
2 Simon Schama, 'The Church of Me', *New Yorker*, 17 February 1997, p.57.
3 Keith Bell with Richard Carline and Andrew Causey, *Stanley Spencer*, exh. cat., Royal Academy with Weidenfeld and Nicolson, London, 1980, p.81.
4 Richard Carline, *Stanley Spencer at War*, Faber and Faber, London, 1978, p.95.
5 Stanley Spencer, Notebook, 1945–7, Tate Archive TGA 733.3.86, cited in Adrian Glew, *Stanley Spencer: Letters and Writings*, Tate, London, 2001, p.111.
6 See David Boyd Haycock, *A Crisis of Brilliance: Five Young British Artists and the Great War*, Old Street, London, 2009.
7 TGA 733.3.1, c.1937.
8 John Ruskin, *Giotto and His Works at Padua*, Levey, Robson and Franklyn, London, 1854, p.52.
9 Commenting on Spencer's religious conviction as opposed to significant form, Eric Gill wrote: 'Oh damn the P.I.'s [Post Impressionists] when there is piety like Spencer's to be worshipped.' Eric Gill to Jacques Raverat, 5 December 1912, quoted in Frances Spalding, '"Working for an imaginary temple": Stanley Spencer, Eric Gill, Jacques and Gwen Raverat', *Burlington Magazine*, vol.143, no.1178, May 2001, p.292.
10 Fry was later to recognise Giotto's ability to combine narrative and formal values, stating in a lecture of 1920 that: 'We can say if we like that Giotto used his astonishing genius as a composer to emphasize & illustrate the dramatic theme – but those who have once grasped the extraordinary significance of his formal designs will be likely perhaps to feel that the drama was the point of departure & the pretext for a profound and moving harmony.' Christopher Green, *Art Made Modern: Roger Fry's Vision of Art*, Merrell Holberton, London, 1999, p.221.
11 Clive Bell, 'Post-Impressionism and Aesthetics', *Burlington Magazine*, January 1913, pp.226–30.
12 See Keith Bell, *Stanley Spencer: A Complete Catalogue of the Paintings*, Phaidon, London, 1992.
13 Stanley Spencer to Henry Lamb, October 1913, in Carline 1978, p.38.
14 Stanley Spencer to Henry Lamb, 1 April 1914, in Carline 1978, p.38.
15 Clive Bell, *Art*, Chatto and Windus, London, 1914.
16 Stanley Spencer to Henry Lamb, quoted in Carline 1978, p.40.
17 Stanley Spencer to Desmond Chute, undated but probably written in May 1916, in Carline 1978, p.58. These comments anticipate Barbara Hepworth's 'Hospital Drawings' created in the late 1940s, which depict surgical operations in a manner that recalls early Renaissance paintings: see Nathaniel Hepburn (ed.), *Barbara Hepworth: The Hospital Drawings*, Tate, London, 2012.
18 Stanley Spencer to James Wood, 27 July 1916, in Carline 1978, p.59.
19 Stanley Spencer to Desmond Chute, May 1916, in Carline 1978, pp.62–3.
20 Stanley Spencer to Florence Spencer, in Carline 1978, p.108.
21 Stanley Spencer to Lady Ottoline Morrell, n.d. Harry Ransom Research Centre, University of Texas, Austin, quoted in David Boyd Haycock, *Nash, Nevinson, Spencer, Gertler, Carrington, Bomberg: A Crisis of Brilliance 1908-1922*, Scala Arts & Heritage Publishers Ltd/ Dulwich Picture Gallery, London, 2013.
22 Carline 1978, p.138.
23 Stanley Spencer, in *Stanley Spencer: A Retrospective Exhibition*, Tate Gallery: London, 1955, p.3.
24 Guide to the Sandham Memorial Chapel, undated (c.1965).
25 Stanley Spencer to Florence Spencer in September 1923, in Carline 1978, p.156.
26 Stanley Spencer to Henry Lamb, Carline 1978, p.158.
27 J.L. Carr, *A Month in the Country*, Penguin, Harmondsworth, 1978.
28 Henry Lamb to Richard Carline, 10 May 1924, Tate Archive Box 8216, quoted in Bell 1992, p.369.
29 Stanley Spencer, in Tate 1955, p.3.

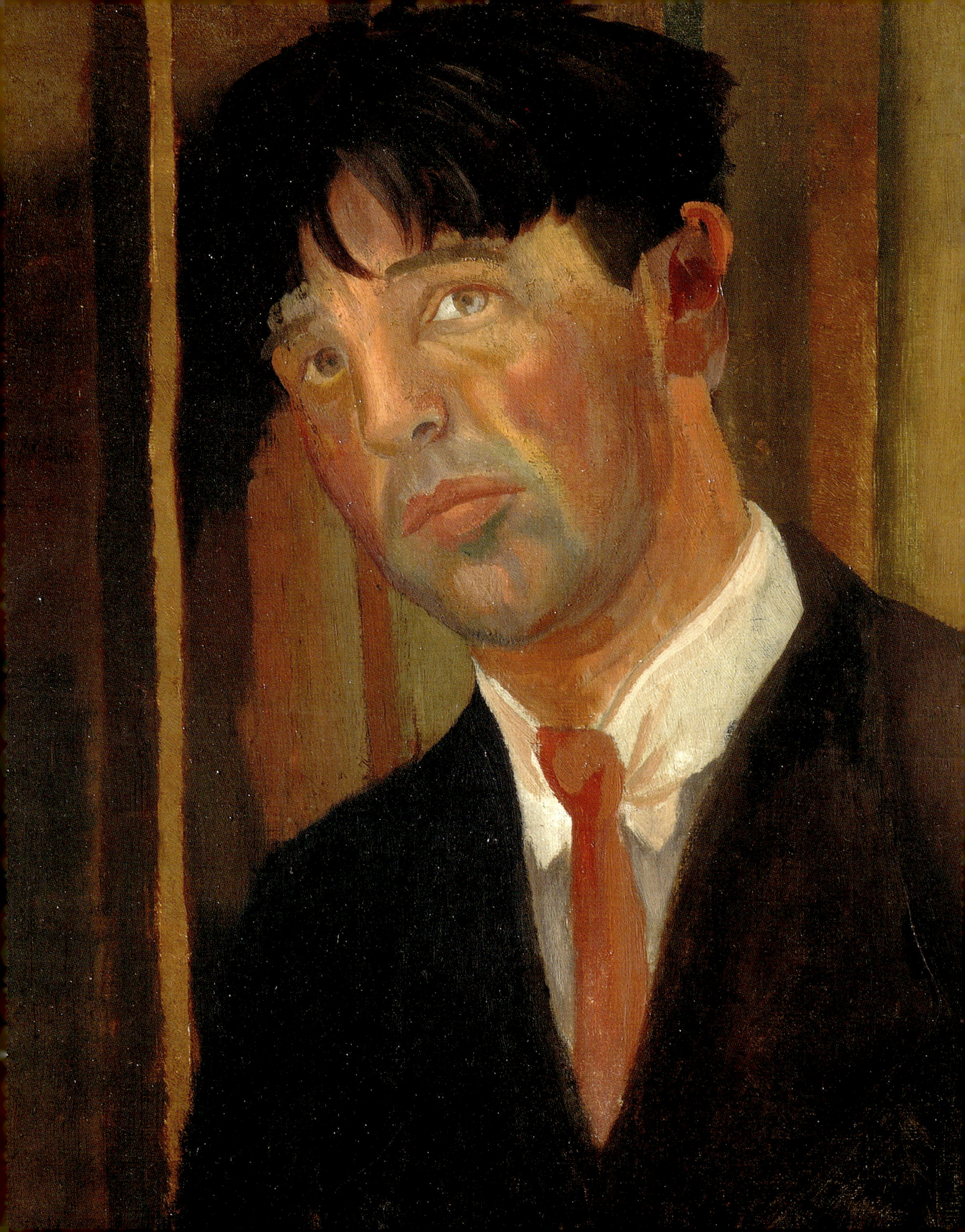

Finding Heaven in a Hell of War: A Psychological Perspective

Jenny Beddington and
Jamie Hacker Hughes

Stanley Spencer (Fig. 1) was born in Cookham, the tenth of eleven children (including twins who died in infancy). During the time of his birth and early childhood, his eldest brother, Will, had a nervous breakdown. Their father, who was a music teacher and church organist, had high hopes for Will in the music world and, according to their mother, put a lot of pressure on him. Will was treated in an expensive mental health institution, causing tremendous financial difficulties for the family. There was no money for a nanny so Stanley and his younger brother, Gilbert, to whom he was close, were looked after by their elder sister, Annie. According to Gilbert, the father never quite got over the disappointment of his elder son and buried himself more and more in his books.

The Spencers could not afford private schooling and did not wish to send the boys to a state school. Instead, their father opened his own school in a tin shed. Together with a few other children, he taught them himself. Later, their elder sisters, Annie and Florence, became their teachers. Stanley's education was therefore limited, as can be seen in his letters, with grammatical and spelling errors, and he would sometimes describe himself as a dunce (he was known to ask people to correct his letters). However, he was well educated in many other ways. The family was artistic and intellectual – musical instruments and books were part of their upbringing. There were long family discussions at meal times on politics, philosophy and so on. Kenneth Pople (one of Spencer's biographers) describes the family as 'acquirers of information'.[1] Importantly, their father would read them the Bible, which Stanley would continue to do for the rest of his life. It was during his childhood that Stanley learnt to use his imagination and began to draw. Like all children he liked to fantasise. For instance, he drew a picture of the Cookham fire brigade riding on the back of snails. This ability to fantasise would remain with him into his adult life and act as a trigger for many of his paintings. He was able to use it to imagine a different reality when in a difficult situation.

Fig. 1
Self-Portrait, 1923
Oil on canvas
Stanley Spencer Gallery
(Barbara Karmel Bequest, 1995)

Fig. 2
Photograph at Fernlea, Cookham c.1900
Stanley (front row) and Gilbert (back row) with the Bailey girls who lived over the road from Fernlea
Stanley Spencer Gallery

Home for Stanley was his sanctuary; it was his 'safe place', and he would think about it in the First World War and return to live there afterwards. Cookham would represent his family for the rest of his life. As a child he would be bullied by the local village boys who mocked his height – he was only five feet two – and was seen as a misfit both here and later in the Army. Inside the home he felt safe from these threats. The family rarely left Cookham and, if they did, would complain of homesickness. They were very close, but over-protected, so going into the outside world, especially in a time of war, was difficult. Pople says that home meant handholding and Stanley continued to find 'handholders' for the rest of his life.[2] These were parental figures, such as Gwen and Jacques Raverat or the Behrends. Often these were couples or families who would support him emotionally and materially, and stimulate his imagination for his paintings.

Due to the large family, financial difficulties, the father's concern about Will and the effect on the mother of losing her twins, Stanley may have missed out on the important stage of having a one-to-one relationship with a parental figure, so vital for emotional development. Whilst the family was close and related well together, this would not protect Stanley if he missed out on this stage. A lack of such a relationship can result in children longing for the 'oneness' they missed. They can sometimes find difference and separation difficult, which can cause problems in their adult relationships. Some become Peter Pan-type figures, always remaining the child. Stanley would later say that his happiest memories were when he was a child in a pram. Others find difference and separation difficult in their adult relationships. Stanley said that, in his relationship with his wife Hilda, he wanted her 'you-ness' fusing with his 'oneness'.[3] This caused them problems; it was only in his relationship with God that he would achieve this.

Stanley was accepted for the Slade School of Fine Art in London but initially needed his father to travel with him as he was frightened, particularly of crossing the Euston Road. When eventually he did travel by himself he had to keep to the same route as he always wanted to know exactly where he was. This need for routine and fear of change remained with him all his life. It was the hospital and military routine, rather than the suffering of the soldiers, that he chose to paint for the Sandham Memorial Chapel.

When war broke out in 1914, Stanley wished to join the Royal Berkshires as an infantryman but his height precluded him and his mother was not keen. Gilbert became a medical orderly and was sent to the Beaufort War Hospital. Stanley, who had passed the St John Ambulance exam, decided to join him. He left the family home, Fernlea in Cookham, by a roundabout route so as to avoid saying goodbye to his family, but when he arrived at Maidenhead Station, his father was there to see him off. Stanley joined the other volunteers but as the train left the station, his father called to the orderly in charge of the group to take care of him as he was 'valuable'.

Stanley was unhappy with his non-combative role and previously had felt embarrassed when a Boer War veteran questioned him on why he had not signed up, made worse by the fact that the barber had given him a non-conformist centre parting.[4] In his letters and writings, Stanley talks of the Beaufort as a place that brought him 'innumerable unanalysable mental shocks that continually beset me' and writes that he was 'horribly fed up'.[5] Yet his paintings of the Beaufort, painted for Sandham, left out all the pain, discomfort and death, instead showing patients and orderlies working together in a calm, serene fashion. The paintings depict routine, humdrum events – scrubbing the floor, washing cabinets, bed-making, sorting the laundry, sorting and moving kitbags, filling tea urns and tea in the hospital ward – occurring quietly in a busy hospital teeming with nearly 1,500 military patients. Only two paintings show anything remotely clinical – patients with frostbite (Cat. 11) with the sheets raised on arches to protect the damaged limbs below, and *Ablutions* (Cat. 3). On first sight the latter appears to show blood on the soldiers' bodies but we later learn that it is iodine being painted on to the skin as an antiseptic.

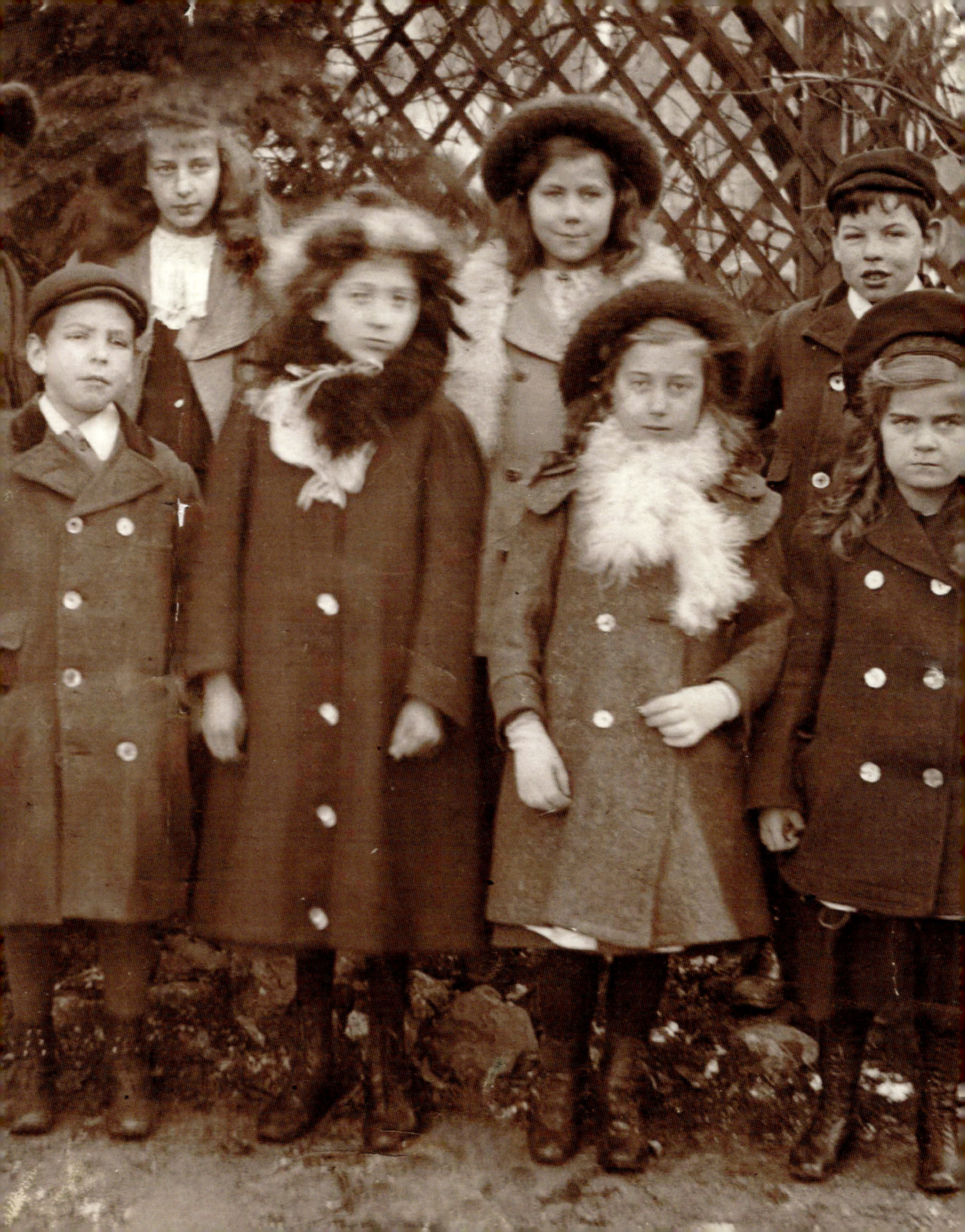

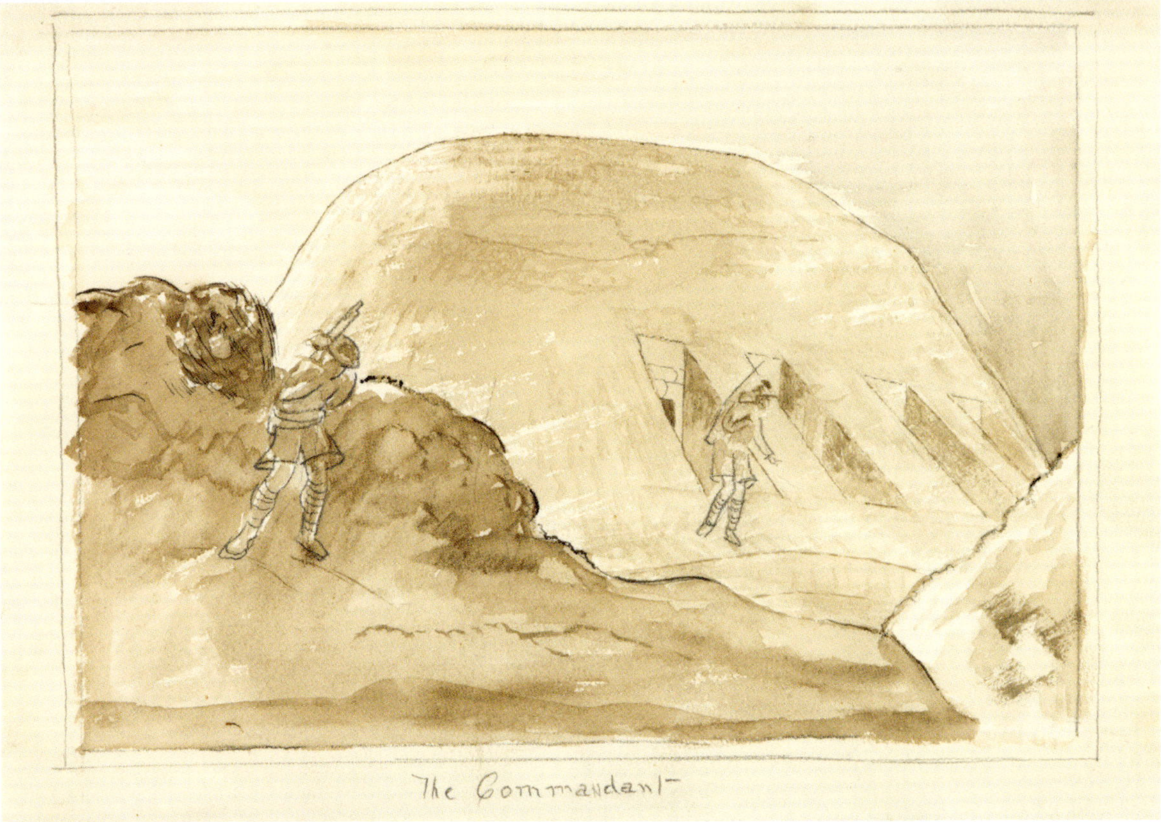

Fig. 3
The Commandant
Pencil and wash on paper
Imperial War Museums

Stanley must have seen terrible injuries during his time at the Beaufort and will have tended many of them himself. No wonder that he described seeking solitude in the linen closets between the larger wards at the Beaufort or hid between the baths. By December 1915, Stanley was at his lowest ebb. It was during his time at the Beaufort, however, that he met the young man who was to become his long-time friend and correspondent, Desmond Chute, who, Spencer wrote, 'appreciated the mental suffering that I was going through'.[6] Chute introduced Stanley, amongst other things, to St Augustine's *Confessions*. For Stanley, this validated the spiritual value of the sort of menial service in which he was involved in for much of his time at the Beaufort. Stanley writes, for example, of the pleasure that he derived from such simple tasks as scrubbing the floor and he depicts a shell-shocked patient, in his blue overall, doing just that (Cat. 2).

After ten months at the Beaufort, Stanley volunteered for overseas service in late autumn 1915 and, in May 1916, was finally sent to Tweseldown Camp, near Farnham, to train and prepare for mobilisation. It was at Tweseldown that he learned the duties of a field medical orderly in a field ambulance unit and became adept at stretcher, mule and wagon-handling, learning to operate water-carts and living in a world of trenches and dugouts. It is clear that, after his time at the Beaufort, Stanley thoroughly enjoyed much of his time at Tweseldown, and focused on the surrounding countryside, whilst longing for his beloved Cookham, perhaps in an attempt, conscious or unconscious, to cope with his forthcoming deployment to a war zone. When he needed to, Stanley 'grounded' himself by recalling the exact layout of his house at Fernlea, and the disposition of the flowerbeds, borders, bushes and trees.

On 23 August 1916, Stanley was posted to Salonika in Macedonia to join the 68th Field Ambulance, Royal Army Medical Corps, as a medical orderly. The role of orderly was lowlier than the one he had hoped for, that of stretcher

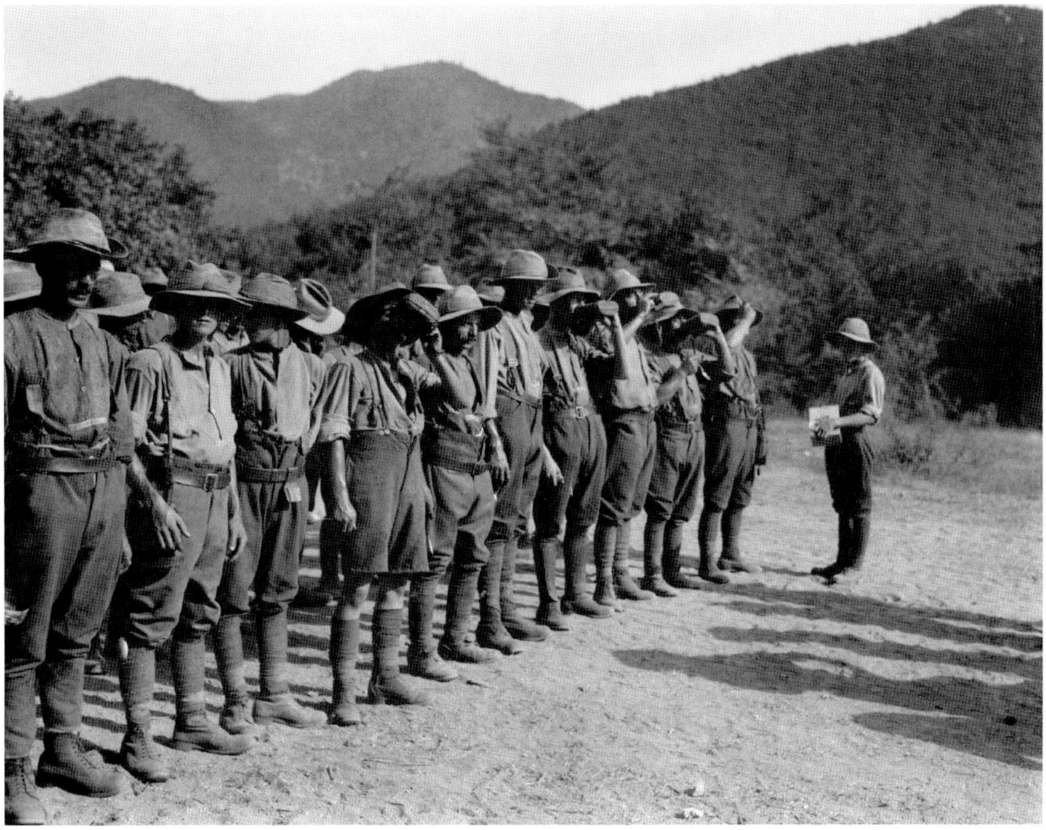

bearer – the men who, with the initials 'SB' emblazoned on brassards on their arms, bore the casualties on their initial journey from the front lines, often under fire. Soon after his arrival in theatre, however, Stanley was exposed to action: the attack on, and capture of, Machine Gun Hill – held for just a day until it was recaptured by the Bulgars.

Stanley, unsurprisingly, found the war difficult to cope with and appears to have had difficulties in acknowledging its darker aspects or 'shadow side'. He wished that he was braver and that he had 'nerves of steel'; he said that the sound of gunfire left him in a state of what he called 'melancholy depression' and he wrote that 'recent experiences' (on which he never elaborated) 'unmanned' him.[7] He doubtless saw innumerable dreadful sights, and many scores of dead, dying and wounded. No small wonder that, having taken part in many burial parties, he wanted to resurrect them all.

Yet, when he painted, the horrors and terrors of war never found their way into the finished works. Death is sanitised so that it is not terrible but, rather, idealised, and trauma is normalised rather than glorified. Stanley's duties as a medic made him among the most vulnerable to psychological trauma, and the same holds true today according to research on troops serving in Iraq and Afghanistan. So how did Stanley protect himself from being affected from the horrors that he must have seen? Part of the answer lies in his ability to have internalised his home environment of Cookham and, through endless rehearsal and repetition, to keep those images fresh. It is of interest that the shapes of the cowls from the Cookham oasthouses found their way into numerous Sandham paintings, *Sorting the Laundry* (Cat. 6), *Reveille* (Cat. 10) and *Firebelt* (Cat. 16). To all intents and purposes, Stanley seems to have taken Cookham with him into the Beaufort and to the Balkans. Bouts of injury and malaria served to give Stanley regular respite from the front, and he was treated according to the principles of proximity, immediacy and

Fig. 4
British soldiers on parade waiting to receive their daily dose of the anti-malaria drug Quinine, in Salonika, 1916–17
Imperial War Museums

expectancy (PIE) which are still the mainstay of front-line medical and mental health care.

During his time in Macedonia, Stanley was often in great danger, real or potential: from the enemy at Machine Gun Hill; in the closing stages of the war, during his time with the Berkshires; and from the humble malarial mosquito. Despite the precautions of the shroud-like mosquito nets shown in *Reveille*, malaria was to play a large role in Stanley's time spent in what Paul Gough describes as the 'rather sorry Macedonia campaign' (Fig. 4).[8] He contracted it three times and, as a result, had several changes of unit (from the 68th, to the 66th and finally to the 143rd Field Ambulance, with stays at the 4th and 5th Canadian Hospital in between), which he found hugely disconcerting and also meant loss of contact with the often good friends that he had made.

In February 1918, Stanley transferred to his home county regiment, C Company, 7th Battalion, the Royal Berkshires, who happened to be serving as a line infantry regiment in the Macedonian theatre. As an infantryman preparing to join an offensive in which 160 officers and 3,000 men had been killed, wounded or taken prisoner within the first 48 hours, Stanley was in great danger and it was only because of a last-minute withdrawal by the Bulgars that Stanley escaped involvement in pitched battle. He also narrowly escaped a bullet taken by the young officer that he was assisting on a reconnaissance mission. Spencer never expected to return home to England or to Cookham. His lengthy return to Southampton from Macedonia via Italy and France in November 1918 served a similar purpose to modern-day decompression where troops do not return directly to the UK from operational theatres but, instead, travel via Cyprus where there is a 36-hour pause before the flight home and reunion with relatives and loved ones.

During and after decompression, soldiers are observed to see if they are suffering from post traumatic stress or other disorders. Symptoms include distress at reminders of traumatic experiences, intense grief at the loss of, or injuries to, their colleagues and/or guilt that they have survived, together with anger and irritability, often affecting their personal relationships. In such cases returning servicemen and women are referred for assessment and therapy, either in a group or individually. Soldiers who are very defended, like Stanley, would be encouraged to discuss their feelings about their experience. Severe cases, such as those suffered by some of Stanley's Slade colleagues, might be admitted as in-patients. With therapy, soldiers who have been traumatised can be helped to readjust to their war experiences so leading to a different future. Initially after the First World War, there was limited therapeutic help available for veterans. Later, the Tavistock Clinic was founded to treat the victims of 'shell shock', as it was then called, so beginning the way to the therapeutic help given to the troops today.

Stanley did manage to return to Cookham, and found a changed world. His mother was unwell, his father aged and most of his siblings had left home. He tried to continue painting *Swan Upping at Cookham* (Tate), which he had started before the war, but could not get back to his previous standard. He said, 'It is not proper or sensible to paint well after such experiences.'[9] Stanley had arrived home to learn of the death of one of his favourite brothers, Sydney, and later his friend from the Slade, Isaac Rosenberg. He had doubts about his faith and found it difficult to settle.[10] There are hints of survivor guilt but no major symptoms of post traumatic stress disorder.

Many of the other artists that Stanley knew at the Slade suffered from the war: Mark Gertler had a mental breakdown (he recovered, but was later certified as insane in 1924, and committed to an asylum where he died in 1955); Dora Carrington committed suicide; and C.R.W. Nevinson found it difficult to paint properly after 1927, possibly because of his experience of seeing injured patients in the French war hospitals. In later life Stanley was to say he 'turned his back'[11] on the Great War. He painted in a completely different way to the other artists. They showed the terrible suffering of the war but instead Stanley removed himself from this, and used his imagination, to show a different image, which caused him less distress than the other artists.

Whilst Stanley had difficulties in relationships, we can summarise the reasons why he did not become as disturbed as his contemporaries. He used the following strategies:

— by making a safe place for himself – be it the thought of Cookham or a space in a room in Burghclere; notably, he ended the latter part of life in his family home, Fernlea, which had been bought back for him by William Astor and Jack Martineau.

— by relating to God. He could become 'one' with God and believed He was there in every action he undertook.

— by fantasising a different image to what actually happened.

— by focusing on the routine aspect of the work, such as eating and washing, rather than the suffering of the soldiers.

— by reading as a diversion – he described books as his 'armour'.

— by sketching or composing, in his mind, future paintings.

— by having supportive parental figures.

— by believing that menial work was spiritual.

— by resurrecting the dead soldiers to be with God in heaven and giving them a happy ending.

Notes

Jenny Beddington is a consultant psychotherapist and Jungian analyst. Jamie Hacker Hughes is a consultant clinical psychologist and psychotherapist. They are both specialists in psychological trauma. They are also consultants to Psychology in the Creative Arts (www.hackerhughesbeddington.com).

1 Kenneth Pople, *Stanley Spencer: A Biography*, Collins, London, 1991, p.9.
2 Pople 1991, p.9.
3 Pople 1991, p.202.
4 David Boyd Haycock, *A Crisis of Brilliance: Five Young British Artists and the Great War*, Old Street, London, 2009, p.212.
5 Paul Gough (ed.), *Your Loving Friend Stanley: The Great War Correspondence between Stanley Spencer and Desmond Chute*, Samson & Co., Bristol, 2011, pp.16 and 17.
6 Tate Archive, TGA 733.3.85, cited in Gough 2011, p.26.
7 Boyd Haycock 2009, p.296.
8 Paul Gough, *Stanley Spencer: Journey to Burghclere*, Sansom & Co., Bristol, 2006, p.89.
9 Boyd Haycock 2009, p.302.
10 Pople 1991, p.185.
11 Pople 1991, p.95.

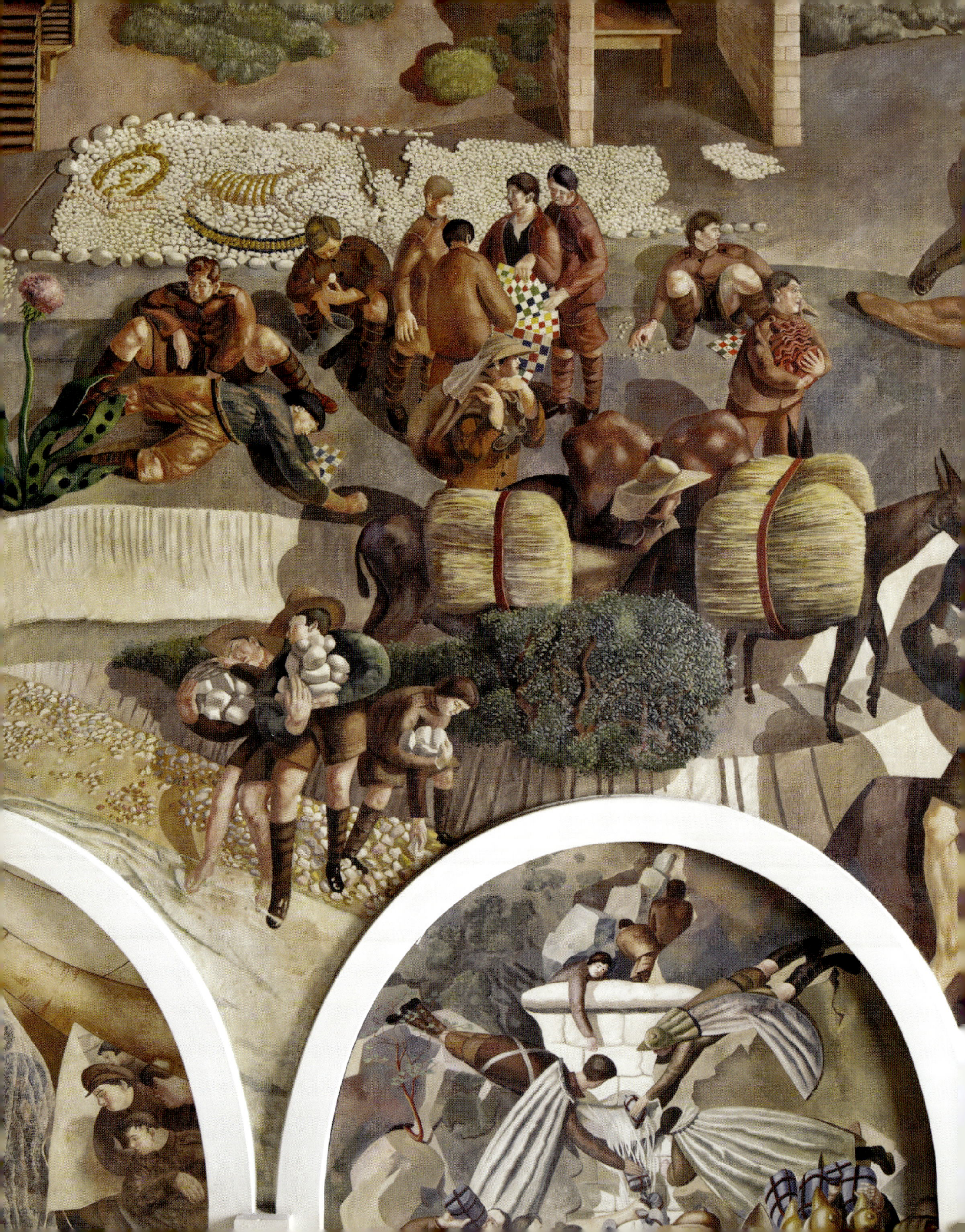

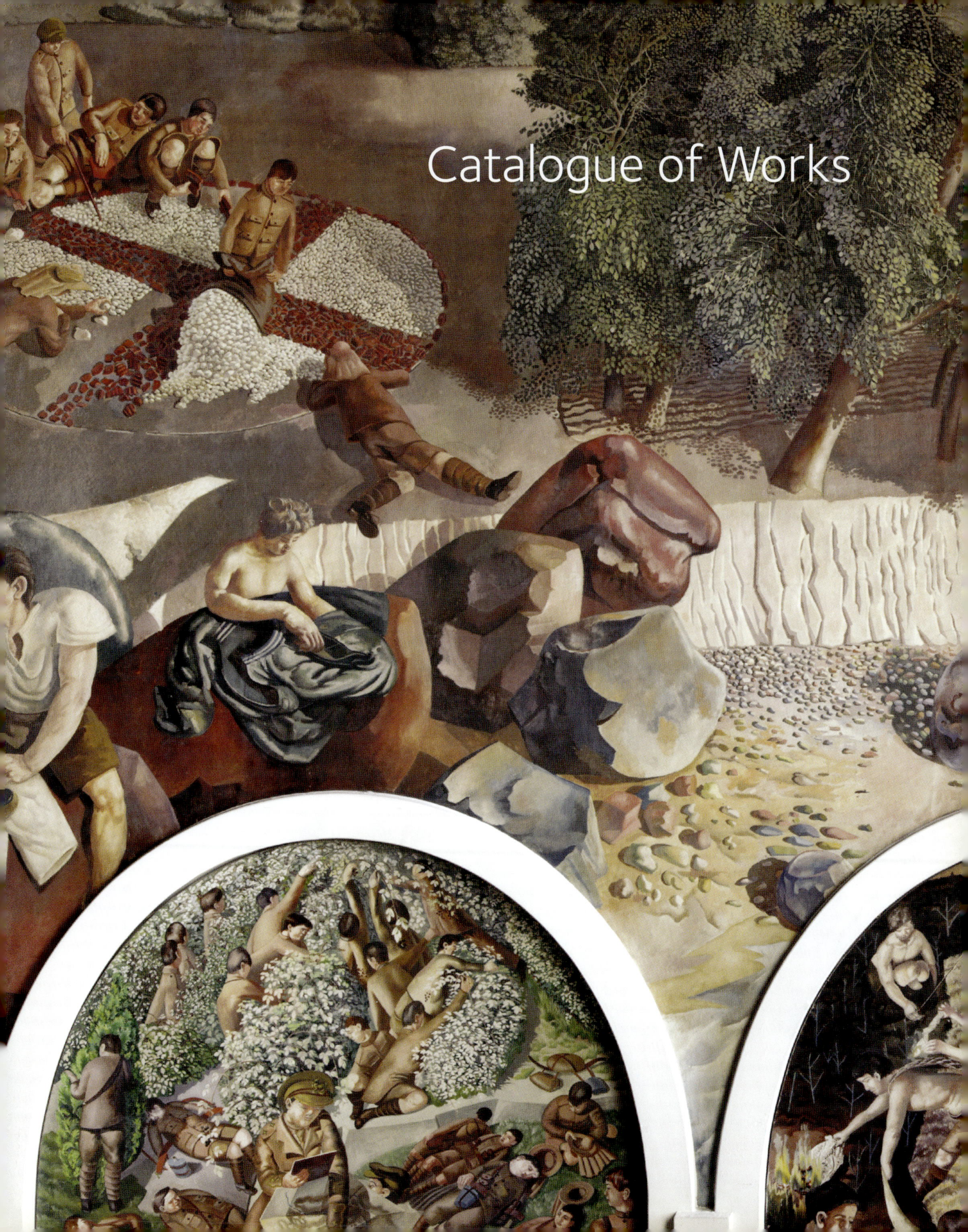

Catalogue of Works

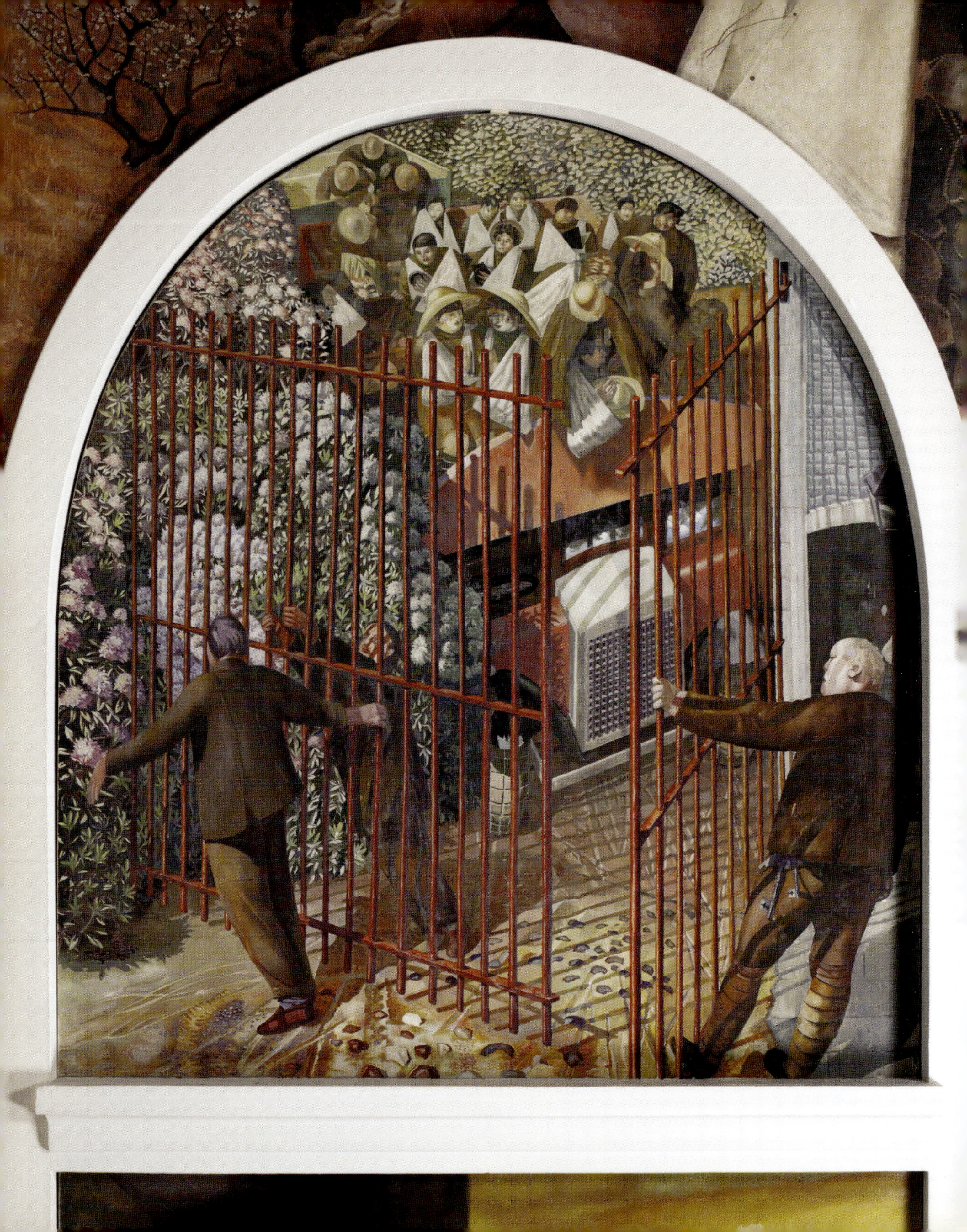

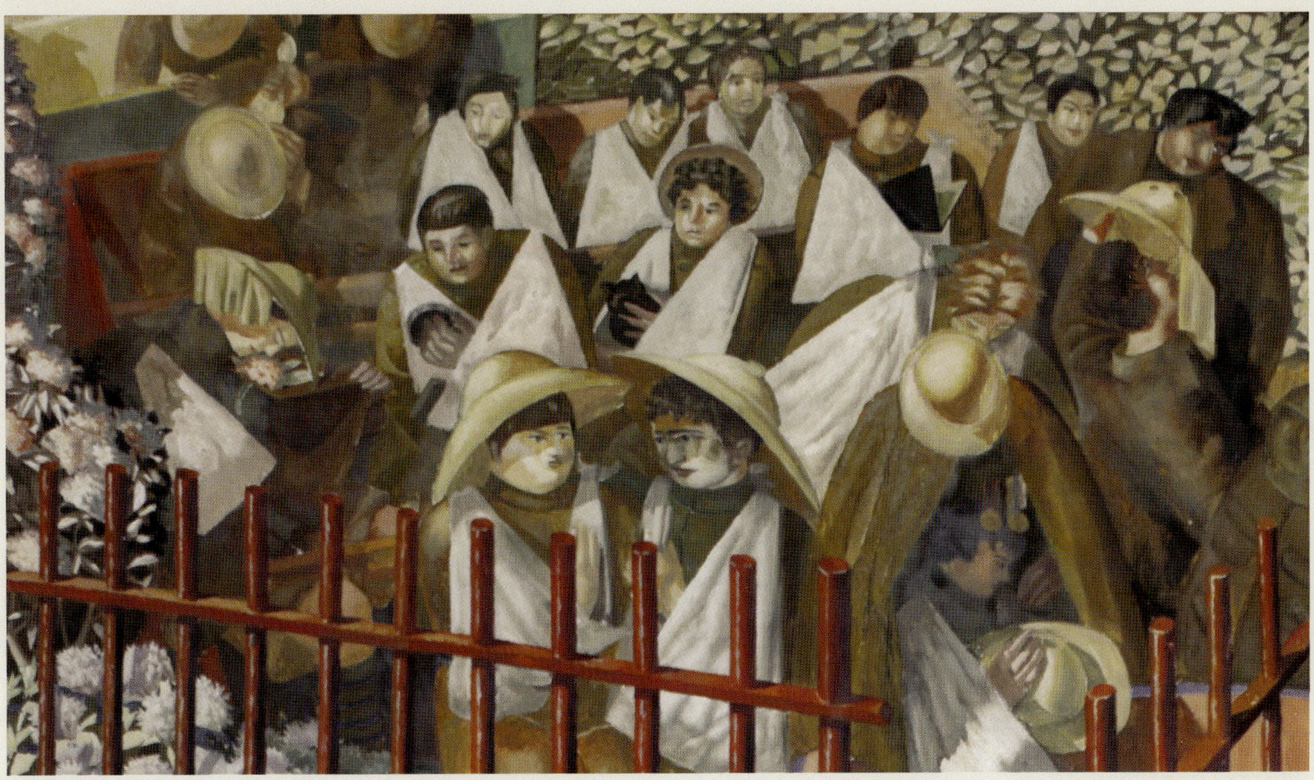

Cat. 1

CONVOY ARRIVING WITH THE WOUNDED

North Wall, Sandham Memorial Chapel,
Burghclere, Hampshire
213.5 × 185.5 cm (84 × 73 in)

The depiction of wounded troops arriving at the Beaufort War Hospital in Bristol was the first of the Sandham canvases that Stanley Spencer painted in the chapel. From a high vantage point, we look down onto an open-top bus, almost engulfed in rhododendrons, pushing its way towards the asylum gates. The wounded soldiers in the bus look at first like day-trippers arriving for a leisurely excursion, until we notice their helmets and bandaged arms.

Spencer found it difficult to remember the specific details of the hospital gateway and so the rhododendrons are those that grew along the roadsides at Burghclere. The gate, 'as massive and as high as the gate of Hell', is shown being pulled open by two civilian hospital workers on the left and, on the right, by a brutish looking man, painted after a gatekeeper that had scared Spencer in the past.[1] The keys at his belt are copied from those to the chapel, rather than the hospital gates, but their purpose in the painting is to link the two buildings – here they serve to emphasise the opening of the gates, which in the narrative of *Convoy Arriving* open into some unknown world, and as such introduces the rest of the canvases in the chapel. *David Taylor*

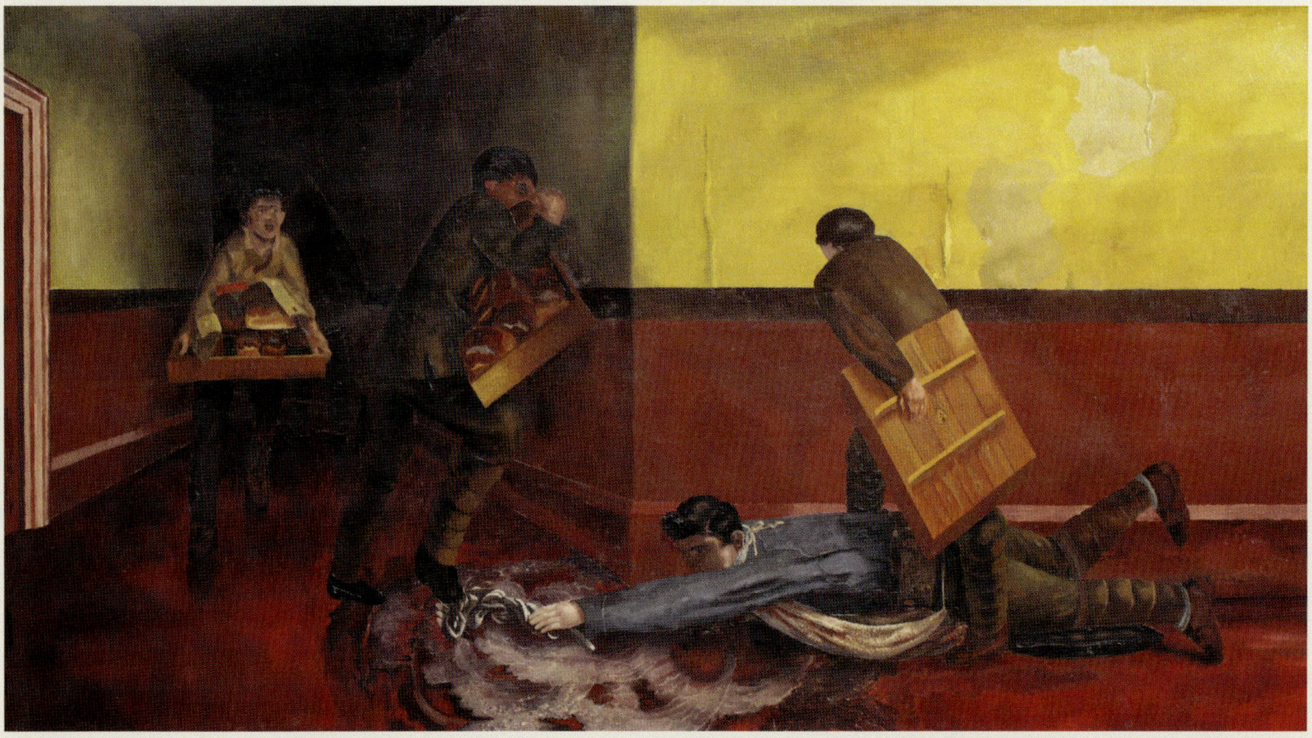

Cat. 2

SCRUBBING THE FLOOR

North Wall, Sandham Memorial Chapel, Burghclere, Hampshire.
105.5 × 185.5 cm (41 ½ × 73 in)

In this, the first of the predella canvases in the sequence, painted in Henry Lamb's studio in Hampstead, we see the corner of a corridor at Beaufort, with an ominous dark passageway to the left. In this regimented, institutional world, a shell-shocked soldier, wearing slippers and an apron, scrubs the floor clean with a rag, his obsessive, circular actions marked out in soap suds. He lies down, prostrate on the floor, while figures above him rush trays of bread from the hospital stores to the wards.

Spencer sometimes envied the quiet, insular lives of the asylum patients, some of whom had been at Beaufort for decades: 'I would like to do things that way ... I felt that in that state, and moving at that speed, I could take things in. I could contemplate. Nothing would disturb me.'[2]

David Taylor

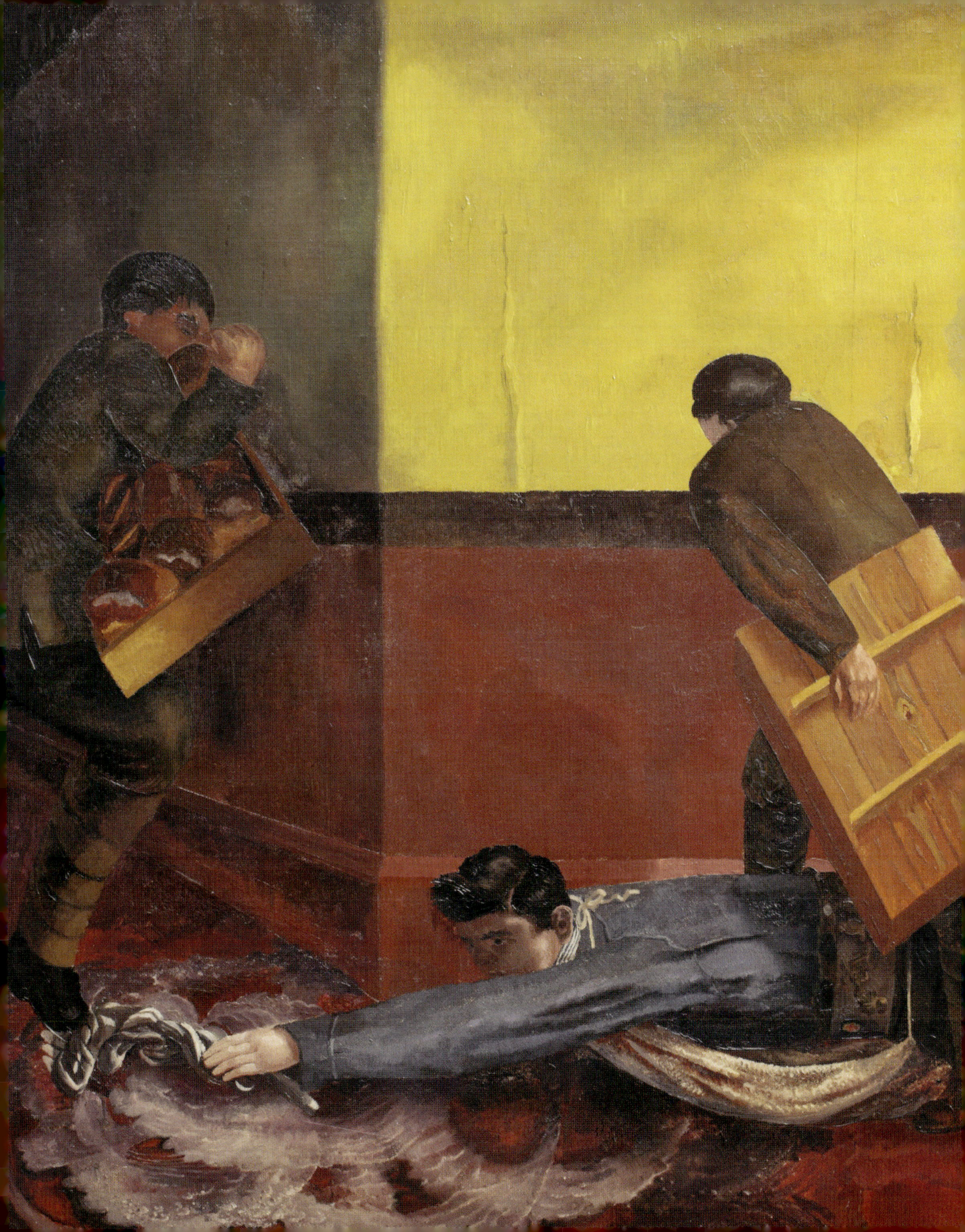

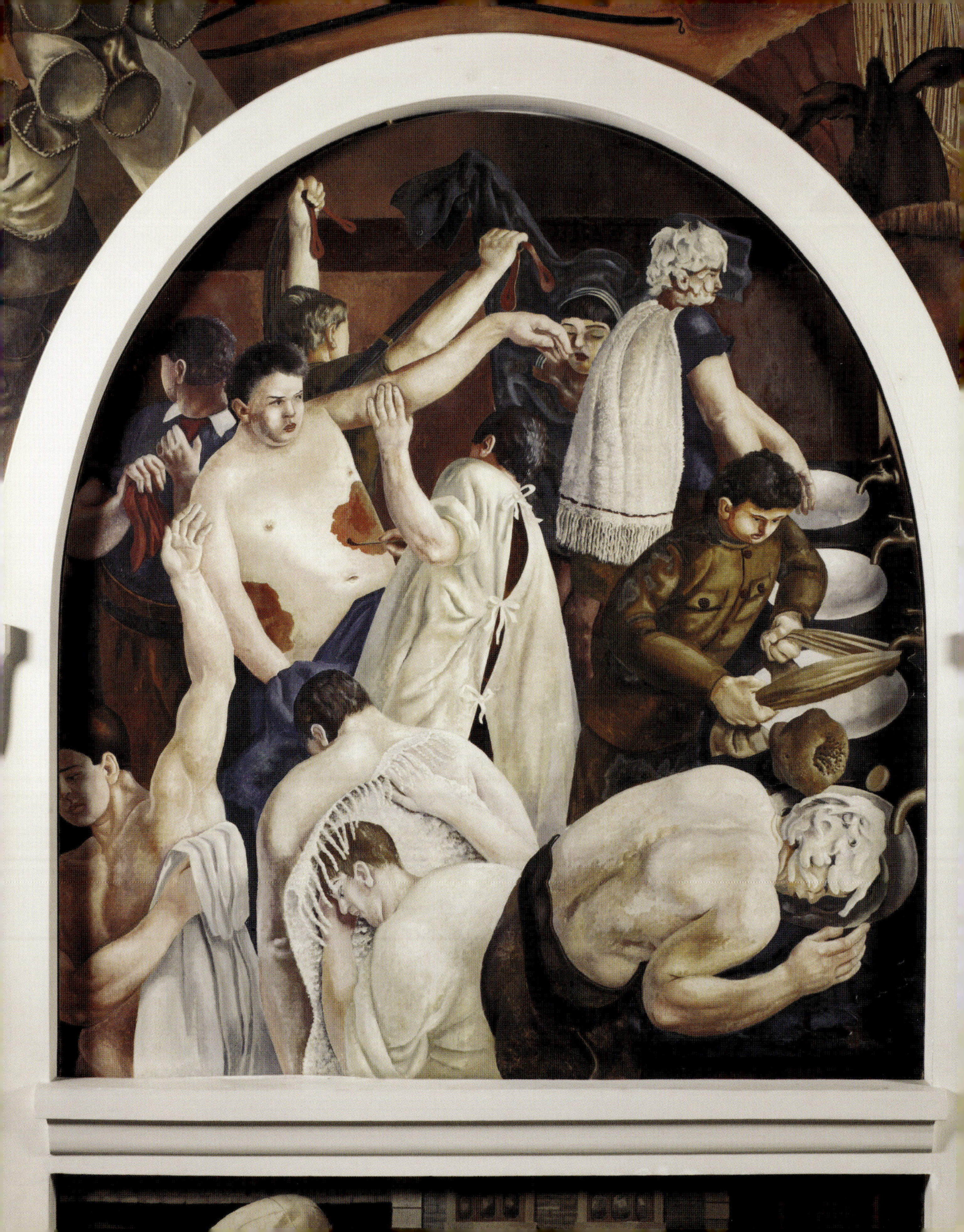

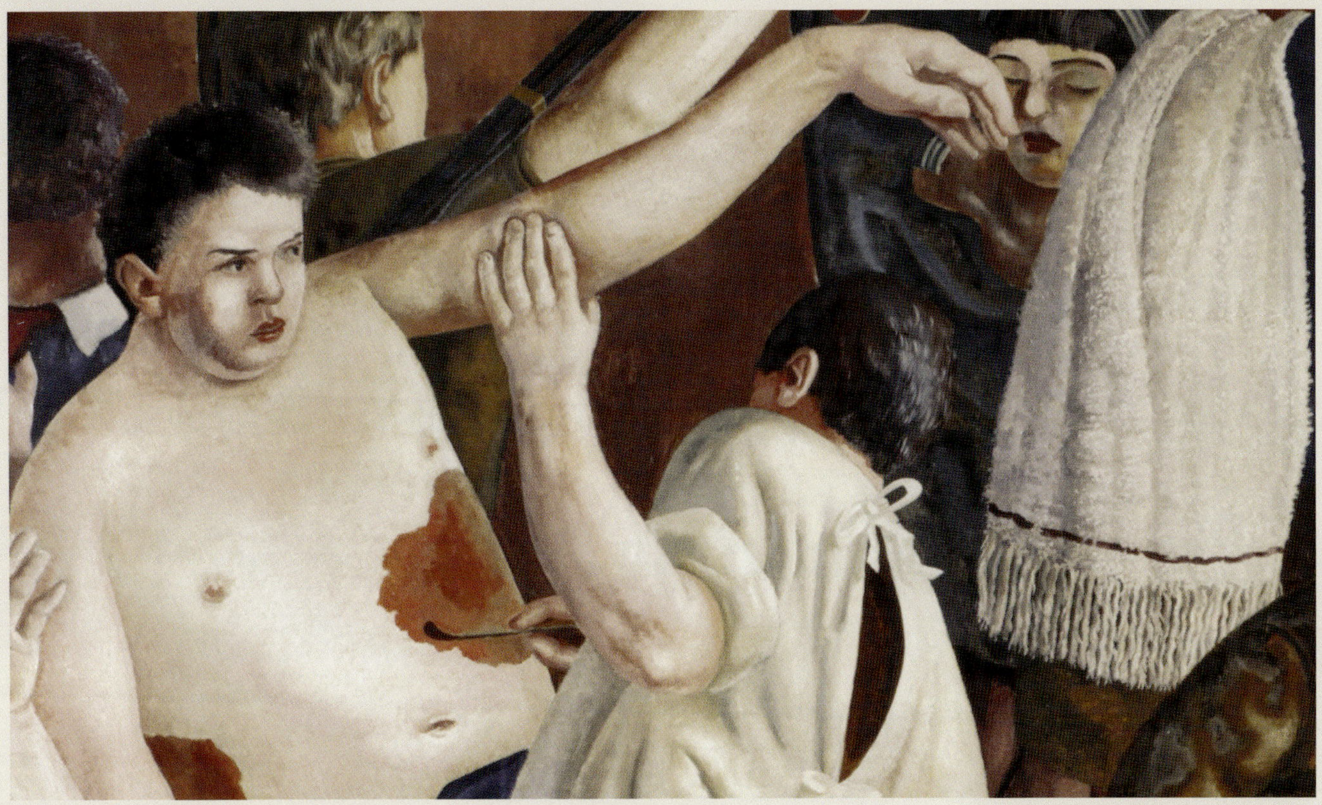

Cat. 3
ABLUTIONS
North Wall, Sandham Memorial Chapel, Burghclere, Hampshire
213.5 × 185.5 cm (84 × 73 in)

The busy composition shows the bathroom at Beaufort, overcrowded with figures, at the centre of which is an orderly, carefully lifting a patient's arm to paint iodine on a wound on his side. The vertical row of basins to the right of the canvas was first depicted by Spencer in a 1921 sketch, *Scrubbing the Floor and Soldiers Washing, Beaufort Hospital, Bristol* (Fitzwilliam Museum, Cambridge) – here two soldiers wash their hair, and a third carefully polishes a tap with a towel, 'on which depends his week-end pass'.[3]

Evidence of Spencer as a brilliant still-life painter is the beautiful depiction of a sponge that seems to float out of the canvas, just below the orderly cleaning the tap, one of the many surfaces in the painting, such as the towels and the soapy hair, that Spencer took great care to paint convincingly. He had difficulties in depicting a convincing sponge, though: 'I sat ... for half an hour, trying to think what a sponge looked like; but it was no good. I had to go home and get mine.'[4]
David Taylor

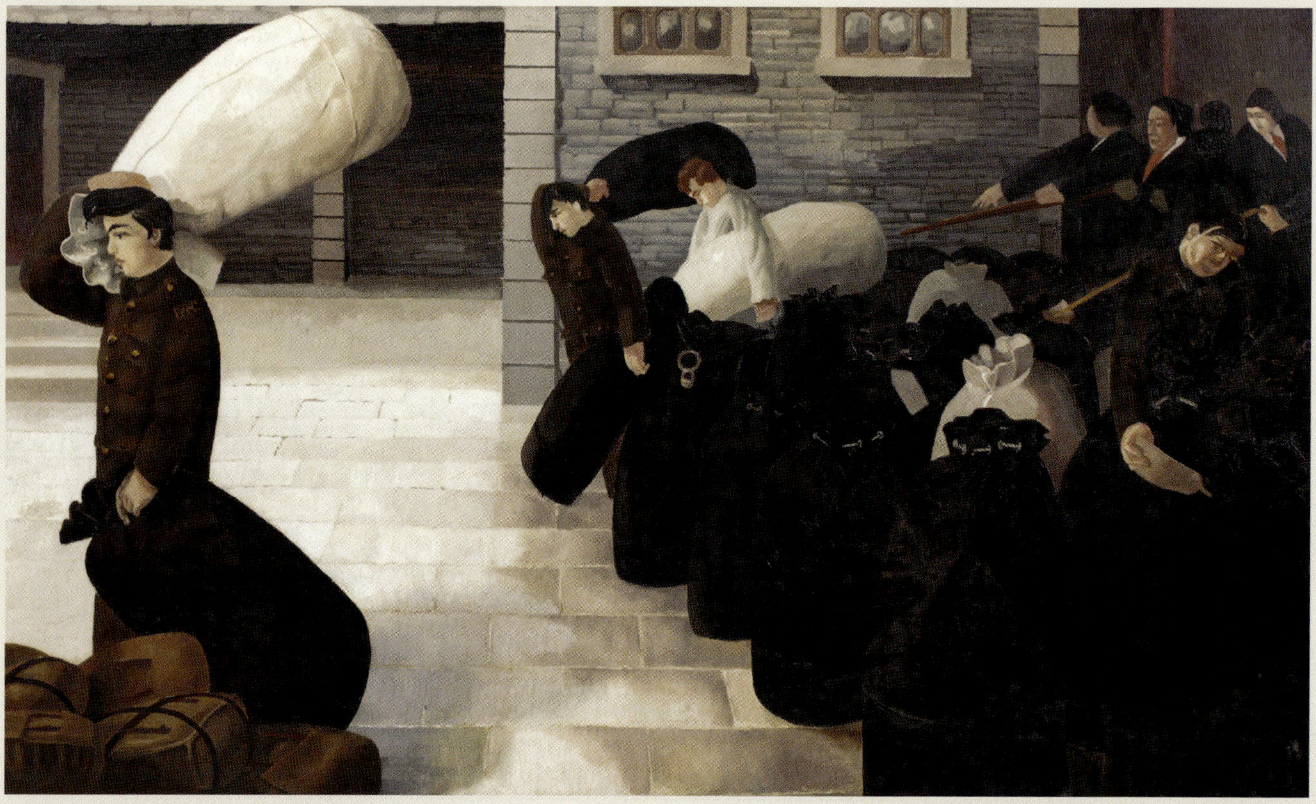

Cat. 4

SORTING AND MOVING KIT-BAGS

North Wall, Sandham Memorial Chapel,
Burghclere, Hampshire
105.5 × 185.5 cm (41 ½ × 73 in)

Another picture painted in Hampstead in 1927, *Sorting and Moving Kit-Bags* shows part of the Beaufort War Hospital that, in essence, survives to this day.

Describing the picture to Richard Carline, Spencer said, 'Immediately on arrival at the hospital the kit-bags of the soldiers just arrived would be stacked all together in the courtyard ... The patients who happened to be not "bed cases" would point out to the orderlies whichever happened to be their respective bags. The orderlies would then carry them to wherever the patient wanted then, or open them if so required. They were all padlocked.'[5]

Mundane activities like this were part of the routine and daily life of the hospital, although the arrival of a convoy must have been of interest to the orderlies: 'New faces to encounter and eager hands to help the suffering, who stand with the blank expression of uncertainty amid new surroundings that are made to look as grim as possible.'[6] *David Taylor*

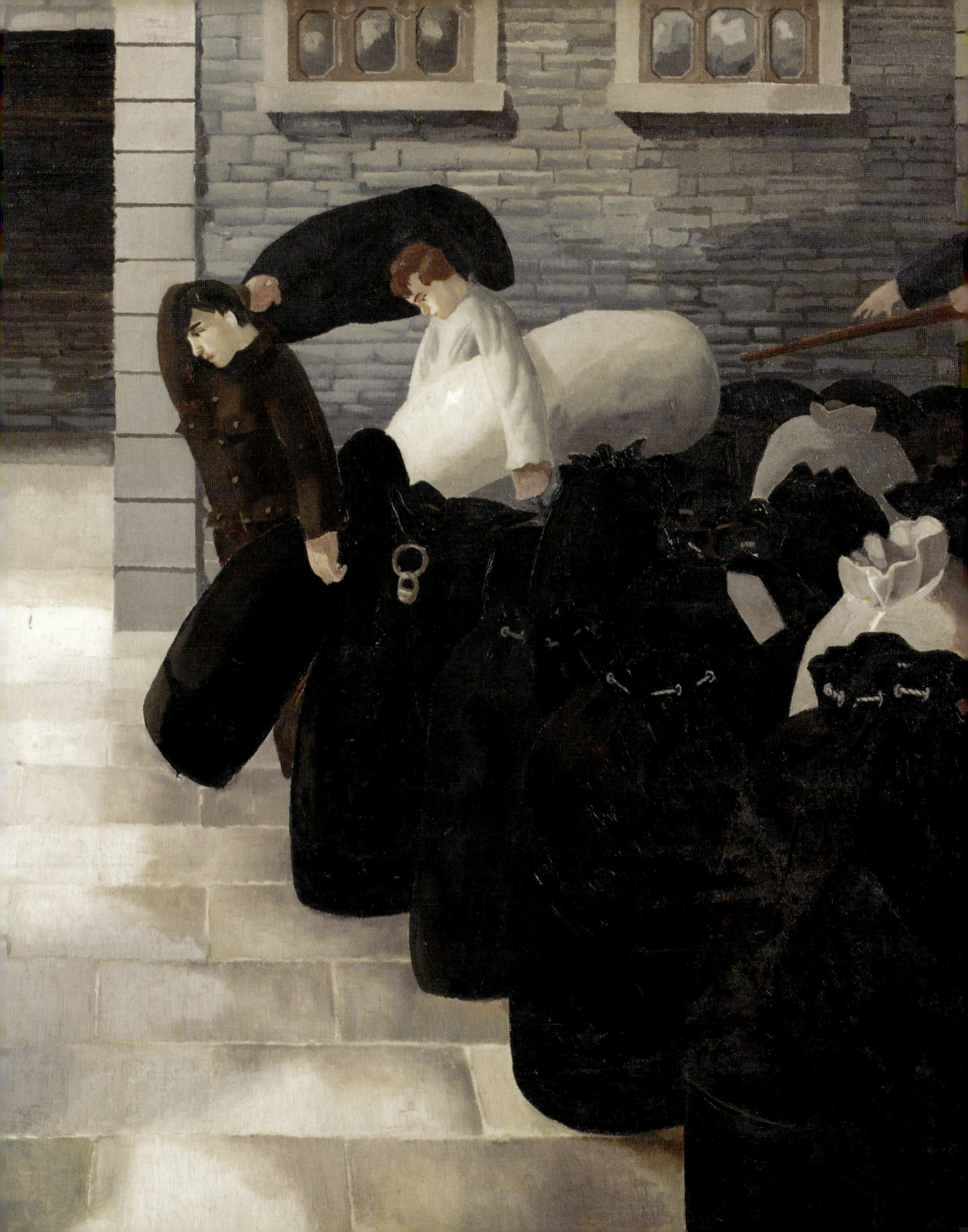

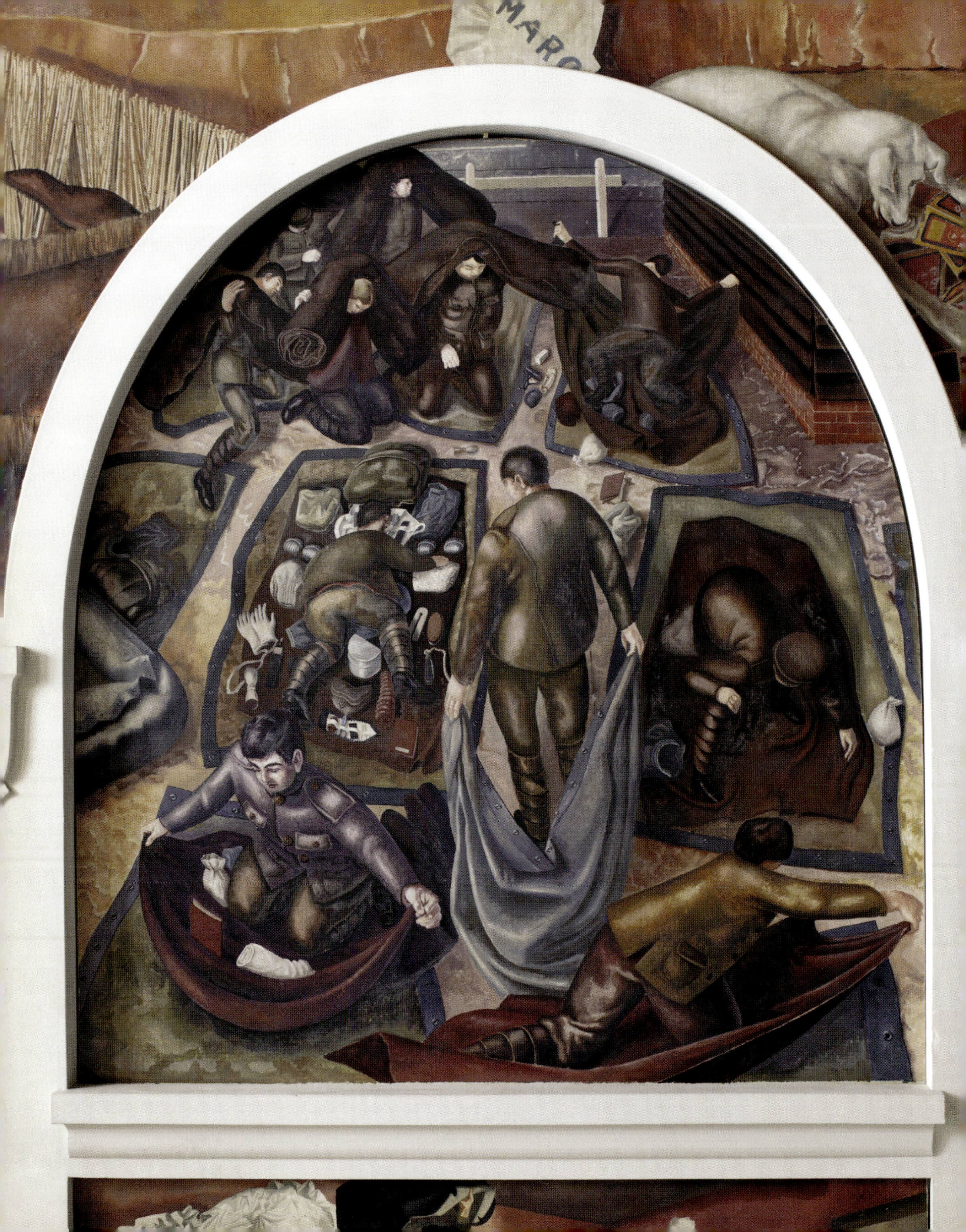

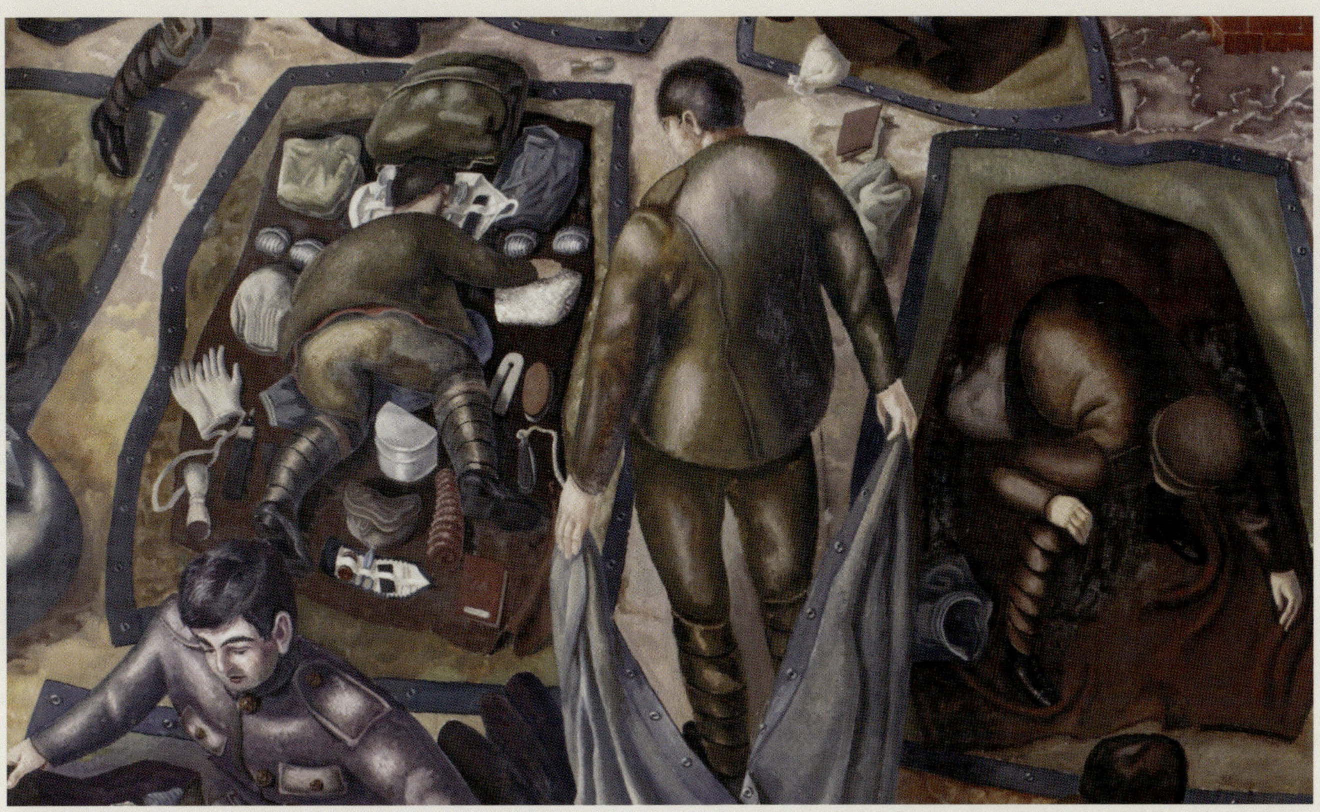

Cat. 5
KIT INSPECTION
North Wall, Sandham Memorial Chapel, Burghclere, Hampshire
213.5 × 185.5 cm (84 × 73 in)

This canvas is the only Sandham picture set at the training ground at Tweseldown Camp, near Farnham in Surrey, where Spencer was sent from the Beaufort War Hospital for training, prior to his leaving for the Macedonian front.

From a high viewpoint we look down on the soldiers laying out their respective kits on blankets on top of canvas ground sheets. Most of the soldiers appear to struggle with flattening out their blankets, and only one solider has successfully laid out his kit, which includes gloves and a shaving brush. Although he is smoothing out a folded towel, it appears as if he has fallen asleep on the job and is lying awkwardly on top of all his work.

It is usually assumed that Spencer, considered an untidy man, would have disliked this particular job: 'Anyone who had ever met him could imagine the trial Spencer found in spreading out his too-large ground sheet and attempting to assemble all the items on it correctly.'[7] *David Taylor*

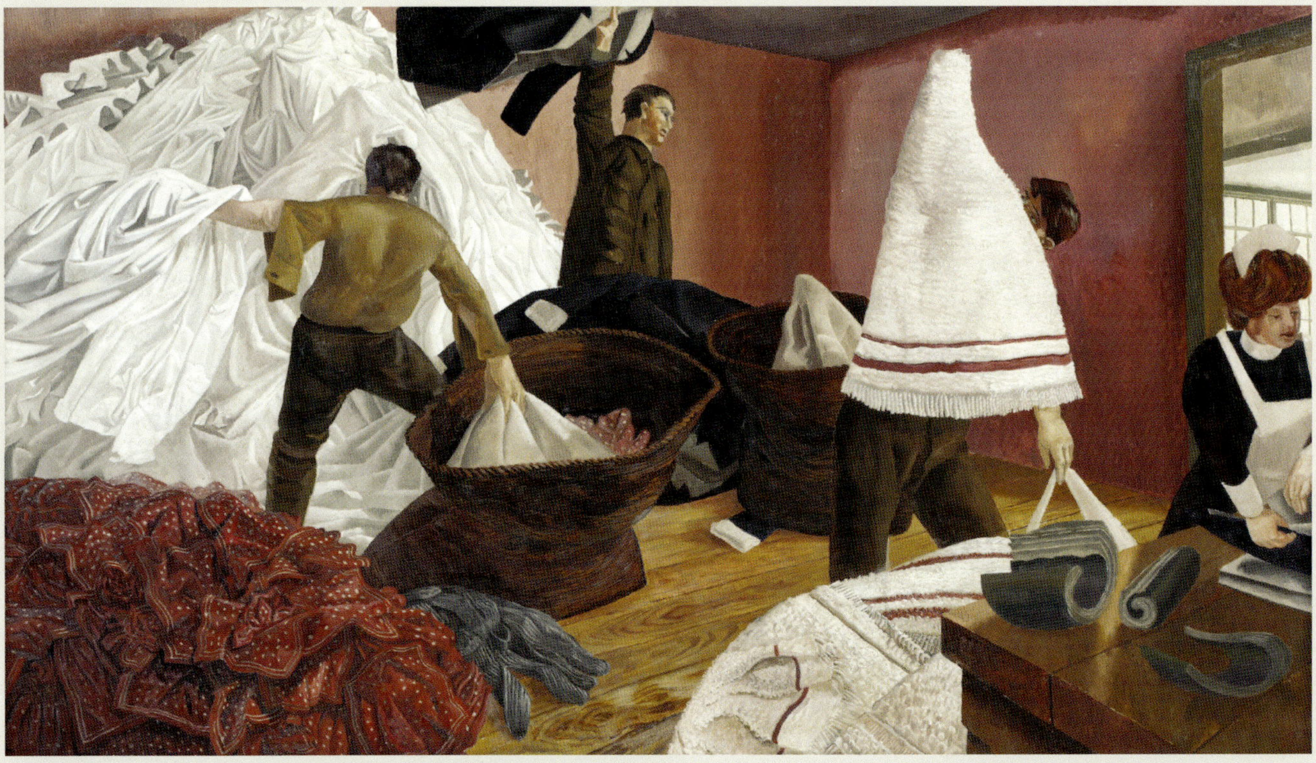

Cat. 6

SORTING THE LAUNDRY

North Wall, Sandham Memorial Chapel, Burghclere, Hampshire

105.5 × 185.5 cm (41 ½ × 73 in)

Spencer's canvas shows the scene in the laundry at Beaufort, described by him to Richard Carline: 'As each orderly called out the name of each article, the laundress would write it down in the respective orderly's "check book".'[8] This was a space in the Beaufort War Hospital where the artist found a haven from the routines of his other daily chores. A nurse, wearing a starched white cap, stands at a table with an open book, as the orderlies sort through the laundry behind her: a huge mountain of white sheets, a jacket held aloft and a towel that adds a humorous touch by almost covering the man who holds it up.

The spotted red handkerchiefs in the bottom left-hand corner belong to the permanent inmates of the asylum and serve as a reminder of the dual purpose of Beaufort during the war. In retrospect, they add a somewhat sinister touch to a canvas that stands out as being particularly cheerful within the series at Sandham, reminding modern viewers of the confiscated and stolen items that were collected en masse in the Nazi concentration camps during the Second World War. *David Taylor*

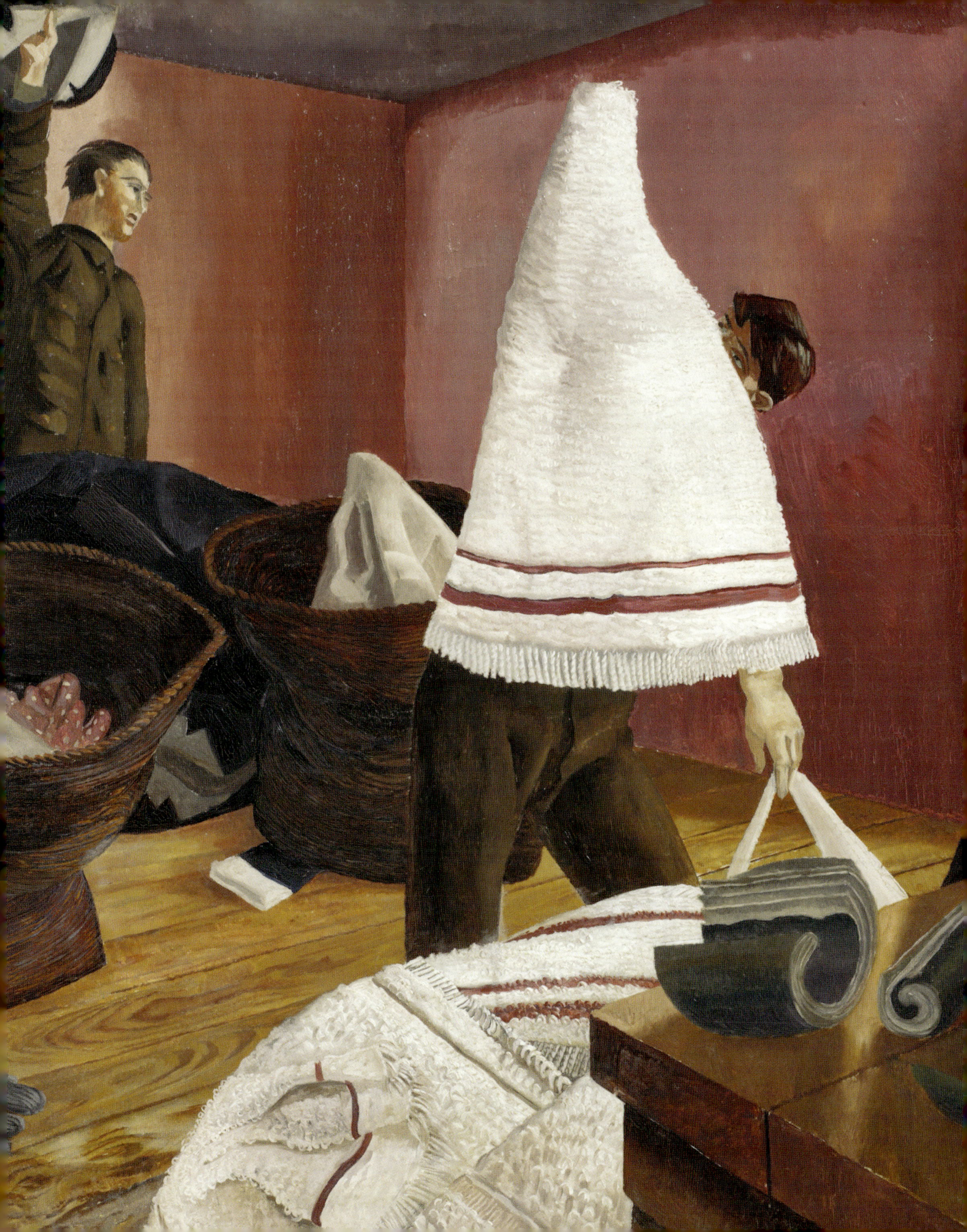

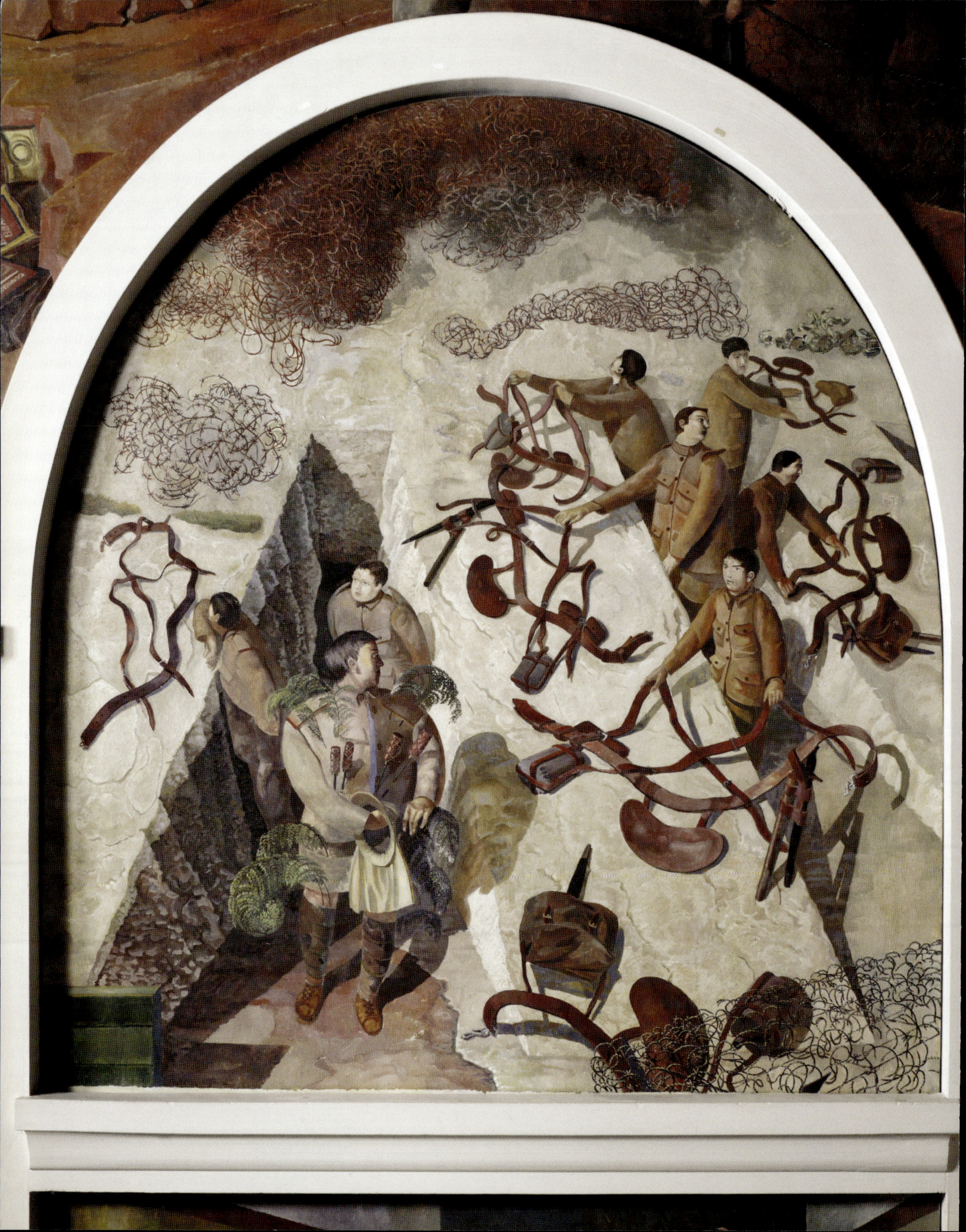

Cat. 7
DUG-OUT (OR STAND-TO)
North Wall, Sandham Memorial Chapel,
Burghclere, Hampshire
213.5 × 185.5 cm (84 × 73 in)

Dug-out is the first in the sequence of the Sandham canvases to show a scene set at the front in Salonika, Macedonia. We look down on two trenches, outside of which the soldiers have placed their equipment in readiness for a 'stand-to' order from their sergeant, who stands in front of the trench on the left, his uniform camouflaged with fern fronds. A study exists for the sergeant (Fig. 1), someone Spencer knew well and who was killed in action in Salonika, and other sketches show soldiers standing at the entrances to trenches or dug-outs (Fig. 2). Under piles of barbed wire, painted like ominous thunderclouds, some of the exhausted soldiers look towards *The Resurrection of the Soldiers* (Cat. 9) on the East Wall of the chapel. Spencer described the inspiration behind the composition: 'The idea ... occurred to me in thinking how marvellous it would be if one morning, when we came out of our dug-outs, we found that somehow everything was peace and that war was no more ... The picture really depicts the scene I had imagined supposing that at the moment of "stand-to", it had suddenly been realised that the war had ceased.'[9]
David Taylor

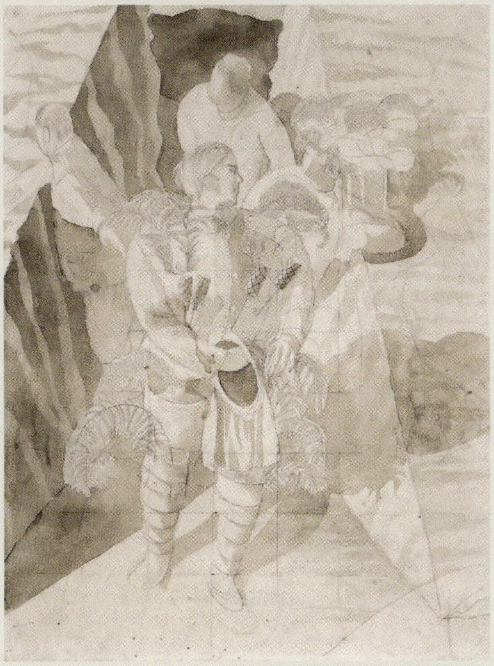

Fig. 1
Camouflaged Grenadier
(Verso: Two Composition Studies for Burghclere Chapel), 1922–3
Graphite and watercolour on paper
Tate, Purchased 1927

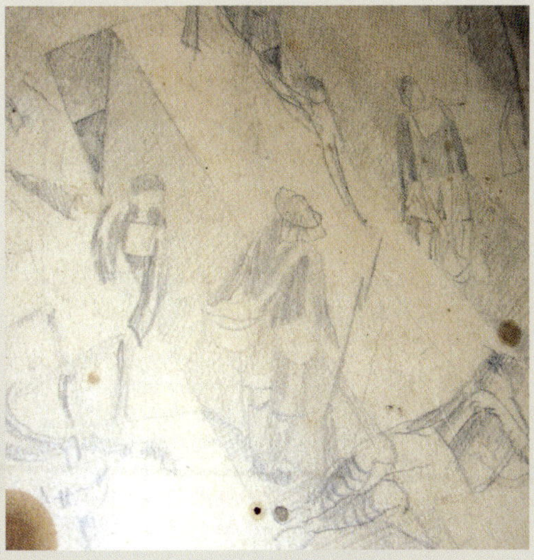

Fig. 2
Sketch for Dug-out
c.1923
Pencil on paper
The Behrend Collection, The Vyne, National Trust

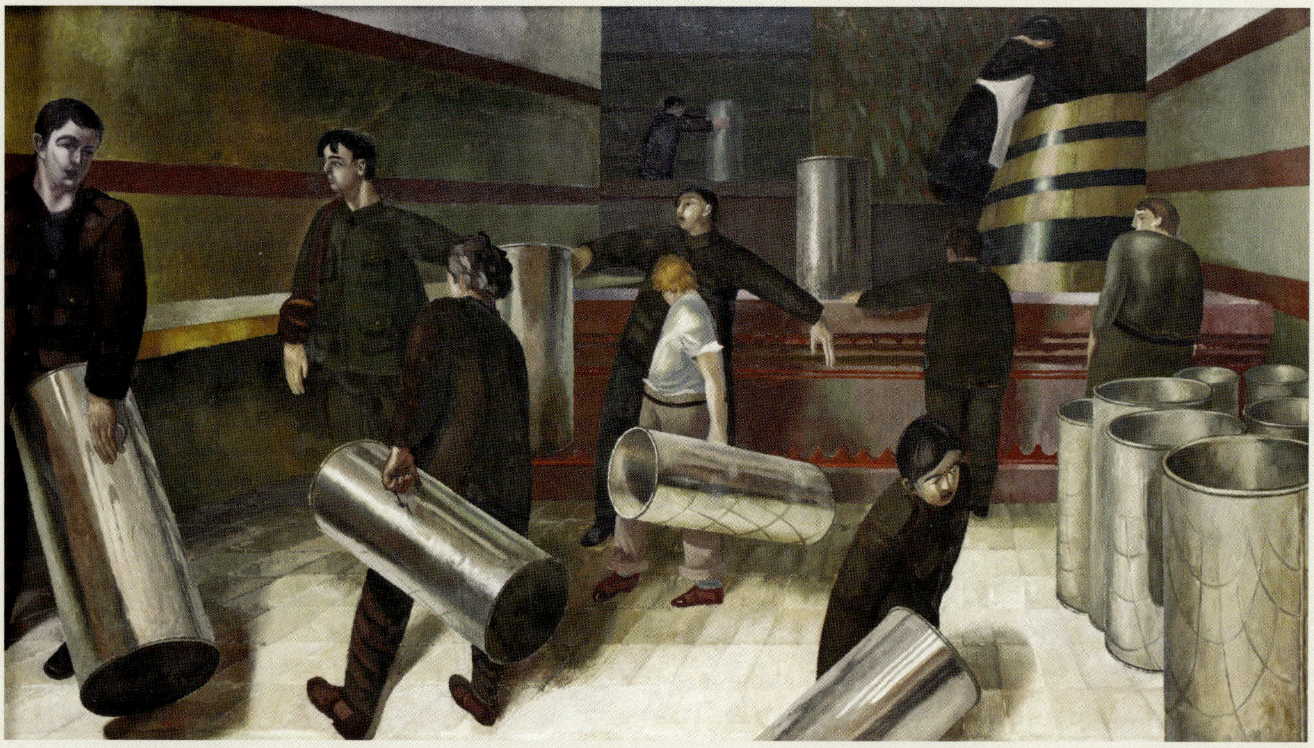

Cat. 8
FILLING TEA URNS
North Wall, Sandham Memorial Chapel, Burghclere, Hampshire
105.5 × 185.5 cm (41 ½ × 73 in)

The last of the predella canvases on the chapel's North Wall shows another scene at the Beaufort War Hospital, in which orderlies fill urns with tea to take back to their respective wards. Spencer was curious about the lives of the mental patients at the hospital, who lived in a separate wing from the soldiers and whom he only saw in the kitchens, separated from the soldiers by counters; 'Spencer saw the inmate who stands with his urn on the far side of the room every day for a year, without discovering who he was, or what lay down the passage behind, into which he disappeared.'[10]

Spencer saw the counter as the marker of a mysterious other world, 'a portentous threshold between two distinct passages of experience, a dividing line between zones of refuge and anxiety'.[11] *David Taylor*

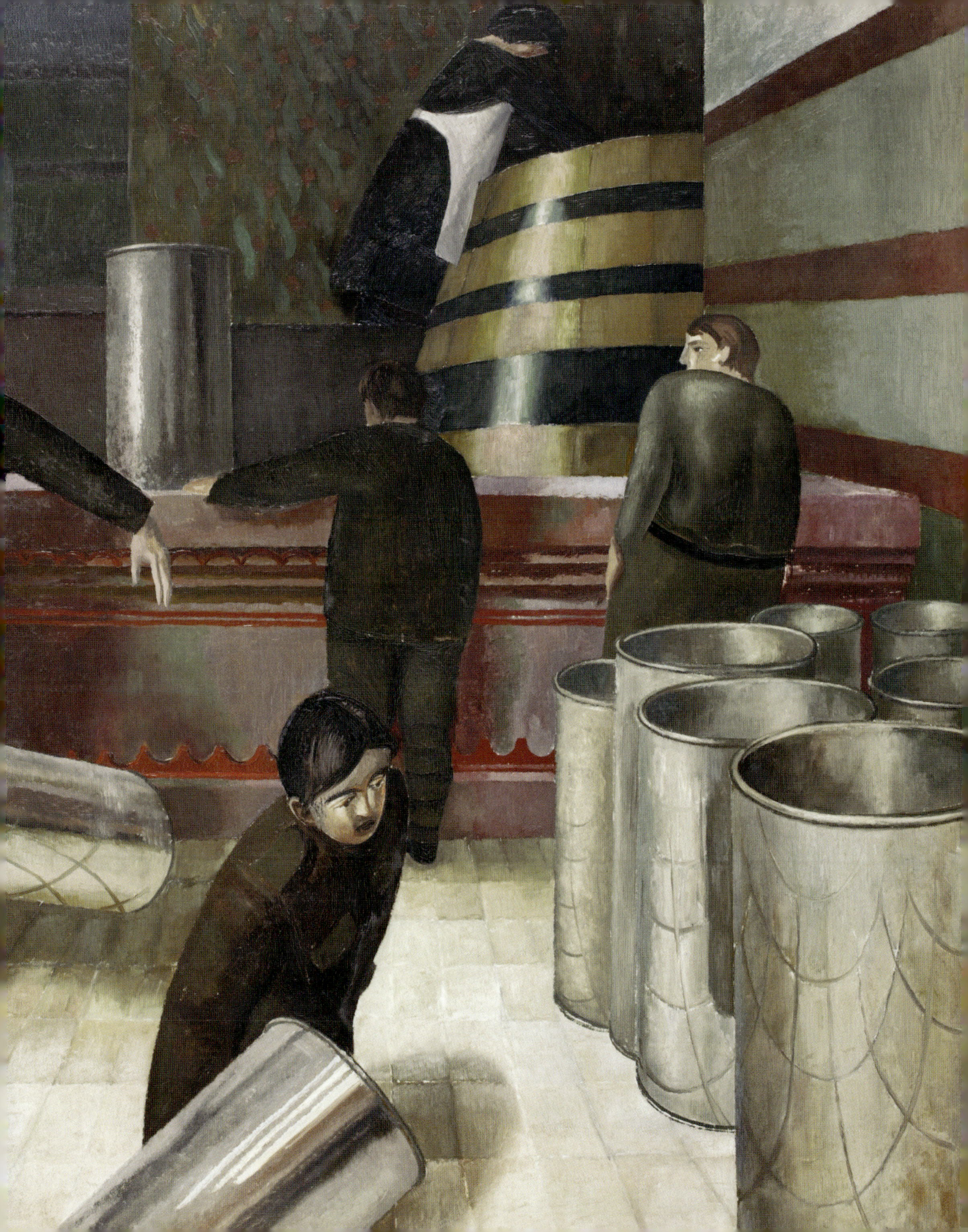

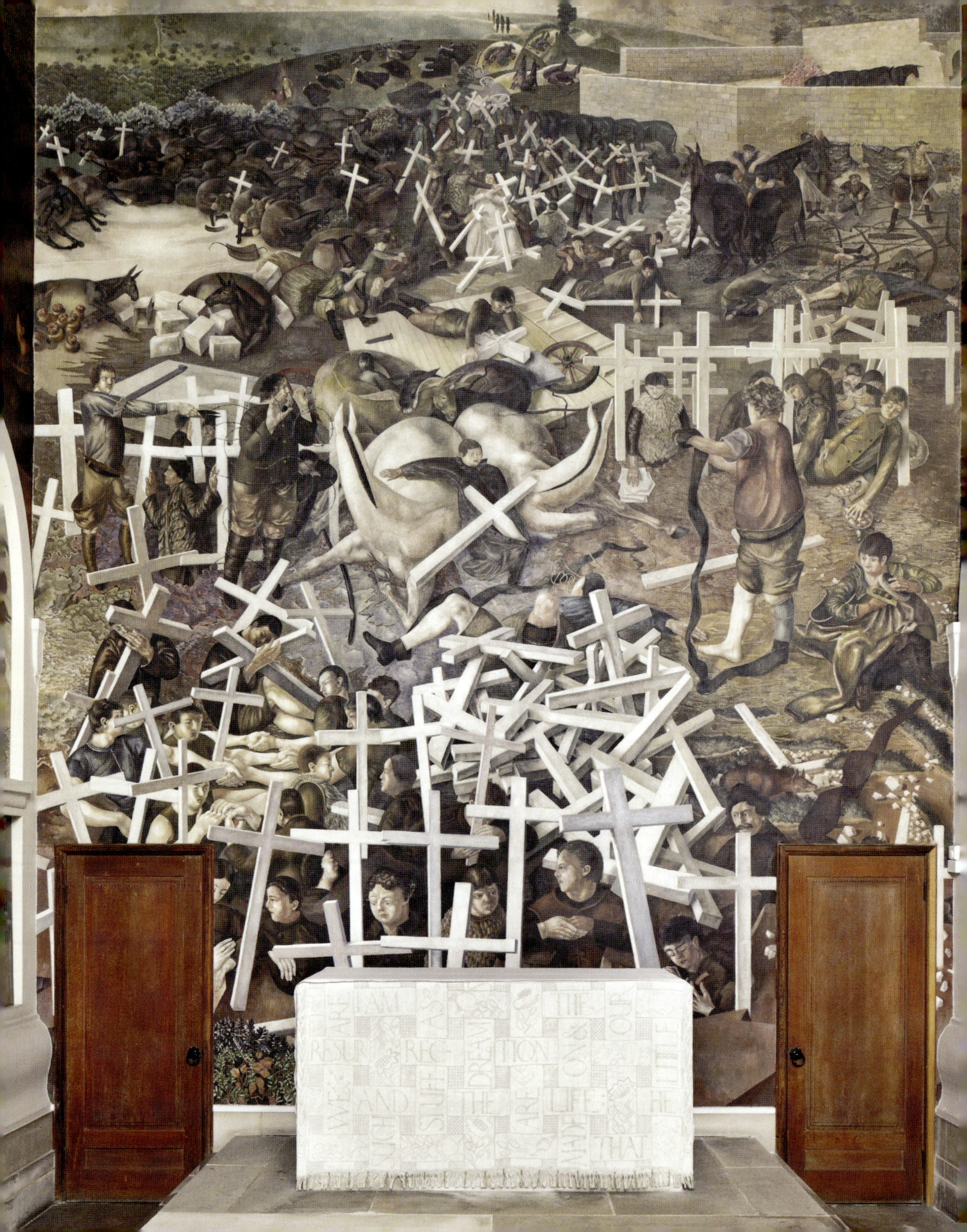

I AM
THE
RESUR
REC
TION
AND
THE
LIFE
THAT

Cat. 9
THE RESURRECTION OF THE SOLDIERS WITH ALTAR
East Wall, Sandham Memorial Chapel, Burghclere, Hampshire
640.5 × 526 cm (252 1/8 × 207 1/8 in)

'And death shall be no more; death shall not die.' [12]

The metaphysics of John Donne's words – well-known to Spencer – are an eloquent summation of the message of *The Resurrection of the Soldiers* (which was painted on canvas adhered to the wall of the high altar at Sandham and is thus presented as a projection in the current exhibition). Contrary to other war artists and poets, Spencer had found his 'heaven in a hell of war'; he 'had buried so many people and saw so many dead bodies that he felt that death could not be the end of everything'.[13] Each cross amongst the astonishing and brave tumble across the canvas serves as an object of devotion (some of which are handed to Christ in the mid-background); or marks a grave from which a soldier emerges; or serves to frame a bewildered face. Spencer noted: 'The truth that the cross is supposed to symbolize in this picture is that nothing is lost where a sacrifice has been the result of a perfect understanding ... it very much influenced me in deciding the behaviour of the men. They are all, for instance, meant to be happy.'[14] Yet no one smiles in this resurrection, perhaps because 'the sudden realization of peace' is dawning upon them 'at a moment when everyone is expecting the opposite'.[15]

Spencer had – characteristically – made prolific sketches for the altarpiece. He abandoned plans for an arched top altarpiece bordered with Giottesque vignettes around the edge, and had also decided not to fill the canvas with swathes of barbed wire – this is limited to a vignette, based on a personal experience, to the left of the canvas, where a soldier cuts free another from the wire.

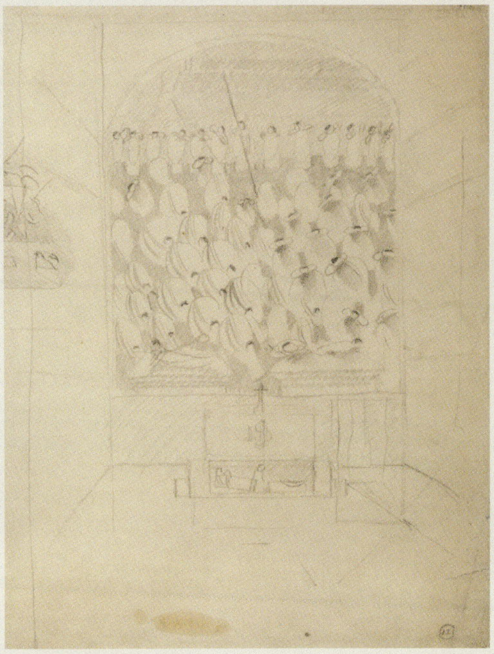

Fig. 1
Study for the Resurrection of Soldiers: Burghclere Chapel
1927–8
Graphite on paper
Tate, presented by the American Fund for the Tate Gallery, courtesy of Robert Littman, in honour of the Director, 1989

The central motif is a pair of fallen mules, still harnessed to their timber wagon, whereas Christ has been unconventionally placed in the far background. This subversiveness – intentional or not – heightens the sense of Mannerist, emotive disarray. Certainly, Spencer's approach was liturgically unconventional, down to the presence of technically un-resurrectable animals. Spencer's was an idiosyncratic and personal faith, which war had only complicated; the notion that 'God is in all things I love' perhaps encapsulated his beliefs. [16] Nevertheless, the sanctity and meaning of the cross on the altar was of great importance to him, for he felt it 'imperative that the top of the altar should be slightly above the bottom of the big picture' so that it might be incorporated visually amongst the mass of his own painted crosses.[17] *Amanda Bradley*

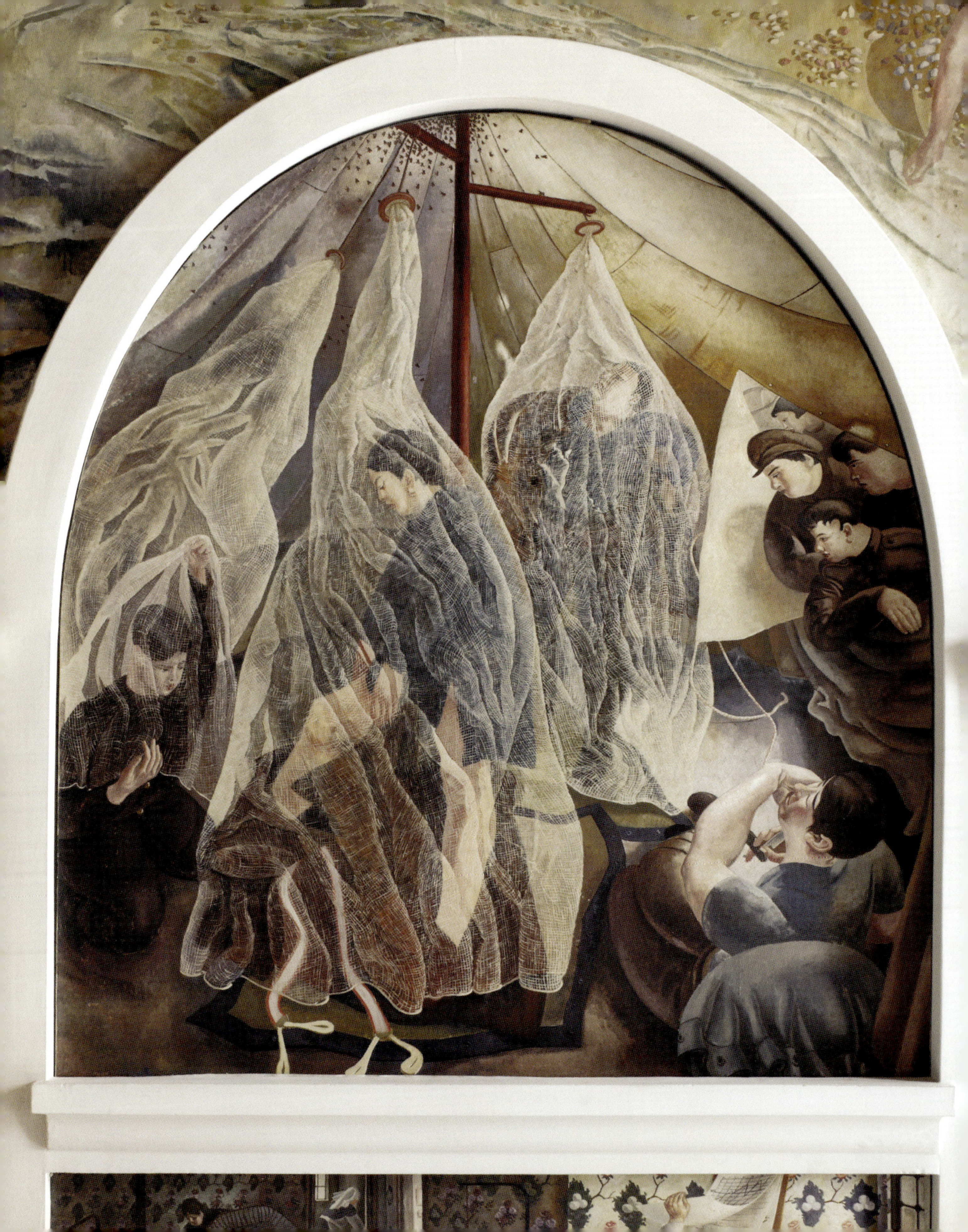

Cat. 10

REVEILLE

South Wall, Sandham Memorial Chapel, Burghclere, Hampshire

213.5 × 185.5 cm (84 × 73 in)

Reveille (the morning wake-up) concludes the pictorial trinity centred on *The Resurrection* altarpiece (Cat. 9). Spencer himself wrote of the soldiers looming into the tent, like angels annunciate, proclaiming 'the fact of the Resurrection' (or, more specifically, that the war was over).[18] He wrote that the scene was a 'mixture of real and spiritual fact ... the idea is again really the resurrection ... there is happiness which is the result of certainty, the certainty in this case being clearly understanding, in the same way as one understands twice one are two, the meaning of He that looseth his life for my sake shall save it'.[19]

The very form of the mosquito nets under which the soldiers are compelled to dress seems to signify a chrysalis-like cocoon from which they shall be reborn. This scene is the only memento mori in the chapel, with the malaria-infested mosquitoes hovering at the top of the tent, although Spencer was undoubtedly more concerned with reminiscences of his own malaria than the disease which supposedly ultimately killed the dedicatee of the chapel.

Again, the spiritual is rooted in the mundane. A soldier shaving in the bottom right-hand corner has been given an expressive form, the arc of his arm creating something eloquent and meaningful; and some striped braces have been given centre-stage, emerging from the mesh of the net.

Spencer seemed to enjoy exploring the pictorial possibilities of spatial depth, as attested in his many sketches of tents and tent openings, which were at one time to feature as a border around the altarpiece. The nets within the tented area evoke a deep three-dimensional space, inverting the studies of tent exteriors. The spatial complexity is accented by the masterly painting of the netting, the expressive folds falling into the leaden seams at the bottom. Their texture forms part of the rhythm of the chapel, and is echoed in other scenes such as the hessian aprons in *Washing Lockers* (Cat. 17).

Amanda Bradley

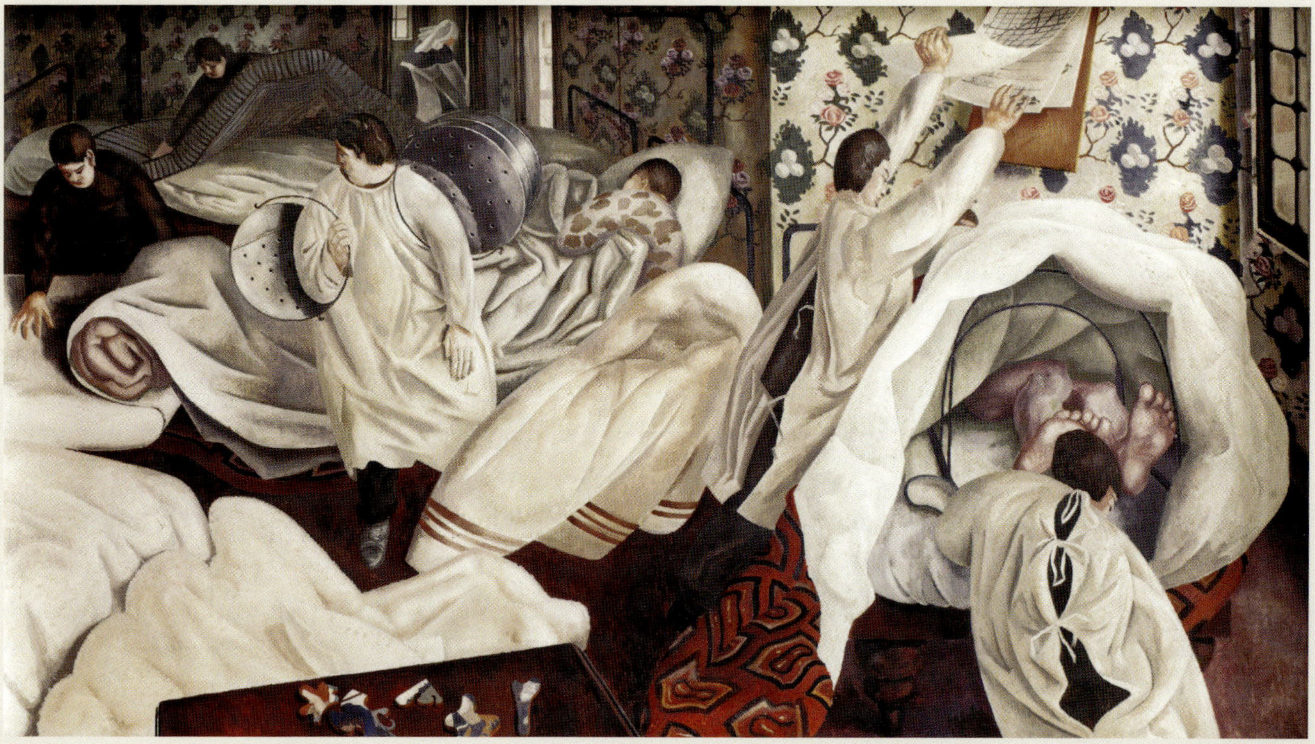

Cat. 11
FROSTBITE
South Wall, Sandham Memorial Chapel,
Burghclere, Hampshire
105.5 x 185.5 cm (41½ x 73 in)

A harsh actuality of war is represented in this scene at the Beaufort War Hospital, for soldiers could easily loose limbs or even die from the effects and complications of frostbite. In one of the busiest canvases in the chapel, a patient's smitten feet are shown protruding from a conical contraption designed to keep the sheets away from his skin. But again, Spencer has presented us with a vignette distinctly positive in its portrayal. One feels that the busy-ness, as specified by St Augustine, is bringing these characters closer to God. One of the orderlies has even sprouted wings in the form of the buckets that he carries.[20] The quintessentially English wallpaper itself roots the scene into the realm of the divine, being something that Spencer had probably seen in his spiritual home of Cookham.

The orderlies are dressed in gowns – not unlike angels – which fasten at the back. They are not dissimilar to the openings of military tents, something which Spencer explored in numerous sketches, including one owned by the National Trust. Various features alliterate with other scenes in the chapel: the cocoon of the bed contraption mirrors the form of the mosquito nets in the picture above; and the reflections in the metal buckets (a passage of great painterly skill) evoke those in the tea urns on the opposite wall.

The use of space is notably recessive, with the nurse in the background reminiscent of a Dutch genre scene or a religious vignette in a Tintoretto. Indeed, the almost Mannerist confusion of space is similar to that found in the work of the Venetian master, and it undoubtedly contributes to the sense of the bustle in the ward. *Amanda Bradley*

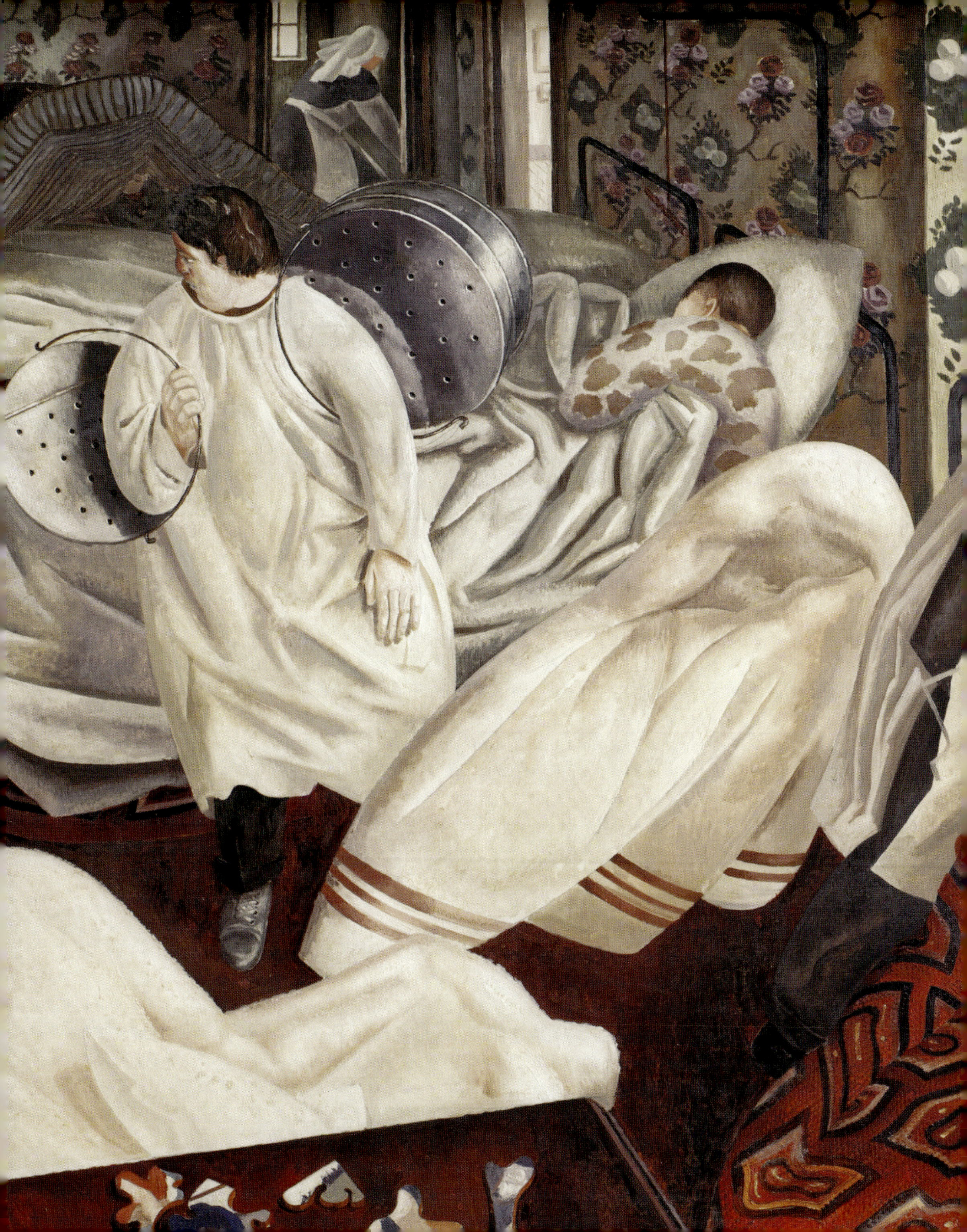

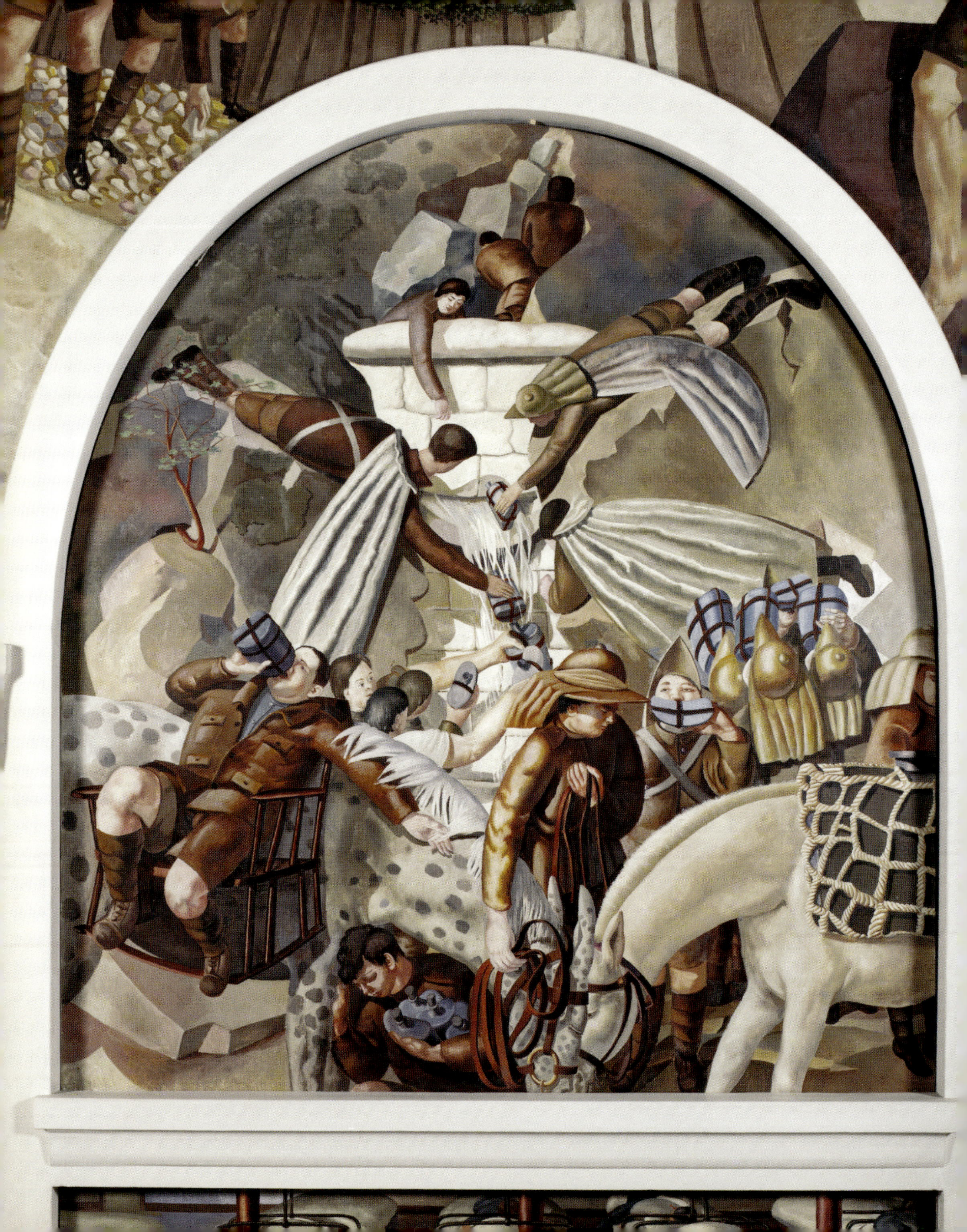

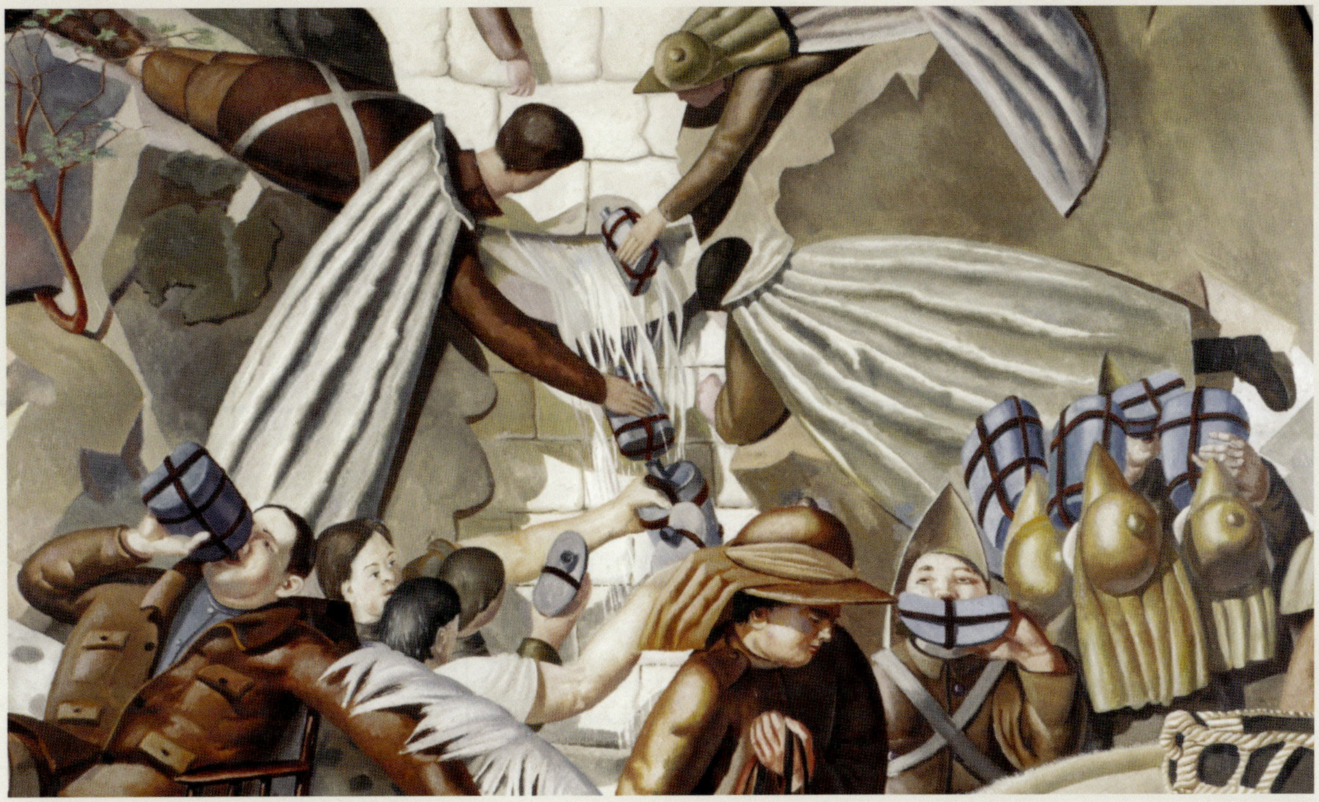

Cat. 12
FILLING WATER-BOTTLES
South Wall, Sandham Memorial Chapel, Burghclere, Hampshire
213.5 × 185.5 cm (84 × 73 in)

The orderly's 'wings' in *Frostbite* (Cat. 11) are echoed here in a different form – in the dramatically flowing 'wings' of the soldier's mackintoshes, as they collect water from a spring.[21] The extreme stylisation, notably in the use of arching curves (the mules' necks, the bottom of the water bottles and human limbs) in some way mirrors the soldiers' desperation to reach the water in the Macedonian heat. The cool tonality of the paint, studded with the gentle blue of the bottles, expresses the freshness of the water they are drinking. The technical skill in evidence here demonstrates how Spencer had matured during his painting of the chapel canvases, for this was one of the last scenes he painted.

Spencer had written about water fountains like this one: 'There is a great crowd of men round a Greek fountain or drinking-water trough (usually two slabs of marble, one set vertically into the side of a hill, having a slit-shaped hole in it which the other slab fits ...). What rather amused me was that often above the fountain, you could see the water trickling down the little groove made by it in the rock.'[22]

There is also a gentle humour in this scene; the leather straps on the water bottle form a Cheshire-like grin on the face of the soldier who drinks from it, and a seated, more rotund, soldier plays with the mane on the mule as he drinks, as a child would hold a comforter. *Amanda Bradley*

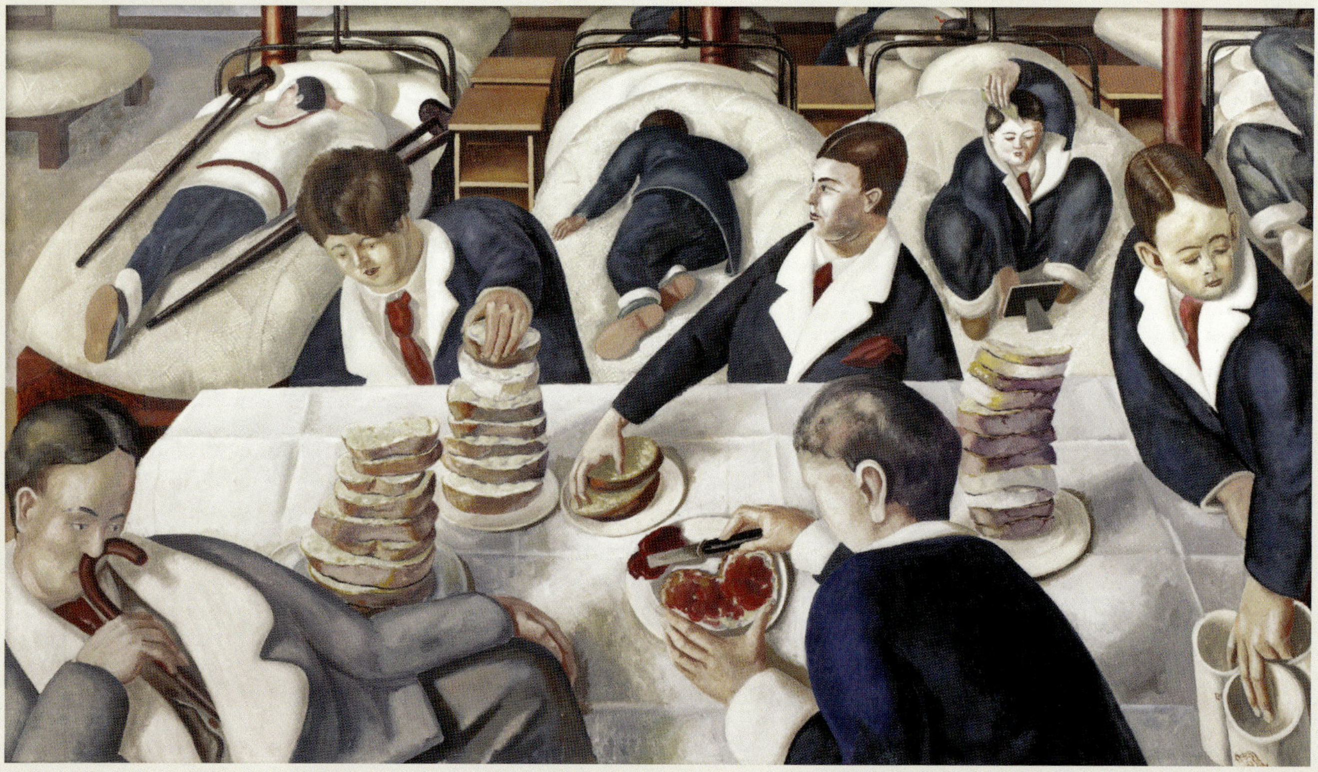

Cat. 13

TEA IN THE HOSPITAL WARD

South Wall, Sandham Memorial Chapel, Burghclere, Hampshire

105.5 × 185.5 cm (41 ½ × 73 in)

Spencer was proud of his brushed-forward fringe, which was a determined stance against sartorial convention. These patients at Beaufort War Hospital are shown with their slickly parted hair, one of them making great attempts to tame it in front of a photograph of a sweetheart.

'I am a boy for bread and butter', wrote Stanley, in a Proustian vein; but it is the jam on these sandwiches that creates a startling tonal effect of red on white – as well as showing his virtuoso still-life skills.[23] Continuing the rhythmical interplay between the canvases, the folds in the linen tablecloth echo the tessellations of the rope on the mule's back in *Filling Water-bottles* (Cat. 12).

Teatime must have been one of the highlights in the daily routine at Beaufort. The contemplative figure in the bottom left-hand corner suggests that it was a quiet time, although a photograph in the Glenside Hospital Museum shows a reality quite different to the cosy scene evoked by Spencer, with formal, serried ranks of patients sitting at trestle tables. In the photograph the patients are wearing the same jackets as those painted by Spencer – grey with white collars. It is extraordinary to think of him recalling details such as this years later, but it was typical of his practice to 'photograph a scene in his mind and then reproduce it long afterwards'.[24] Also in his memory must have been the way in which the table was more efficiently cleared by gathering up three cups at a time by the fingers (bottom right).

This scene did not feature in Spencer's original scheme and was the last of the predella canvases to be painted in 1932.
Amanda Bradley

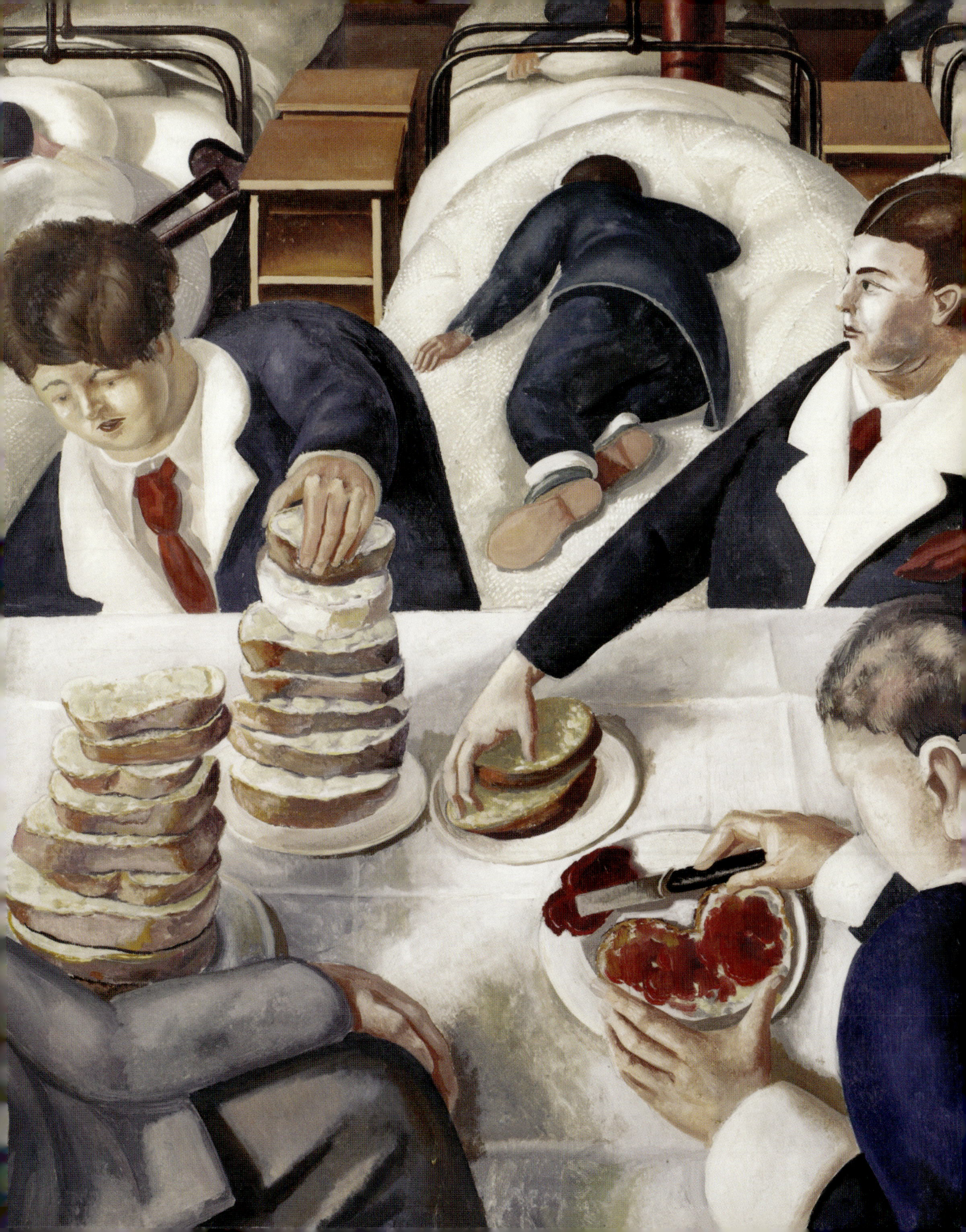

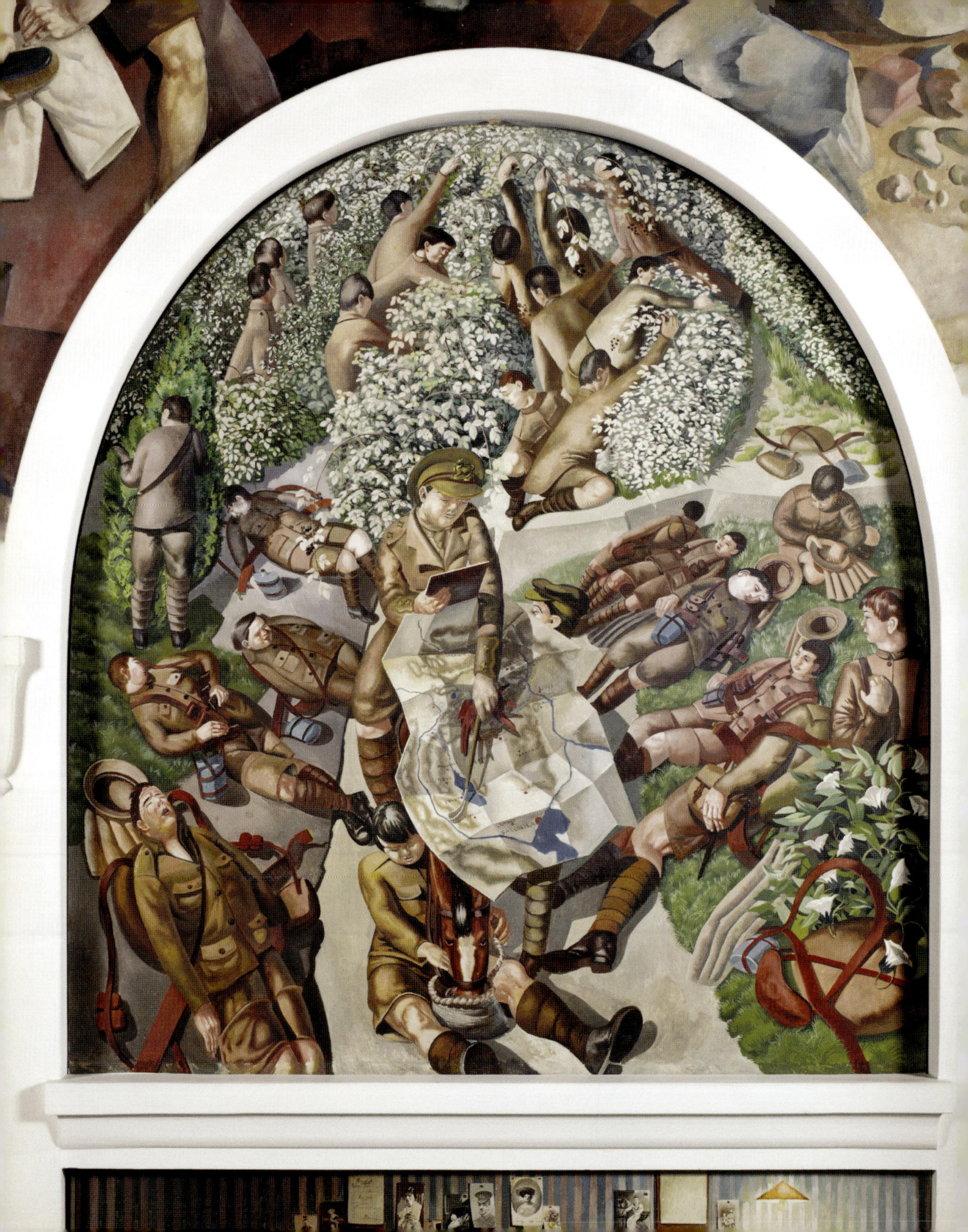

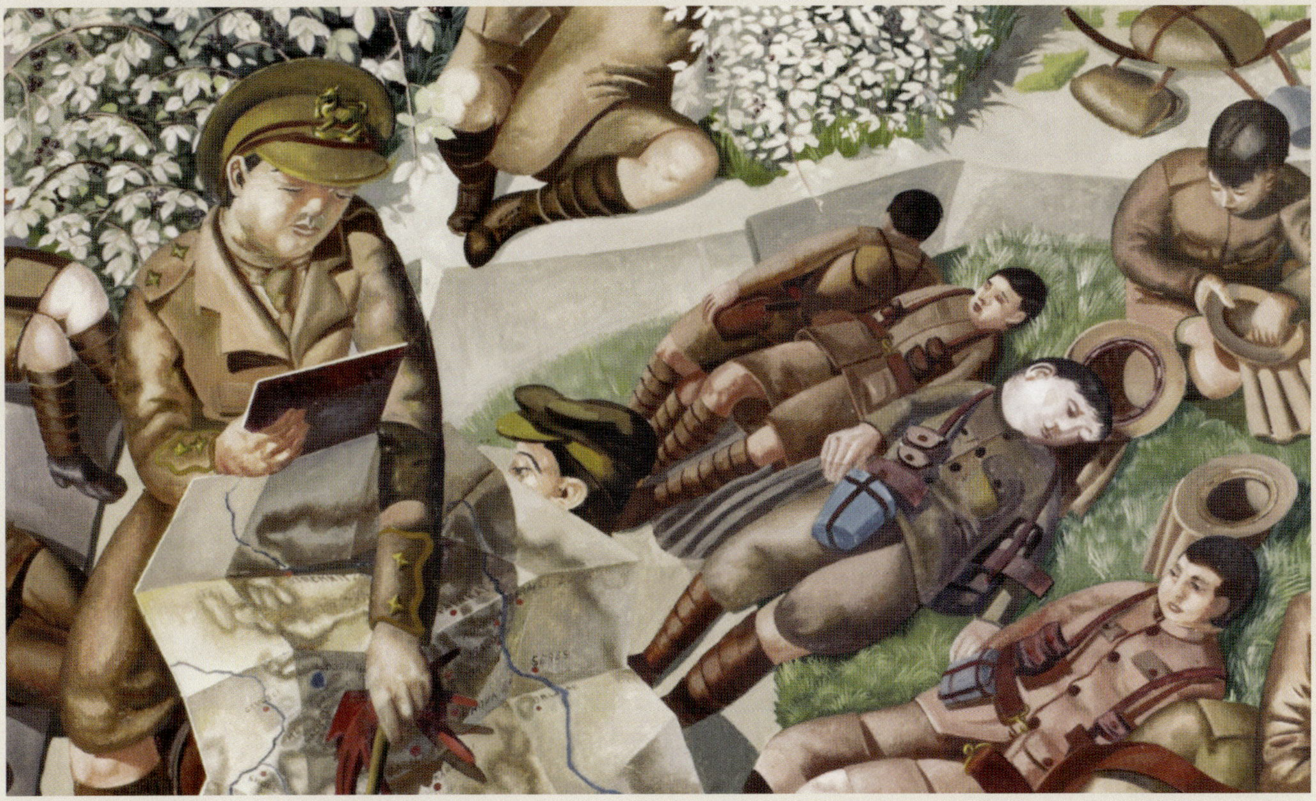

Cat. 14
MAP READING
South Wall, Sandham Memorial Chapel, Burghclere, Hampshire
213.5 × 185.5 cm (84 × 73 in)

The recuperative tone of this scene is redolent of a lazy summer day. The soldiers feasting on bilberries in the background might almost be in Cookham. The map held by the officer, however, is a key narrative device, locating the soldiers in Macedonia, and on it Spencer has noted all the places that he could remember visiting there. The officer is the only soldier in command represented in the cycle and it is pertinent that it is he who is holding the map, which along with any strategic information, remained in the hands of the officer class.[25] Spencer often complained that he did not know what was going on or where he was being sent. 'Be careful what you say about this picture,' wrote Spencer, 'it's got an officer in it.'[26]

This scene features in the original 1923 sketches for the chapel and has been developed into a mature piece of pictorial complexity. The central axis of the pathway, with soldiers falling either side, mirrors the angle of those either side of the water fountain in the adjacent panel. The rendering of landscape and greenery typifies Spencer's skill in landscape and still-life, and contributes to the rhythms of the space, reflecting the rhododendrons by the Beaufort gatehouse in *Convoy Arriving with the Wounded* (Cat. 1), and the rolling landscape above *The Resurrection of the Soldiers* (Cat. 9).
Amanda Bradley

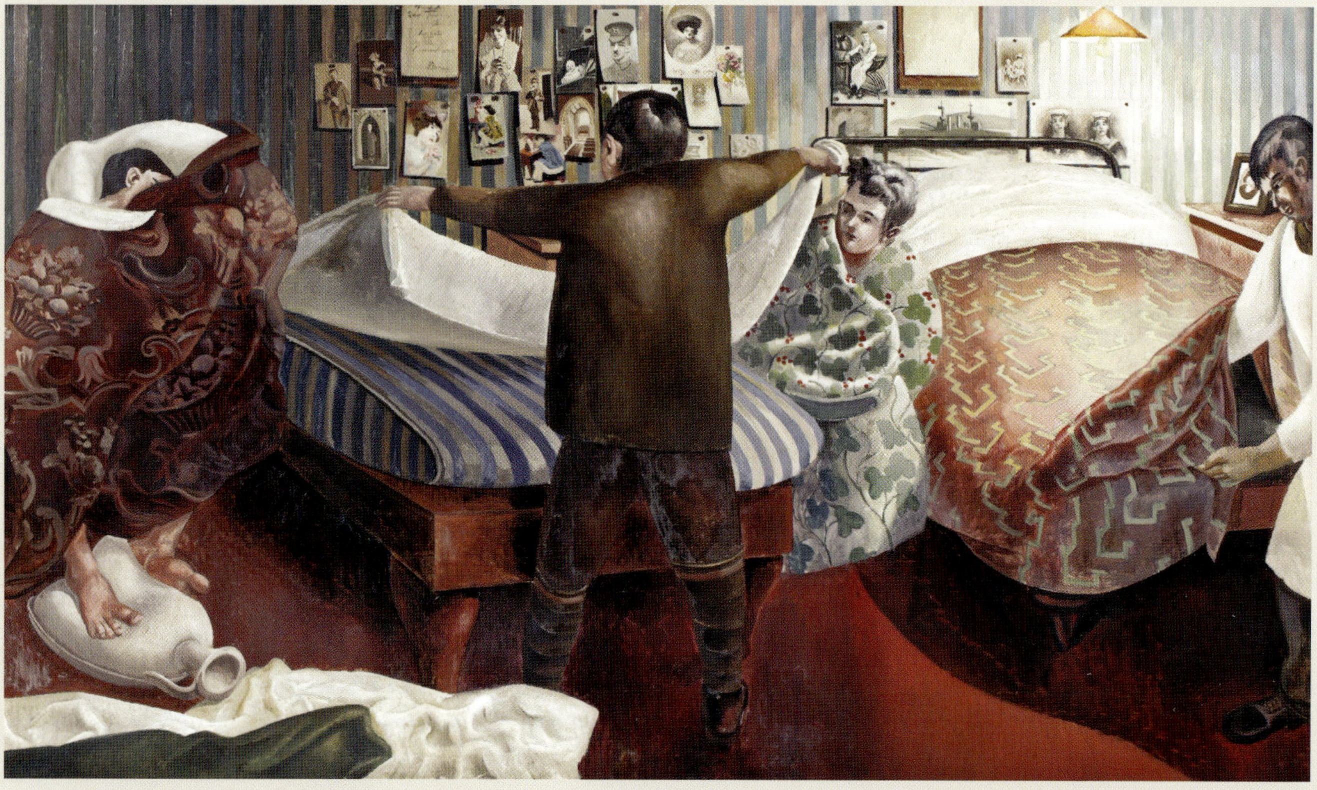

Cat. 15
BEDMAKING
South Wall, Sandham Memorial Chapel, Burghclere, Hampshire
105.5 × 185.5 cm (41 ½ × 73 in)

Even the lifting of the sheet above the bed has beauty in its form and a sacredness in its action, with the orderly's arms outstretched like the crucified Christ. A figure – perhaps Spencer himself – is cocooned inside his blankets, but unlike his companions in *Frostbite* (Cat. 11), he is upright, his expressive, oversized toes dancing on the urn-like form of the hot-water bottle. Spencer has recalled with remarkable accuracy the process of bed-making, the figure on the right shown making 'hospital corners'. The placement of the figures and even some of the decorative details remain close to an early sketch owned by the National Trust.

Somehow it seems a quintessentially English scene, with the mismatched fabrics, stripy wallpaper and pinned-up images above the bed (both Hilda and Spencer's father are shown). It has been suggested that the scene shows a hospital ward in a requisitioned house in Salonika, but it is more likely to be a fusion of memories of the Beaufort and Macedonia, where Spencer had been a patient himself.[27] With intermittent chills amongst the fever brought on by malaria, patients would have been unwilling to extricate themselves from the warmth of their bedclothes.

In the pre-war mental hospital days, each ward at the Beaufort was a self-contained unit with the day rooms furnished in a more homely fashion. During the war, the pressure of capacity meant that all areas were used as medical wards.[28]
Amanda Bradley

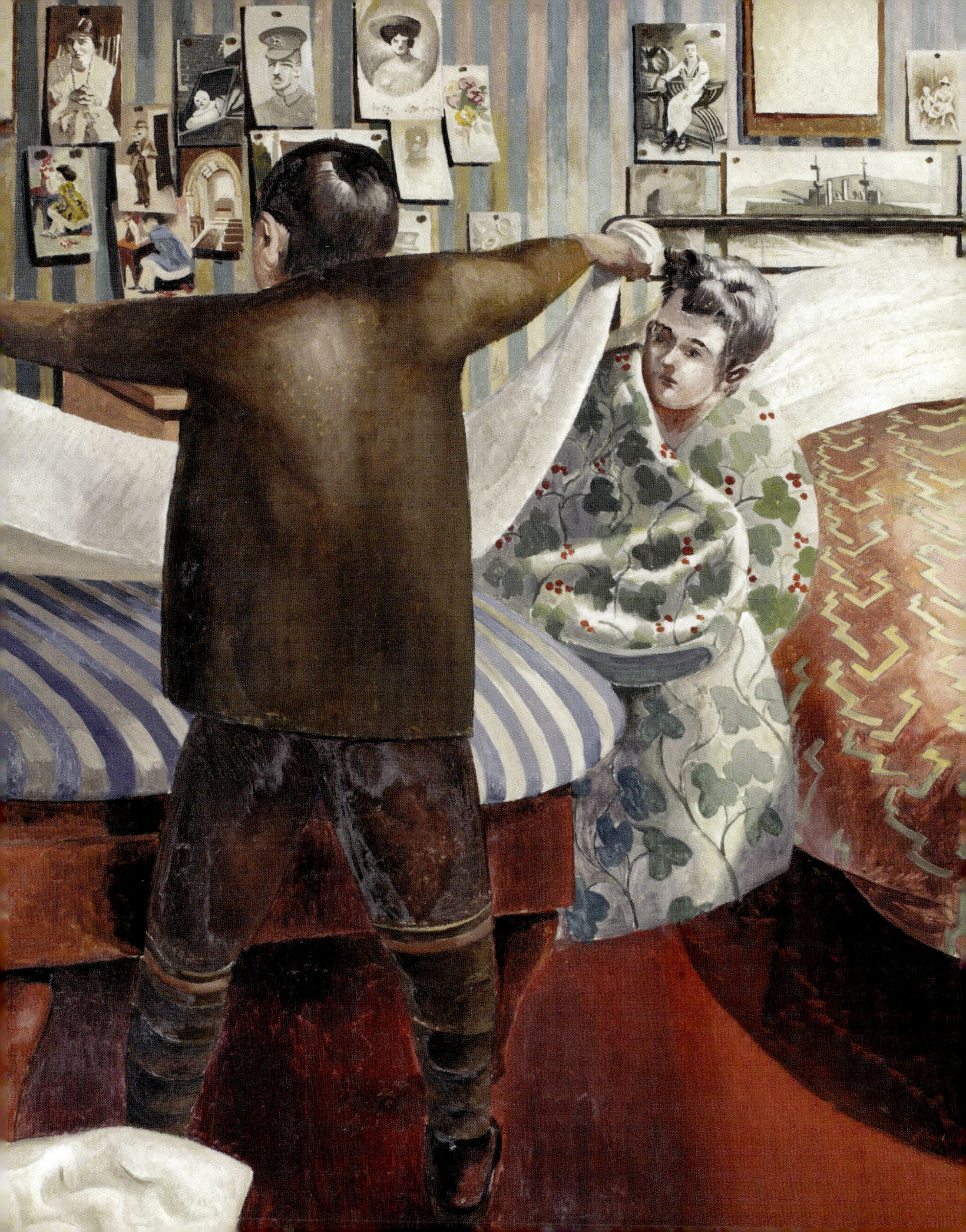

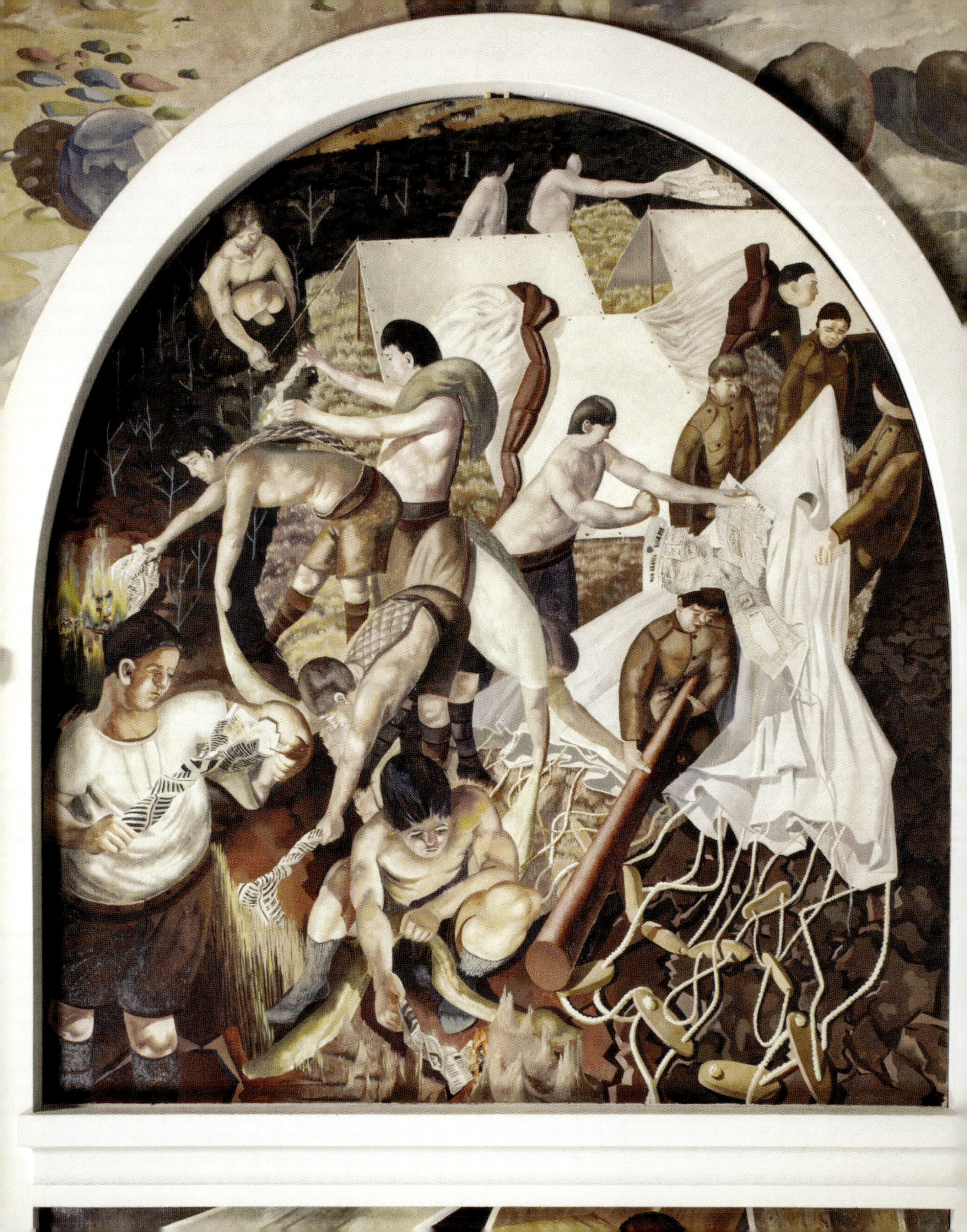

Cat. 16

FIREBELT

South Wall, Sandham Memorial Chapel, Burghclere, Hampshire
213.5 × 185.5 cm (84 × 73 in)

'Of the last three arched pictures, I like [this] the best', Spencer wrote to Mary Behrend.[29] The tangle of pulleys and complicated interplay of figures, including a Spencer-esque figure in uniform, holding a tent pole, does indeed make for a complex but resoundingly successful composition. The play of firelight on the face of the figure crouching in the foreground is akin to a modern-day Schalcken. The creation of a firebelt entailed the burning off of grass around the camp in order to create a protective fire barrier; here the soldiers are using copies of the *Balkan News* as firelighters.

Two sketches owned by the National Trust (Figs 1 and 2) show how Spencer developed a *primo pensiero* (exploring the position of the tent pole) into a fuller sketch. In both sketches he has, typically, squared the paper – a technique derived from his tutelage at the Slade under Henry Tonks. *Amanda Bradley*

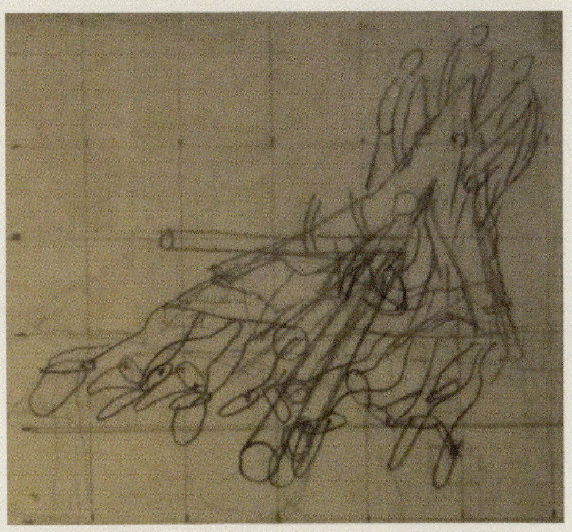

Fig. 1
Study for Firebelt (detail)
c.1923
Pencil on paper, partly squared
The Behrend Collection, The Vyne, National Trust

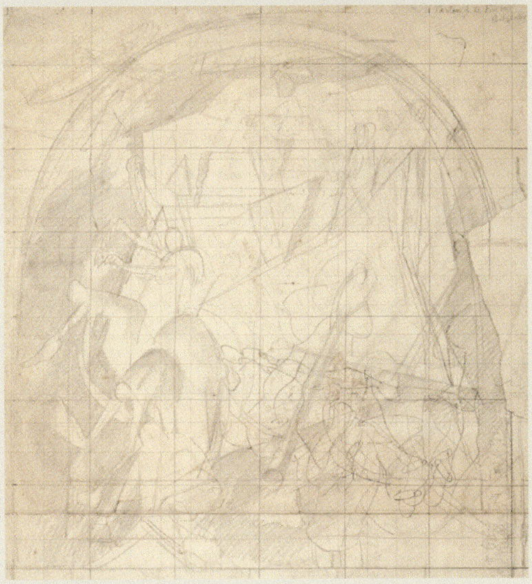

Fig. 2
Study for Firebelt
c.1923
Pencil on squared paper, squared for transfer
Sandham Memorial Chapel, National Trust

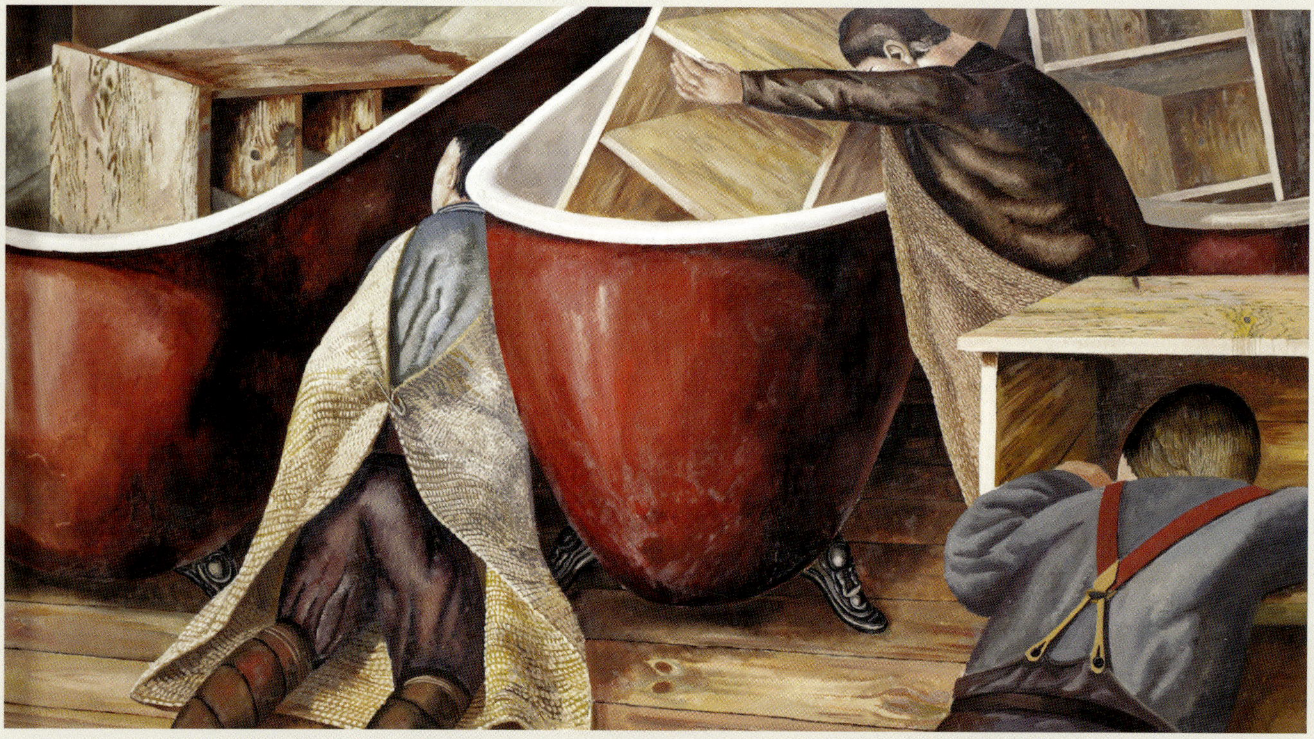

Cat. 17

WASHING LOCKERS

South Wall, Sandham Memorial Chapel, Burghclere, Hampshire

105.5 × 185.5 cm (41 ½ × 73 in)

On the back of a sketch for this predella, Spencer had written: 'Me scrubbing: I say "me", because I have only to mentally place myself between the baths to feel at once inspired.'[30] This ritual of scrubbing bedside lockers at the Beaufort War Hospital took place in the bathroom of Ward 4; one can still see today the striking sequence of water pipes emanating from this part of the building – it contained around six baths and about 20 hand basins.[31] This duty was often overseen by the fearsome Sister Hunter, who once caught Stanley's brother, Gilbert, cleaning the floor with a mop instead of a scrubbing brush. 'There are no corners to Spencer's Ward,' she admonished.[32]

By squeezing himself between these 'deep sort of magenta ... marvellous' tubs, Spencer was able to find some all-too-elusive personal space: 'Of course one had to realise that five minutes of being by oneself during the war was a great spiritual experience.'[33] Typically for Spencer the menial and the ordinary became a transubstantive experience.

Spencer has enjoyed the visual interplay between rounded and angular form, and exploring the concept of hollow forms and empty space. The play of the neutral tones of the masterfully painted hessian aprons against the red bath tubs echoes the similar contrast of colour in *Tea in the Hospital Ward* (jam against bread, Cat. 13) and *Sorting the Laundry* (white sheets and red handkerchiefs, Cat. 6).

Amanda Bradley

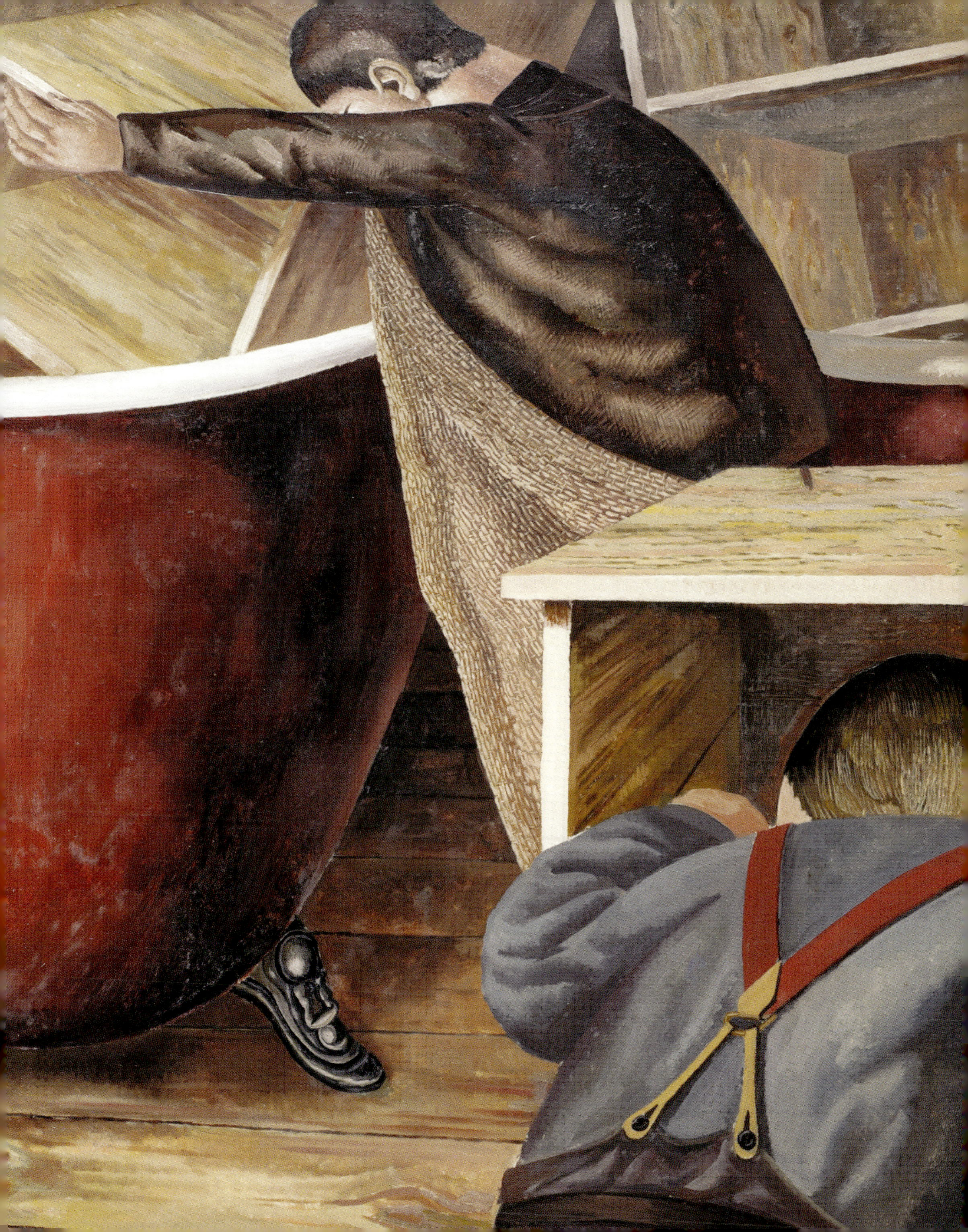

Study for the Resurrection of the Soldiers at Burghclere
c.1927
Graphite, blue and grey wash on paper laid down on card
Fitzwilliam Museum, Cambridge

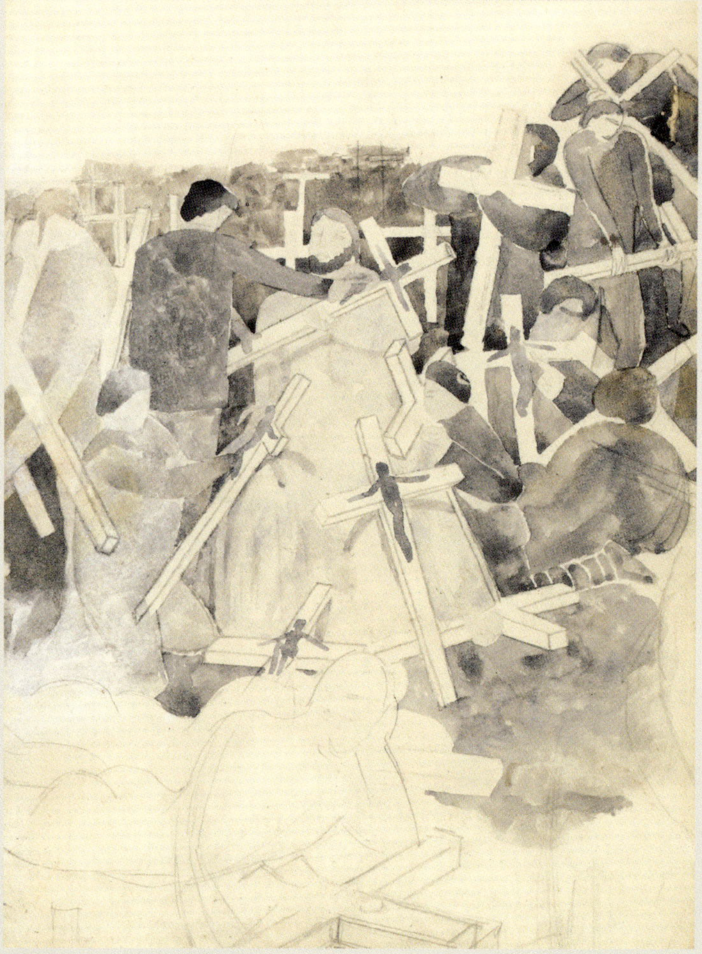

Notes

1 Paul Gough, *Stanley Spencer: Journey to Burghclere*, Samson & Co., Bristol, 2006, p.114.
2 Gough 2006, p.117.
3 George Behrend, *Stanley Spencer at Burghclere*, Macdonald, London, 1965, p.8.
4 Behrend 1965, p.8.
5 Keith Bell with Richard Carline and Andrew Causey, *Stanley Spencer*, exh. cat. Royal Academy with Weidenfeld and Nicolson, London, 1980, p.104.
6 Behrend 1965, p.6.
7 Behrend 1965, p.8.
8 Bell 1980, p.106.
9 Bell 1980, p.106.
10 Bell 1980, p.106.
11 Gough 2006, p.127.
12 Cited in Gough 2006, p.168; see Gough's chapter, 'Resurrection: 'God in the real bare things', pp.156 ff. for a full account of the altarpiece.
13 Words spoken by Spencer to a reporter in 1927; cited in Gough 2006, p.152.
14 Quoted in Richard Carline, *Stanley Spencer at War*, Faber and Faber, London, 1978, p.162.
15 Tate Archive TGA 825.21 (W7).
16 Gough 2006, p.175.
17 TGA 825.21 (W6).
18 TGA 825.21 (W24).
19 TGA 825.21 (W9–13).
20 Gough 2006, p.133.
21 Spencer himself alluded to the wing-like form of Army mackintoshes; TGA 825.21 (W22).
22 Cited in Carline 1978, p.183.
23 TGA 756.12.
24 Noted in Edward Beddington-Behrens, *Look Back, Look Forward*, Macmillan, London, 1963, p.93, in relation to Beddington-Behrens' Saas-Fee commissions.
25 Gough 2006, p.148.
26 Stanley Spencer to John Louis Behrend, TGA 882.5.
27 Duncan Robinson, *Stanley Spencer at Burghclere*, National Trust, London, 1991, p.27; Gough 2006, p.130 has suggested the idea that it is a fusion of memories.
28 Correspondence between Kenneth Pople and Sarah Hook (National Trust), 14 December 1999, Cookham Gallery Archive (51.01).
29 Stanley Spencer to Mary Behrend, 3 October 1932, TGA 882.4.
30 Cited in Carline 1978, p.182.
31 Pointed out by Paul Gough.
32 Gilbert Spencer, *Stanley Spencer by His Brother Gilbert*, Gollancz, London, 1961, p.139.
33 TGA 825.21 (W26).

Additional Loans

Preparatory Sketches

1
STUDY FOR THE RESURRECTION ALTARPIECE
*c.*1923
Pencil and wash on paper, partly squared for transfer (upper left)
56 × 45 cm (22 × 17 7/8 in)
The Behrend Collection, The Vyne, National Trust

2
STUDY FOR DRYING WASHING
*c.*1923
Pencil and wash on paper
35 × 25 cm (13 3/4 × 9 7/8 in)
Inscribed bottom right: drying washing
The Behrend Collection, The Vyne, National Trust

3
STUDY FOR 'BEDMAKING', WITH A SQUARED ARCH, A MULE AND AUXILIARY SKETCHES
*c.*1923
Pencil on paper
35 × 25 cm (13 3/4 × 9 7/8 in)
verso: study for an arch
The Behrend Collection, The Vyne, National Trust

4
STUDY FOR 'FIREBELT'
*c.*1923
Pencil on paper, partly squared
35 × 25 cm (13 3/4 × 9 7/8 in)
verso: sketches for *Firebelt*, a predella scene showing bathing, auxiliary sketches for bath scenes, a squared arch and a landscape detail
The Behrend Collection, The Vyne, National Trust

5
SKETCH FOR 'FIREBELT'
*c.*1923
Pencil on squared paper, squared for transfer
49.9 × 45.7 cm (19 5/8 × 18 in).
Inscribed upper right: Cartoon for the Fire belt Burghcler [*sic*]
Sandham Memorial Chapel, National Trust

6
LETTER FROM STANLEY SPENCER TO JOHN LOUIS BEHREND
23 November 1925, sent from the Vale Hotel Studio, Hampstead

7
LETTER FROM STANLEY SPENCER TO JOHN LOUIS BEHREND
20 December 1926, sent from the Vale Hotel Studio, Hampstead

8
LETTER FROM STANLEY SPENCER TO JOHN LOUIS BEHREND
16 January 1931, sent from Chapel View, Burghclere

9
RECEIPT FOR MONIES RECEIVED FROM JOHN LOUIS BEHREND
21 January 1932, sent from Cookham

10
HILDA STUDYING A MODEL FOR BURGHCLERE
*c.*1930
Pencil on paper, with brown oil paint
18.5 × 10.2 cm (7 1/4 × 4 in)
circa 1930
Sandham Memorial Chapel, National Trust

11
HILDA STUDYING A MODEL FOR BURGHCLERE
*c.*1930
Oil on paper
24.5 × 35.5 cm (9 5/8 × 14 in)
Collection of Catherine and William MacDougall

12
SKETCHES FOR THE CHAPEL EXTERIOR AND INTERIOR
*c.*1923
Pencil on paper
29.8 × 22.9 cm (11 3/4 × 9 in)
Inscribed, bottom left, in Spencer's own hand: I rather like these proportions as it retains Pearsons [*sic*] roof & our parapet & is a nice big window
Sandham Memorial Chapel, National Trust

13
SKETCH FOR THE FALLEN MULE DRIVER IN THE 'RESURRECTION'
*c.*1923
Pencil on torn paper
21.5 × 27.9 cm (8 1/2 × 11 in)
Inscribed upper right: The Mules, End Wall, Burghclere
Sandham Memorial Chapel, National Trust

14
CAMOUFLAGED GRENADIER
1922–3
Pencil and watercolour on paper
50.5 × 37.1 cm (19 7/8 × 14 5/8 in)
verso: two compositions for the Chapel
Tate (N04245), purchased 1927

15
STUDY FOR THE RESURRECTION OF THE SOLDIERS
1927–8
Pencil on paper
30.4 × 23 cm (12 × 9 in)
Tate (T05526), presented by the American Fund for the Tate Gallery, courtesy of Robert Littman, in honour of the Director, 1989

16
PORTRAIT OF LOUIS BEHREND
Date unknown
Pencil on paper
29.2 × 22.5 cm (11 1/2 × 8 7/8 in)
Tate (T03337), presented by Mrs Nancy Carline in memory of her husband Richard Carline, 1982

17
TWO STUDIES FOR THE SIDE WALLS AT BURGHCLERE
*c.*1923
pencil and wash on paper
North Wall 55.9 × 71.4 cm (22 × 28 1/8 in);
South Wall 30.5 × 45.7 cm (12 × 18 in)
Cookham, Stanley Spencer Gallery

18
STUDY FOR RESURRECTION
*c.*1927
Pencil, blue and grey wash on paper
35.6 x 25.4 cm (14 × 10 in)
The Fitzwilliam Museum, Cambridge

19
THE COMMANDANT
1919
Pencil and wash on paper
18.2 × 25.2 cm (7 1/8 × 9 7/8 in)
Imperial War Museum (ART 3880)

20
TRAVOYS PASSING UP SEDOMLI RAVINE ON THE WAY TO LE NAZE
1919
Pencil and wash on paper
21.5 × 25.4 cm (8 1/2 × 10 in)
Imperial War Museum (ART 3878)

21
STRETCHER BEARERS, MACEDONIA
1919
Pencil and wash on paper
21.5 × 14.6 cm (8 1/2 × 5 3/4 in)
Imperial War Museum (ART 3879)

22
GOWANS & GRAY 'GIOTTO'
1909 edition
Private Collection

Paintings

23
Henry Lamb
THE BEHREND FAMILY
1927
Oil on canvas
53.5 x 67.5 cm (21 1/8 × 26 5/8 in)
Brighton and Hove Museums

24
Henry Lamb
SIR STANLEY SPENCER
1928
Oil on canvas
50.8 × 40.6 cm (20 × 16 in)
National Portrait Gallery, London (NPG 4527)

25
SELF PORTRAIT
1923
Oil on canvas
50.8 × 40.6 cm (20 × 16 in)
Stanley Spencer Gallery, Cookham
(Barbara Karmel Bequest, 1995)

26
POPPIES
1938
Oil on canvas
44.5 × 58.5 cm (17 1/2 × 23 in)
Town Hall Museum, Newark

27
Henry Lamb
TROOPS BATHING AT SALONIKA
1917
Oil on canvas
153 × 122.5 cm (60 1/4 × 48 1/4 in)
Private Collection; on loan to
Southampton City Art Gallery

28
Henry Lamb
IRISH TROOPS IN THE JUDEAN HILLS SURPRISED BY A TURKISH BOMBARDMENT
1919
Oil on canvas
184.6 × 220.5 cm (72 5/8 × 86 3/4 in)
Imperial War Museum (ART 2746)

Select Bibliography

Behrend, George, *Stanley Spencer at Burghclere*, Macdonald, London, 1965

Bell, Keith, *Stanley Spencer: A Complete Catalogue of the Paintings*, Phaidon, London, 1992

Bell, Keith with Richard Carline and Andrew Causey, *Stanley Spencer*, exh. cat., Royal Academy with Weidenfeld and Nicolson, London, 1980

Bell, Keith, Martin Hammer, James and Julie Lawson, Andrew Patrizio and Duncan Thomson, *Men of the Clyde: Stanley Spencer's Vision at Port Glasgow*, exh. cat., Scottish National Portrait Gallery, Edinburgh, 2000

Boyd Haycock, David, *A Crisis of Brilliance: Five Young British Artists and the Great War*, Old Street, London, 2009

Boyd Haycock, David, *Nash Nevinson Spencer Gertler Carrington Bomberg: A Crisis of Brilliance, 1908–1922*, exh. cat., Dulwich Picture Gallery, London, 2013

Carline, Richard, 'New Mural Paintings by Stanley Spencer', *Studio*, no.96, November 1928, pp.316–23

Carline, Richard, *Stanley Spencer at War*, Faber and Faber, London, 1978

Clements, Keith, *Henry Lamb, The Artist and His Friends*, Redcliffe Press, Bristol, 1985

Collis, Maurice, *Stanley Spencer: A Biography*, Harvill, London, 1962

Glew, Adrian (ed.), *Stanley Spencer: Letters and Writings*, Tate, London, 2001

Gormley, Anthony, 'The Sacred and the Profane in the Art of Stanley Spencer', *Stanley Spencer*, exh. cat., Arts Council, London, 1976, pp.21–2

Gough, Paul, *A Terrible Beauty: British Artists in the First World War*, Samson & Co., Bristol, 2010

Gough, Paul, *Stanley Spencer: Journey to Burghclere*, Samson & Co., Bristol, 2006

Gough, Paul. (ed.), *Your Loving Friend, Stanley: The Great War Correspondence Between Stanley Spencer and Desmond Chute*, Samson & Co., Bristol, 2011

Hauser, Kitty, *Stanley Spencer*, Tate, London, 2001

Henry Lamb, exh. cat., Manchester City Art Gallery, Manchester, 1984

Hyman, Timothy and Patrick Wright, *Stanley Spencer*, exh. cat., Tate, London, 2001

Newton, Eric, *Stanley Spencer* (Penguin Modern Painters), Penguin, Harmondsworth, 1947

Parissien, Steven (ed.), *Stanley Spencer and the English Garden*, Compton Verney in association with Paul Holberton, London

Pople, Kenneth, *Stanley Spencer: A Biography*, Collins, London, 1991

Robinson, Duncan, *Stanley Spencer*, Phaidon, Oxford, 1990

Robinson, Duncan, *Stanley Spencer at Burghclere*, National Trust, London, 1991

Rothenstein, Elizabeth, *Stanley Spencer*, Phaidon, Oxford, 1947

Rothenstein, Elizabeth, *Stanley Spencer*, Purnell, London, 1967

Rothenstein, John (ed.), *Stanley Spencer: The Man, Correspondence and Reminiscences*, Paul Elek, London, 1979

Rutherston, Albert (ed.), *Henry Lamb*, Ernest Benn, London, 1924

Spencer, Gilbert, *Stanley Spencer by His Brother Gilbert*, Gollancz, London, 1961 (reprinted 1991)

Wilenski, R.H., *Stanley Spencer*, Ernest Benn, London, 1924

Picture Credits

Unless otherwise indicated all images are
© The Estate of Stanley Spencer 2013.
All rights reserved DACS.
National Trust/ John Hammond

© The Estate of Stanley Spencer 2013.
All rights reserved DACS: p. 26, p. 54 (left), p. 58 (both), p. 62, p. 85 (both), p. 89, p.103 (both), p. 106, back cover.

© Paul Blatchford: p. 16.

© The National Trust: p. 20 (both), p. 24 (bottom).

© Christie's Images Limited, 2013: p. 24 (top).

© Imperial War Museums: p. 33 (ART 2746), p. 46 (HU 102285), p. 49 (ART 2273), p. 66 (ART 3880), p. 67 (Q 32159).

© Courtesy of the Estate of Henry Lamb: p. 27, p. 34, p. 35, p. 36.

© National Portrait Gallery, London: p. 37 (NPG 4527).

© Crown copyright: UK Government Art Collection: p. 39 (GAC140).

© Tate, London 2013: p. 48 (right).

© The Fitzwilliam Museum, Cambridge: p. 50.

© Stanley Spencer Gallery, Cookham, Photograph Archive: p. 64.

Image supply:
The Bridgeman Art Library: p. 54 (both), p. 55.
The Public Catalogue Foundation: back cover.

Acknowledgements

This exhibition represents the team effort of many National Trust staff, past and present. We should like to thank in particular: the Sandham project board, led by James Taylor; the Regional Curator, James Rothwell; the Property Manager, Dave Green; staff at Sandham Memorial Chapel, and especially, Alison Paton and Tom Bromwell; the conservation team, including Nigel Blades, Andrew Bush, Ylva Dahnsjo, Tina Sitwell and their assistants; our London Director, Ivo Dawnay; on the press and PR team, Alison Dalby and Jo Dyson; Claire Forbes and Oliver Garnett in Specialist Publications; and also our Registrar, Fernanda Torrente, assisted by Holly Lopez, without whom none of this would have been possible. David Adshead, our Head Curator, has been a pillar of support and reason throughout. We should also like to thank: Harriet Judd (Project Manager of the catalogue), Howard Watson (copy editor) and David Wynn (designer); and the contributors to the catalogue – Jenny Beddington, Paul Gough, Jamie Hacker Hughes, Simon Martin and Katy Norris. We are also indebted to numerous external scholars, advisers and friends: Claudia Coates (Christie's), Ann Danks (Stanley Spencer Gallery), Jennifer Fletcher, Adrian Glew and staff at Tate Archive, Carolyn Leder (Stanley Spencer Gallery), Jane Martineau, Jeff Pilkington (Christie's archive), and Graham Southern (Blain Southern). The exhibition would not have been possible without the generosity of lending institutions and private collectors, or without the blessing of the Spencer family, Unity, Shirin and John, for which we are grateful.